THE DYNAMIC LAWS

OF PROSPERITY

Other Books by Catherine Ponder

A PROSPERITY LOVE STORY
A Memoir

THE DYNAMIC LAWS OF PROSPERITY

THE DYNAMIC LAWS OF HEALING

THE PROSPERITY SECRET OF THE AGES

THE DYNAMIC LAWS OF PRAYER

THE HEALING SECRET OF THE AGES

OPEN YOUR MIND TO PROSPERITY

DARE TO PROSPER

THE SECRET OF UNLIMITED PROSPERITY

OPEN YOUR MIND TO RECEIVE

THE PROSPERING POWER OF PRAYER

<u>The Millionaires of the Bible Series:</u>

THE MILLIONAIRES OF GENESIS

THE MILLIONAIRE MOSES

THE MILLIONAIRE JOSHUA

THE MILLIONAIRE FROM NAZARETH

THE
DYNAMIC LAWS
OF
PROSPERITY

by

Catherine Ponder

DeVorss Publications
Camarillo, California

The Dynamic Laws of Prosperity
Copyright © 1962 by Prentice-Hall, Inc.
Copyright transferred in 1984 to Catherine Ponder

ISBN: 0-87516-551-6
ISBN13: 978-087516-551-6
Library of Congress Catalog Card: 62-18836
Fourteenth Printing, 2006

DeVorss & Company, Publisher
PO Box 1389
Camarillo CA 93011-1389
www.devorss.com

Printed in the United States of America

CONTENTS

PART I

BASIC PROSPERITY LAWS
That Can Bring Riches to You

The birth of prosperous thinking. The salesman with the golden touch. The laws of prosperity. How the laws have worked for others. Prosperity brings "new look" and new health. Your whole outlook changes. The salesman was right.

You should desire prosperity. Poverty is a sin. Prosperity is your divine heritage. Success is divinely ordained. The Bible is a prosperity textbook. Why poverty is not spiritual. Right attitudes will pay your bills. How to stabilize your finances. The link between thought and supply. Success adores the prosperous attitude.

PART II

OTHER PROSPERITY LAWS
That Can Bring Riches to You

important. Sex, an important expression of love. Express love to children. Children thrive on encouragement. Discipline with love. Begin where you are, expressing love.

trust dissolves indebtedness. Discord causes indebtedness. There is a way out of indebtedness. Keep quiet about indebtedness. Speak only in prosperous terms. No one can withhold your prosperity. Deliberately think big. Begin to pay cash for more items. Dismiss financial mistakes of the past. Ask for prosperous ideas. Indebtedness can be a blessing in disguise. How to gain financial freedom.

Prosperous thinking is healthy thinking. Inharmony causes ill health. Healthy thinking is an ancient art. Attitudes can heal. An emotional cause of cancer. Forgiveness heals. Happiness heals. Therapy for female trouble. The *first* step in healing. How to lose weight. The *second* step in healing. The Lord's Prayer has healing power. Griping can make you sick. Your prayers for another's healing have power. The *third* step in healing. Make a wheel of fortune for health. Reduce through mental images. How to stop smoking. This method is effective for overcoming alcoholism. The Bible teaches this healing technique. A healing prophecy.

Persistence is your "can-do" attitude. Don't surrender to defeat. Persistence produces success. Failure can be a prelude to success. Refuse "no" as an answer. Persistence works both ways. One right attitude is enough. Meet hard experiences with persistence. Revise your success plans. Plod on to victory. Don't look back—look forward. Persistence alone is all-powerful. Be prepared if success comes suddenly.

PART I

BASIC PROSPERITY LAWS THAT CAN BRING RICHES TO YOU

Introduction . . . .

THERE'S GOLD DUST IN THE AIR FOR YOU!

This book is the result of several recent recessions and many years of lean living. Nobody likes recessions and nobody likes lean living — and indeed nobody should like them.

For fifteen years I tried to find such a book as this one. During those years of searching the book shelves, I found that there are many books which give various success ideas, but in none of them did I find a set of compact, simple laws for assuring success.

I began searching for a book such as this after having been widowed and left with a small son to rear and educate. Since I had no training for work and no means of income, I would have given anything to have known then about the power of prosperous thinking.

For a while I experienced depression, ill health, loneliness, financial lack and a sense of complete failure. It seemed that the whole world was against me, and that everything I did went wrong. But with my son to provide for, I could not settle for failure. I had to succeed for his sake as well as for my own.

Finally, when I was at my lowest ebb emotionally, physically, and financially, I learned about the power of thought as an instrument for successs or failure. I came to realize that failure is basically the result of failure thinking. I learned that the right use of my mind could become the key to healthy, happy, prosperous, successful living.

As soon as I grasped this wonderful success secret, the tide began to change!

THE BIRTH OF PROSPEROUS THINKING

You've heard much in recent years about positive thinking. Out of the recessions and lean years another term has been born—"prosperous thinking." The word "prosper" means "to flourish, succeed, thrive, to experience favorable results."

You are prosperous to the degree that you are experiencing peace, health, and plenty in your world. While prosperous thinking means many things to people, basically it gives you the power to make your dreams come true, whether those dreams are concerned with better health, increased financial success, a happier personal life, more education and travel, or a deeper spiritual life.

This book plainly shows how prosperous thinking has helped people in every walk of life to experience these results. Furthermore, it shows how prosperous thinking can do these things for you, too! As you read this book, chapter by chapter, you will automatically begin to develop the power of prosperous thinking and, almost as easily, you can begin to reap a harvest of prosperous results.

THE SALESMAN WITH THE GOLDEN TOUCH

Years ago, a salesman used the power of prosperous thinking, although he may not consciously have been aware of it. When people asked him, "How's business?" he always gave this standard answer: "Business is wonderful because there's gold dust in the air!" For him it certainly seemed to be so—every contact became a sale. After a while, whenever his name was mentioned, people always said, "Yes, everything he touches turns to gold."

THE LAWS OF PROSPERITY

During my first year in the ministry, one of the most severe business recessions since World War II hit this country. Members of my congregation began asking for lectures on ways to survive this difficult period. It was then that these dynamic laws of prosperity began to take form. And, with breathtaking rapidity, these ideas worked—for all types of people!

The word "dynamic" has the same root as the word "dynamite." That which is dynamic is powerful, forceful, filled with energy, and leads to change. That which is dynamic tends to blast you out of a rut!

A "law" is a principle that works. Sir William Blackstone, well-known writer of the law, pointed out many years ago, that a "law" is a settled rule of action. The word "law" usually suggests a desire for order. People experiencing limitation need just that— *order* in their thinking, emotions, bodies, financial affairs and in all phases of their lives.

The brilliant scientist, Sir Isaac Newton, an early researcher of nature's laws, once said that there is one set of natural laws for the physical world. But let us go further: *There are also higher mental and spiritual laws than those usually used on the physical plane of life. Jesus knew and used them constantly. These higher mental and spiritual laws are so powerful that they can be used to multiply, neutralize, or even reverse natural laws! It is when these higher mental and spiritual laws are used by the mind of man, that they often produce results that seem miraculous on the physical plane.*

HOW THE LAWS HAVE WORKED FOR OTHERS

Within a week after the first lecture, two secretaries had received raises in pay, one with a promotion and new title. A stockbroker soon reported that he had more business than he had dared hope for, although most of his fellow workers were comparatively idle. One client whom he had not seen for several years appeared and handed him a check to invest for $200,000! A month after beginning to deliberatly invoke prosperous thinking, his income was four times its usual amount.

A lawyer, who had several industrial clients then on strike or out of work, reported that the recession was suddenly over for him. His income zoomed upward into the $2,000-a-month bracket, which at the time seemed a great increase, though later, after he had established a definite pattern of prosperous thinking, it seemed only normal.

A steel manufacturer's agent, whose business was affected by recession, reported that he unexpectedly received an order amounting to $4,500 which he had not solicited. One woman was a saleslady in a department store which employed more than 100 people. All of her fellow workers had been thinking and talking hard times. At the end of the month, after this woman began to deliberately think prosperously, out of more than 100 employees, she was the only one in the store who received a commission check for having oversold her quota for the month. The other employees had decreed hard times and had gotten such results for themselves.

The owner of an electrical business had an outstanding account of $750 owing his company. As he began to think of those owing him as prosperous, the account was quietly paid.

A jeweler had an indebtedness owing him which he tried every means he knew to collect, including the use of unkind letters, all to no avail. When he, too, decided to think in prosperous terms about himself and the one owing him, to his amazement the creditor quickly paid up. One family that desired freedom from indebtedness suddenly inherited a nice sum of money.

A government employee received a raise in pay that had been pending in Congress for several years. A telephone company employee also received a general raise that had been promised months earlier. A construction engineer received a new assignment to a 15.5 million dollar construction job, after having served on a million-and-a-half dollar construction job. One couple even received an all-expense-paid trip abroad!

These are but a few examples of the power of prosperous thinking.

PROSPERITY BRINGS "NEW LOOK" AND NEW HEALTH

But more than financial returns appeared. As I weekly lectured on prosperous thinking, I began to realize that the people in attendance were beginning to blossom forth with a "new look"—a look of inner peace, poise, happiness, security and stability not previously apparent. The failure look of depression and discouragement was replaced with the look of success, self-confidence and inner happiness. The look of defeat was replaced with a look of dominion, authority, victory. It was wonderful to behold!

New mental and physical health appeared for a number of people, too. One businessman had been told most of his life that he had a serious heart condition that would have to be pampered constantly. As he began to apply the power of prosperous thinking in every phase of his world, he relaxed more and more in mind and body. Tension, both conscious and subconscious, gradually eased. After a time, his doctor stated that his earlier heart trouble had vanished. Now, several years later, he remains healthier and happier than ever before.

Several people with nervous conditions found new health, serenity and peace of mind. A housewife in this group had for years visited a series of doctors who could find nothing organically wrong with her. As she began deliberately to practice prosperous thinking, she began to think more lovingly of others—including her husband! Her new attitude of appreciation gave him a feeling of approval he had not had from his wife in many a year. This, in turn, added to his self-confidence and was reflected as new success in his work. His new job success brought a happiness and satisfaction to their marriage that had long been missing. This woman's health improved so much that she soon appeared years younger, and her aches and pains faded as happiness came into the various departments of her life.

YOUR WHOLE OUTLOOK CHANGES

A lonely, unhappy businesswoman, who had often threatened suicide, became so intensely interested in the laws of prosperity that she found interests outside herself. This led to a happier, more balanced life. The suicide talk stopped. A housewife and also a businessman, whose secret drinking had become serious problems, found new hope in their practice of prosperous thinking. They began to realize that their drinking problems *could* be overcome. As they gained this victorious expectation, they were able to begin resolving and dissolving inner hostilities and conflicts. Their drinking gradually diminished.

Several marriages were saved, after one or other of the marriage partners began to invoke these laws of prosperity. One person's divorced partner returned and they were remarried. Several lonely, unmarried people happily married, one after having been widowed for 20 years.

A businessman who had always detested his work found, as he began using these ideas, that he got a whole new perspective on his job, and in due time he no longer disliked it.

As a result of the over-all success of that prosperity class, some of its members came to my aid: A businessman helped me pray this book into print, a stockbroker named it, and a public relations consultant located a literary agent and publisher for the book.

THE SALESMAN WAS RIGHT

That salesman was right! There *is* gold dust in the air — for you, for me, for everyone! The scientists know that there's gold dust in the air because they declare this universe to be composed of nothing but radiant substance or ether, to which man has unlimited access. Psychologists and metaphysicians know about the gold dust. They declare that man forms his world from the rich, unlimited substance within him and around him through his thoughts, emotions, words and actions.

And so let us proceed in confidence, knowing that there is gold dust in the air — and that there is gold dust everywhere. As you begin reading this book, no matter what the conditions of your life may now be, do so in this attitude of mind: *"There is gold dust in the air—for me. Through definite, deliberate prosperous thinking, I now begin assimilating that gold dust. And even now I am beginning to experience gold dust results!"*

Now proceed quickly to the following pages where you will learn the exciting gold dust secrets of countless others.

Catherine Ponder

THE SHOCKING TRUTH
ABOUT PROSPERITY

— Chapter 1 —

The shocking truth about prosperity is that it is shockingly right instead of shockingly wrong for you to be prosperous!

Russell H. Conwell emphasized this in his famous "Acres of Diamonds" lecture:

> I say you ought to be rich; you have no right to be poor. To live and not be rich is a misfortune and it is doubly a misfortune because you could have been rich just as well as being poor. . . . We ought to get rich if we can by honorable methods, and these are the only methods that sweep us quickly toward the goal of riches.[1]

---

1. Russell Conwell, *Acres of Diamonds* (California: DeVorss & Company)

Please note that the word "rich" means having an abundance of good or living a fuller, more satisfying life. Indeed, you are prosperous to the degree that you are experiencing peace, health, happiness and plenty in your world. There *are* honorable methods that can carry you quickly toward that goal. It is easier to accomplish than you may now think. That, too, is the shocking truth about prosperity.

Several decades ago a businessman predicted that the religious leaders of the future would be forced to give more attention to helping their followers solve their economic and personal problems of the present; and they would be less concerned with the dead past or the unborn future. I agree with that businessman and I wish to help you do just that—solve your present economic and personal problems. As you do, your dead past and your unborn future will surely be taken care of.

YOU SHOULD DESIRE PROSPERITY

Perhaps one of the greatest shocks I ever received was the one that became apparent when I began lecturing on prosperity. I soon realized that many of the people attending the lectures were still trying to resolve that old conflict of whether they should desire to be prosperous. Of course, they wanted prosperity; every normal person does. But they appeared to secretly wonder whether they should seek it or not, especially from a spiritual standpoint. Most of the business people attending the lectures seemed to feel guilty about wanting to be prosperous, though of course they were working hard every day in their jobs to do so. The question, obviously, was still in their minds: whether poverty was a spiritual virtue or a common vice. That conflict in their thinking was setting up a conflicting result in their affairs, which neutralized their efforts to succeed, no matter how hard they were working.

Soon it became apparent that it would take the expression of some bold, even shocking ideas on the subject to blast out the limited beliefs that had bound these people to mediocre living for years. Realizing this, I spent several lecture periods explaining how God, man and prosperity are all divinely related. After the initial shock of these ideas had passed, these fine people were greatly relieved and very happy that, at last, they no longer had to feel guilty about wanting to be prosperous. It was then that they began to experience prosperous results in rapid time.

I find that the same idea still persists. Perfectly wonderful people seem quite confused about whether prosperity should be considered a spiritual blessing. How relieved they are when shown that it definitely is!

POVERTY IS A SIN

And so again I say: It is shockingly right instead of shockingly wrong for you to be prosperous. Obviously, you cannot be very happy if you are poor, and *you need not be poor. It is a sin.* Poverty is a form of hell caused by man's blindness to God's unlimited good for him. Poverty is a dirty, uncomfortable, degrading experience. Poverty is actually a form of disease and in its acute phases, it seems to be a form of insanity.

Poverty fills prisons with thieves and murderers. It drives men and women to drink, prostitution, drug addiction, suicide. It drives potentially fine, talented, intelligent children to delinquency and crime. It makes people do things they otherwise would never dream of doing. Communism, one of the most dreaded movements in the world today, often gets a stronghold as the direct result of poverty. The governments which have become Communist dominated have usually done so for financial reasons, believing it a way to financial security. The sinful results of poverty know no bounds. That is one of the reasons why, as a minister, I have felt so strongly led to do whatever I can to help people learn how to eradicate the sin of poverty from their lives.

A doctor I know has said that he would have few patients if it were not for financial problems which cause them worry, strain and tension, all of which lead to ill health. He states that our mental hospitals are filled with people who have found that financial strain over a long period impaired their minds and bodies to the point of incapacity. It has even been estimated that nine-tenths of mankind's ills are caused by the strain, misery and unhappiness of poverty.

Let us be done with thinking of poverty as a virtue. It is a common vice. If you have been living in financial lack and limitation, you have literally been living in vice. That, too, is the shocking truth about prosperity. But you need not continue living in financial vice. There is a way out.

PROSPERITY IS YOUR DIVINE HERITAGE

The Bible is filled with rich promises regarding your potential prosperity as a child of God. You *should* be prosperous, well supplied and have an abundance of good because it is your divine heritage. Your Creator wants you that way! *That* is the shockingly nice truth about prosperity.

Besides, you can't be much good to yourself or to anyone else unless you are prosperous. The person who does not desire to be prosperous is abnormal, because without prosperity you live abnormally. You cannot live fully on the *physical plane* without proper food, comfortable clothing, warm shelter and without freedom from excessive toil. Rest and recreation are also needed for your physical life.

You cannot live fully on the *mental plane* without satisfying creative mental activity; without books and time to enjoy them; without time to enjoy music, art and other cultural interests; without opportunity and money for travel and intellectual association with others of similar interests.

To live fully on the *spiritual plane* of life, you need time for quiet contemplation; for meditation, prayer, spiritual study, attendance at churches, lectures and satisfying association with others on the spiritual path. It is, therefore, of supreme importance that you be prosperous for your physical, mental and spiritual welfare and development.

Make no excuses for putting up with lack or accepting it as a permanent arrangement in your life. Do not go to the other extreme either, and talk of wanting to be prosperous for the good you can do. That is secondary. You want to be prosperous mainly because it is right that you should be. Prosperity is your divine heritage as the child of a King, as a son of God.

SUCCESS IS DIVINELY ORDAINED

There is no reason for you to think of prosperity as something separate from your spiritual life or "beyond the pale" of religion. You do not have to try to live in two worlds where you run things for six days and then on the seventh give God a chance to show what He can do. Take God as a rich, loving, understanding Father into all your affairs each day of your week. Ask His divine instruction and guidance about all your affairs, financial and otherwise, and you will be pleasantly surprised how much better every phase of your life will become. "All things are yours" is the divine promise. (I Corinthians 3:21)[2]

An analyst once declared to me that he had found the most common cause of failure in people to be conflicting ideas about whether success is divinely ordained or divinely damned. He stated that many had assured him that failure was more spiritually approved than success by quoting the words of Jesus, "You cannot serve God and mammon." (Matthew 6:24) This doctor further said that he has spent many an hour explaining to people who are not succeeding that being success-minded is not serving mammon, and that they should stop using God as an excuse for their failures.

The dictionary describes mammon as "riches regarded as an object of worship or as a false god." People serve mammon who leave God out of their financial affairs and try to go it alone. When you realize that God wants you to be prosperous and that God, as the Creator of this rich universe, is indeed the Source of your prosperity, then you are not worshipping mammon. You are not making prosperity a false god. You are simply claiming your prosperous heritage from the Source of all your blessings. Jehovah pointed out the

---

2. Bible passages quoted herein are from the American Standard Version or the King James Version of the Holy Bible.

right spiritual attitude toward prosperity when He told Moses to remind the Children of Israel: "But thou shalt remember Jehovah thy God, for it is He that giveth thee power to get wealth." (Deuteronomy 8:18) The word "wealth" means grand living and that is what a prosperous thinker should be working toward and should be expecting as his spiritual right.

Perhaps you are recalling, at this point, a statement I also heard as a child which confused me about prosperity being a spiritual blessing. People often said, "I am poor but I'm a good Christian." Even though I come from a family that has produced ministers, I always shuddered when I heard that statement. My immediate reaction was, "Why should Christians or any other group have to be poor? God isn't poor and He is our loving Father." Then, too, that statement made it sound as if all the rich folks were bound for hell. Somehow I could not figure out why rich people had to go to hell just because they were prosperous. It seemed rather inconsistent to me.

THE BIBLE IS A PROSPERITY TEXTBOOK

Upon entering the ministry, I decided to settle the issue within my own mind by studying the Biblical view of prosperity versus poverty. It was a pleasant surprise to discover that the Bible is the greatest textbook on prosperity ever written![3]

---

8 See the author's series of books on the millionaires of the Bible, published by DeVorss & Co., Marina del Rey, CA 90294: *The Millionaires of Genesis* (1976), *The Millionaire Moses* (1977), *The Millionaire Joshua* (1978), and *The Millionaire from Nazareth* (1979).

The Bible clearly shows that you have not been pleasing God by settling for lack and limitation in your life, any more than you have been pleasing yourself. The very first chapter describes the rich universe created for man; the last book of the Bible symbolically describes heaven in rich terms. Most of the great men of the Bible were either born prosperous, became prosperous or had access to riches whenever the need arose. Among them were Abraham, Jacob, Joseph, Moses, David, Solomon, Isaiah, Jeremiah, Nehemiah, Elijah and Elisha of the Old Testament; and Jesus and Paul of the New Testament.

Jesus' life and teachings bear clear evidence of His understanding of prosperity laws. As a baby, He was presented with rich gifts by the Wise Men. Although Jesus has been described as being poor, with no place to lay His head, He had a home with His parents in Nazareth, and was gladly welcomed into the homes of both rich and poor all over Palestine. His first miracle produced a rich gift of the finest wine for His host at a wedding feast. He unhesitatingly used the laws of prosperity to feed thousands in a desert place. His parable of the Prodigal Son contains a fine prosperity lesson.

When Jesus declared, "Blessed are the poor in spirit, for theirs is the kingdom." (Matthew 5:3) He was not referring to those living in poverty. "Poor in spirit" means those who are humble and receptive, not prideful and self-important. When the rich man came to Jesus to inquire about eternal life, it is recorded that "Jesus, looking upon him, loved him." (Mark 10:21) Jesus told him to sell what he had to inherit eternal life, for He saw that the man was possessed by his possessions, rather than being in control of them. Later Jesus commented compassionately, "How hard it is for them that *trust* in riches to enter the kingdom." (Mark 10:24)

His interest in and contact with the financial world included calling a tax collector to be one of His apostles, appointing a treasurer among the apostles to handle their finances, and His paying taxes to the Roman government. Even his seamless robe was considered so valuable that Roman soldiers cast lots for it at the cross. It was a man of wealth, Joseph of Arimathea, who begged for Jesus' body from Pilate and who buried it in his own tomb. Even after the Resurrection, Jesus showed an interest in the prosperity of His followers, instructing the fishermen where to fish successfully, after they had previously failed to catch anything.

WHY POVERTY IS NOT SPIRITUAL

You may wonder why there has been so much talk of sacrifice, persecution and hard times as necessary phases of the spiritual way of life. History reveals that the inspired yet practical teachings of the Bible continued to be observed during the early centuries after Christ. But soon religion became more secularized, leading to variations and departures from Jesus' original teachings. Later, the feudal systems during the Middle Ages assured wealth only for the privileged few. During this period, the teachings of "poverty and penance" were offered to the masses as the only way to salvation, in order to keep people in poverty, and to make lack and privation a supposed "Christian virtue." Unsuspecting millions were led to believe that it was "pious to be poor," a belief which was useful in forestalling revolution among the masses. Some of those old feudal ideas about poverty as a spiritual virtue have persisted until today, but they are false, man-made ideas and not God's rich Truth for you and me.

Thus, make no further excuses to yourself or others for wanting to be prosperous. It is a divine desire that should be given divine expression. You can boldly give thanks that prosperity is your divine heritage; that the Father's desire for you is unlimited good, not merely the means of a meager existence.

RIGHT ATTITUDES WILL PAY YOUR BILLS

Now, in order to help you establish the all-important prosperous attitude, that God is the Source of man's supply as the Creator of this rich universe, and that God's will for you is therefore the wealth of the universe, I suggest that you paraphrase the words of Jehovah to Moses: "I will remember Jehovah God, for He it is that giveth me power to experience wealth." (Deuteronomy 8:18)

Perhaps you are thinking, "Yes, but is this kind of thinking practical? Can such attitudes actually help put shoes on the baby, food on the table and pay the rent?" Yes it can!

I once talked with a young woman who seemed to have everything against her. When stricken with paralysis, her drinking, gambling, non-working husband deserted her, leaving several children to support and educate. Though she had a roof over her head, it was mortgaged. Though her husband was required by court order to provide a small monthly allowance for support of the children, it was insufficient to meet their needs. However, each time that I visited this woman, who for many months was bedridden and later confined to a wheel chair, she always joyously reported new channels of supply which had opened to her.

On one visit, she stated that she had been given enough canned food to last several months; and money had appeared as needed for clothes for her children from some relatives in a distant state; that her own medical expenses were being met by a friend who was overseas; that, indeed, every financial need was being met. Fresh paint had even arrived for the outside of the house and a neighbor was busily repainting it!

When I asked what her prosperity secret was and how she had been able to meet every bill on time, while she was in a wheel chair with no ample or steady income, she said that one prayer had been her great source of strength and supply: Whenever a financial need was near, she would quietly meditate over and over upon this promise from the 46th Psalm: "Be still, and know that I am God." (Psalms 46:10)

One day the mortgage payment was due on the house in the amount of $40. She had not a cent of the money, so she quietly began to think on these words: "BE STILL, AND KNOW THAT I AM GOD. BE STILL, AND KNOW THAT I AM GOD AT WORK IN THIS SITUATION NOW." Around noon she got a sense of peace about the situation and so completed her meditation period. About an hour later, as she was being served lunch by a relative, in walked a neighbor who placed some money in her hand. He said, "Our Sunday School class got to thinking about you. There was some extra money in the treasury and we decided we would like to share it with you." The amount he handed her was $40.

This woman, recognizing God as the Source of her supply, has proved that this Source will never fail her, even under extreme conditions of ill health, marital disappointment and financial uncertainty. Of course, her great desire is to become self-supporting and financially independent of gifts from relatives, neighbors and friends. Surely she will realize this desire as she perseveres in prosperous thinking. She is now beginning to walk again for the first time in several years and will soon be able to work, too. Meanwhile, she is proving that God's rich supply can come in many unforeseen ways to meet the needs of the moment, regardless of life's hard conditions.

The Psalmist was recognizing God as the Source of his supply when he declared, "The Lord is my shepherd, I shall not want." (Psalms 23:1) It is a good prosperity prayer to declare often. A housewife needed $100 to cover two bills that were due by the end of the week. Early that week, whenever fear tried to creep in as to how she would pay those bills, she declared over and over, "THE LORD IS MY SHEPHERD, I SHALL NOT WANT." On Friday morning, the day the bills were due, a check arrived in the mail for $110! It was from a company her husband had worked for several years previously. They wrote a letter saying that they had just "found" in her husband's account that this amount was still due him; and that they were enclosing it to clear his records with them.

A businessman with a large family was getting toward the end of the month financially, and it was still a week until payday. The groceries were running low. On Friday, before Saturday morning grocery shopping time, he and his wife agreed to look to God for their supply and to affirm guidance. They did so by constantly affirming, "OUR SUFFICIENCY IS FROM GOD." (II Corinthians 3:5) Saturday morning a check arrived from the State revenue department: an income tax refund in the amount of $150! The amount covered their needs nicely until payday.

A saleswoman who had had a lot of financial expense and whose sales had fallen off decided to look to God as the Source of her supply by affirming over and over from the Lord's Prayer. "GIVE ME THIS DAY MY DAILY BREAD." It was like a landslide. Her sales picked up tremendously so that the commission checks started coming in again, plus her salary. Neighbors brought her prepared dishes of food as a token of their esteem for her. She was given several lovely items of new clothing by a friend. Some of her customers brought her gifts in appreciation for her loving service to them. A number of dinner invitations were enjoyed. Daily her needs were supplied, as she had prayed they would be. Her daily bread appeared in many satisfying forms.

HOW TO STABILIZE YOUR FINANCES

Of course, the wonderful thing about recognizing God as the Source of all riches, and taking Him into your financial affairs and into every department of your life, is that the more you do so, the more stabilized every phase of your life becomes. In due time, there are no stringent financial emergencies to be dramatically met with instant manna from heaven. Instead, things just get better and better financially, so that there is always substance on hand to meet your needs.

The Psalmist pointed out what happens when you consistently think of God as the Source of your supply: "But his delight is in the law of Jehovah. And on his law doth he meditate day and night. And he shall be like a tree planted by the streams of water, that bringeth forth its fruit in its season, whose leaf also doth not wither; and whatsoever he doeth shall prosper." (Psalms 1:2, 3)

But it is good to know that, until you develop a proper understanding to bring forth the substance of the universe in an abundant, unbroken stream of supply, the financial needs of the moment can be met by looking to the Source of all riches, a rich, Heavenly Father.

THE LINK BETWEEN THOUGHT AND SUPPLY

Perhaps you are thinking, "If my prosperity comes basically from God; if He is the Source of my supply, then why all the talk about 'prosperous thinking'? What does prosperous thinking have to do with my supply?"

God's rich supply is all around you universally, as well as innately within you, as talents and abilities and ideas longing for expression. But that rich supply and substance must be contacted and used. Your mind is your connecting link with it. Your attitudes, your mental concepts, beliefs, and outlook are your connecting links with God's rich substance and your access to it. God can only do *for* you what He can do *through* you, by means of your thoughts and ideas which lead to your reactions. Thus, prosperous thinking opens the way to prosperous results.

Begin making contact with the rich, universal substance around you and with the rich substance within you by declaring often: "I STIR UP THE GIFTS OF GOD

WITHIN ME AND AROUND ME, AND I AM BLESSED ON EVERY HAND WITH HAPPINESS, SUCCESS AND TRUE ACHIEVEMENT." Just by declaring this idea, you will begin stirring up the riches of the universe, attracting them to you and expressing them through you.

SUCCESS ADORES THE PROSPEROUS ATTITUDE

Another of the shocking truths about prosperity is that thoughts of your mind have made you what you are, and thoughts of your mind will make you whatever you become from this day forward. The more you realize this, the more you will come to know that people, places, conditions and events cannot keep your God-given prosperity and success from you, once you decide to deliberately employ prosperous thinking as your ally for success. Indeed, you will discover that the things, people and events that have previously worked against you will either begin to work for and with you, or they will fade out of your life, and new people and events will appear to help you succeed. That is the power of prosperous thinking.

Meanwhile, remind yourself often that God is the Source of all your supply and then make spiritual contact with Him, His rich substance and rich ideas that await your appropriation: "I AM THE RICH CHILD OF A LOVING FATHER. I NOW ACCEPT AND CLAIM HIS RICH GOOD FOR ME IN EVERY PHASE OF MY LIFE. MY OWN GOD-GIVEN SUCCESS IN THE FORM OF RICH IDEAS AND RICH RESULTS NOW APPEARS!"

Remind yourself often of these shocking truths about prosperity: That it is shockingly right instead of shockingly wrong to be prosperous. That God created a rich universe for you and wants you to enjoy it. That prosperity can come quickly through your deliberate use of prosperous thinking, which leads to the expression of rich ideas, rich actions and rich results. Thus, dare to ask a friendly, interested, rich, loving Father for guidance often. And with Moses, *remember Jehovah God, for He it is that giveth thee power to get wealth.*

Now launch forth happily and expectantly into the dynamic laws of prosperity — the spiritual and mental laws which can and will transform your life. Solomon realized the need for exploring them when he explained, "Poverty and shame shall be to him that refuseth instruction." (Proverbs 13:18) You can, from this page forward, begin freeing yourself of limitation, lack and failure. As you accept and use the simple but powerful ideas given in this chapter and in the pages to come, you will find it a pleasant experience that produces satisfying results.

That is the power of prosperous thinking and *that* is the shockingly nice truth about it.

THE BASIC LAW
OF PROSPERITY

— Chapter 2 —

I learned the basic law of prosperity the hard way. I have been earning the right to tell you about it for a long time. Several decades ago, life looked hopeless for me. Widowed and with an infant son, I had no training for any type of work and, therefore, no means of income. My family during that period was not able to offer much financial assistance. If you could have seen me then, you would doubtless have said, "Prosperous thinking or no prosperous thinking, there goes a hopeless case."

It was during this miserable period that I learned about the power of our thinking as an instrument for success or failure. It soon became plain to me that my previous failures were due largely to my previous failure thinking; but that same power of thought, when rightly directed, could be the key to healthy, happy, successful living.

What a realization it was on the day I read the words of Solomon, "As a man thinketh within himself, so is he." (Proverbs 23:7) And later the words of Job: "Thou shalt decree a thing and it shall be established unto thee and light shall shine upon thy way." (Job 22:28) From the philosopher, James Allen, I learned:

> Through his thoughts, man holds the key to every situation and contains within himself that transforming and regenerative agency by which he may make himself what he wills.[1]

I then excitedly surmised that my potential wealth, health and happiness were actually *within* me, waiting to be radiated outward into my world as healthy, wealthy, happy thoughts, feelings, expectations and decrees, which in turn would attract like results into my life.

As soon as I grasped this simple but all-powerful success secret and began applying it, the tide changed and my ships began to come in!

The way soon opened for me to literally work my way through business school. I then became secretary to a young lawyer who became mayor of our town, a candidate for Congress, and who later expanded his law firm to include several attorneys and secretaries who served a number of prosperous clients. At the height of my work with this attorney, I felt led to go into the ministry so that I might help others to realize and apply the spiritual and mental keys to healthy,

---

1. James Allen, *As a Man Thinketh* (Marina del Rey, CA: DeVorss & Co.).

happy, prosperous living that had meant so much to me.

Upon thinking back, I now realize that consciously and unconsciously I invoked the basic prosperity law of radiation and attraction every step of the way. It is because of my own personal use of this basic law that I feel so strongly about it, and emphatically believe that it can work for you in even greater ways than it has for me! A number of people who have attended my prosperity lectures have used it with astounding success.

THE LAW OF LAWS

Truly the laws that govern prosperity are just as sure and workable as the laws that govern mathematics, music, physics, and the other sciences. The Bible describes that basic law of prosperity when it speaks of sowing and reaping, or giving and receiving. The scientists describe it as action and reaction. By some it has been termed the law of supply and demand. Emerson described it as the law of compensation, whereby like attracts like. He declared that the law of compensation is the "law of laws!"

YOU CANNOT GET SOMETHING FOR NOTHING

I agree with Emerson that it is time the law of compensation was emphasized as life's basic law. I like to think of this basic law of prosperity as radiation and attraction: that what you radiate outward in your thoughts, feelings, mental pictures and words, you attract into your life and affairs. But you cannot get something for nothing.

The reason why there is still poverty in this universe of lavish abundance is that many people still do not understand this basic law of life; they do not yet realize that they must radiate in order to attract, and that what they do radiate they constantly attract. Most people today still have to learn that they cannot get something for nothing, but must give before receiving or must sow before reaping. When they do not give or sow in terms of prosperity, they make no contact with God's lavish abundance, and so there is no channel formed through which the rich, unlimited substance of the universe can pour forth its riches to them.

The truth of this was recently brought to my attention when I had contact with some people in a poverty-stricken area. I soon discovered that these people only wanted a "hand-out." They were not interested in invoking the basic law of prosperity by giving or sowing first. Instead, they were trying to get something for nothing, which simply cannot be done. Thus, they continued to live in poverty.

YOU CAN ALWAYS GIVE SOMETHING

Perhaps you are thinking, "What could such a person give when he seems so in lack?" There is *always* something a person can give, either tangibly or intangibly, that will put him in touch with God's rich supply. A widow with a house full of children once telephoned a counselor. She had no money or food for her children. It was lunch time and her children had not eaten since the day before. She was desperate. The counselor who took the call knew well what it was like to find oneself in such a predicament. The power of prosperous thinking

had literally supplied "manna from heaven" at a financially desperate period in her own life. With great
compassion she explained the magic power of giving in
some way, which would start the substance flowing back
in appropriate form.

Of course, when she explained that the widow must
give in order to receive, the widow's first reaction was
much the same that yours or mine might be the first
time we were told we must give to receive. She lamented,
"But that's just it—I have nothing to give." To which
the counselor gently replied, "My dear, of course you
have something to give. We always have something to
give. Indeed, we always have more to give than we at
first realize." She then urged this frantic widow to look
about her and to ask for divine guidance concerning
what she could give.

The widow was assured that this counselor would be
praying with her in the faith that she would be divinely
led as to how to give and how to receive thereafter. The
counselor also told her that, after starting the flow of
substance by giving, she was then to get ready to receive
by preparing her table for that meal she so wished for
her children; and by preparing her grocery list with
which to shop, in the assurance that the money would
manifest very soon for those groceries.

In faith the widow sat down and prayerfully asked
what she had that she could give. Suddenly she
remembered flowers growing in her yard, which she
happily cut and gave to a sick neighbor who was overjoyed to receive them. Next she set her table with the
best china, silver and linens in the house. This caused
pleasure and excitement among her children, who
then expectantly awaited a good meal. Just as she was
completing her grocery list someone who had been owing her money for a long time, dropped by and paid

her $30 on her debt! Thirty dollars which she had long
since given up ever getting back.

If I could shout only one message to the whole world
regarding life's secrets, it would be this: *You cannot
get something for nothing, but you can have the best
of everything when you give full measure for the good
you wish to receive.* Since I have been writing about
prosperity, I have received a number of letters from
people who do not yet understand this law and who are
still trying to get something for nothing. One woman
asked that $30,000 be sent to her immediately to pay
off old debts. She didn't write once or twice, but three
times before she was convinced she must use this basic
law of prosperity and bring in her own supply.

RADIATE AND YOU WILL ATTRACT

Emerson might have been describing this law of giving and receiving or radiation and attraction when he
wrote, "Great hearts send forth steadily the secret
forces that incessantly draw great events." And who
are the "great hearts"? Those people who dare to think
and radiate great thoughts and expectancies of success
and prosperity instead of failure, trouble and limitation. There's nothing great, unusual, or praisewor-
thy about failure, trouble and limitation. Anyone can
experience those things by following the line of
least resistance and by entertaining the usual failure
thoughts that one constantly hears every day.

How often one hears the complaint, "Everything
happens to me. I just can't win for losing. This is a
tough world. The other fellow gets the breaks." This
beginning usually leads into a conversation filled with

unpleasant experiences of the day, criticism of jobs, co-workers, families, the governments, world leaders, war, crime, disease and hard times, hard times, hard times.

Each of us constantly uses the law of radiation and attraction whether we are aware of it or not. But if you wish to enjoy more prosperity and success in life, you have to consciously, boldly and deliberately take hold of your thoughts and feelings and redirect them toward prosperity and success. It is up to you to dare to choose and radiate outward through your thinking what you really wish to experience in life, rather than to get bogged down in unpleasant or failure experiences of the moment. These conditions can change as quickly as you can change your thinking about them.

A friend in the public relations business recently used the law of radiation and attraction with successful results. For some time he had desired a certain out-of-state account and had made every reasonable effort to obtain it. Finally, he decided that he would definitely entertain and mentally radiate the desire for that account strongly, deliberately and boldly; feeling that surely in due time he would receive that account or a bigger one.

He sat down and quietly thought about that account as though he were already handling it. He went over that account in his mind and thought of all the ways he would attempt to serve that client's best interests if he were handling their public relations. He thought about the account and the people involved for a long time and in great detail. He also declared over and over for a time: "I AM NOT DISCOURAGED. I AM PERSISTENT. I GO FORWARD. I AM DETERMINED TO ACHIEVE SUCCESS IN GOD'S OWN WONDERFUL WAY FOR ME." When a sense of peace came over him, he dismissed the matter from his mind.

A few weeks later he attended a convention in which a number of his clients were involved. While swimming with several of them in a motel pool, he met the man whom he had been trying for months to meet who had charge of that out-of-state account. Right there in the pool they negotiated! When he joyously related his experience to me he declared, "It was doubtless that prosperity law of radiation and attraction that brought the happy results."

I have observed in talking with hundreds of people who have gone from failure to success that it is what we really think deep within ourselves most of the time, rather than the "big front" we may put up to others, that unconsciously attracts like results to us. There is an age-old maxim that says, "We are where we are because we are what we are, and we are what we are because of our habitual thinking."

Many people work hard to attract greater good in superficial ways without first habitually radiating its mental equivalent, and then they are sorely disappointed when their great efforts result in failure and disappointment. Once when I was talking with a lady who felt she would like to be married, I suggested that she invoke the law of radiation and attraction. After explaining that she must radiate before she could attract, I suggested that she prayerfully radiate these ideas over and over: "DIVINE LOVE EXPRESSING THROUGH ME NOW DRAWS TO ME ALL THAT IS NEEDED TO MAKE ME HAPPY AND MY LIFE COMPLETE."

A little later I began receiving reports from mutual friends that she was working hard on the attracting angle, but was radiating nothing more than telephone calls and obvious invitations to all the men of her acquaintance. Later she returned and reported that the suggested prayer method had not worked. Gently I reminded her that she had not radiated the "prayer method" suggested, but had radiated the "scare method," which had not been suggested. The method had worked in reverse, because she had reversed the process.

A middle-aged widow more recently dared to try the radiation and attraction method for the same purpose. While floating in a swimming pool she silently affirmed over and over: "DIVINE LOVE EXPRESSING THROUGH ME NOW DRAWS TO ME ALL THAT IS NEEDED TO MAKE ME HAPPY AND MY LIFE COMPLETE." Presently she heard a man's voice calling to her from the side of the pool, inquiring about the water which she assured him was wonderful. Soon he was in the water and a little later he was in her life as her husband.

MENTAL PREPARATION COMES FIRST

What a thrill it is to realize that all things can be accomplished within the mind first; that your mind is your divine power for good! The reason all things can be accomplished mentally first is that the mind is the connecting link between the formed and unformed world.

It's up to you in this wonderful age to claim your spiritual dominion of great good over everything, and to dare to subdue, change or reform your world as you wish! Of course, you have been given all of this power to produce good and only good. Man's difficulties come when he uses this power in reverse.

But what a sense of freedom it gives you to realize that whatever you center your attention upon steadily, constantly and deliberately in your thoughts, feelings and expectancies, forms the experiences of your life. When you realize this, life becomes easier, simpler and more richly satisfying. You then no longer feel that you have to argue, beg, reason, plead, or appeal to anyone for your desired good. Instead, you quietly go to work in your thinking to mentally choose, mentally accept and mentally radiate what you wish to experience in life. It gives you a victorous feeling even before the rich results begin to pour in.

BE DELIBERATE ABOUT WEALTH

You've got to radiate deliberately in order to attract the good you desire; otherwise, you get into a limited trend of thought and produce limited results. What you do radiate or deliberately entertain mentally, you constantly attract. It may not appear that this law works in this exact way when you look at people who seem to be succeeding who apparently do not deserve it; but in due season their health, wealth and happiness crumble if they are not supported by a firm foundation of right thought and feeling. It is just a matter of the mills of the gods grinding slowly. Instead of fretting about whether the law of radiation and attraction is working rightly in the lives of others, proceed quietly to prove the laws of prosperous thinking for yourself.

A stockbroker whose business associates were watching the market reports and declaring how slow things were, slipped into a private office and quietly relaxed. As he did so, he began to radiate this thought: "EVERYTHING AND EVERYBODY PROSPERS ME NOW." Suddenly, the telephone began to ring and ring. Within a short time he had received more business by telephone than he had received through any channel in several days.

A watch repairman's business was slow. As he boarded an early morning bus, he, too, remembered the prosperity law of radiation and attraction and began to silently declare: "EVERYTHING AND EVERYBODY PROSPERS ME NOW." For the next few days he had many new customers come into his store to have watches and jewelry repaired. Soon he had received enough repair work to keep him busy for many weeks.

YOU ARE MAGNETIC

Each of us is a magnet! And as a magnet, you do not have to force success and prosperity to yourself. Instead, you can develop that exalted, expectant, prosperous state of mind that is a magnet for all good things of the universe to hasten to you, rather than entertaining the tense, critical, anxious, depressed, unforgiving, possessive state of mind that is a magnet for all kinds of trouble and failure.

Since you can have the tangible and intangible equivalent of whatever you dare to choose, mentally entertain and radiate, stop thinking of things as apart from or outside yourself. Stop thinking that people, things, circumstances and conditions have power to hurt or harm you. Start realizing that nothing can stand between you and that good that you dare to choose mentally and radiate outward through your thoughts, feelings, words and expectancies.

Choose and radiate mentally; choose and radiate emotionally; choose and radiate constantly and persistently to attract your own good and good for others.

A woman once told me that since she had been deliberately invoking the power of prosperous thinking, everyone in her family had received wonderful blessings: Her husband received several raises in pay; her brother became president of his company; two sisters retired with handsome incomes; another sister became the first woman ever to hold a certain type of executive position for her company; another brother received a managerial position. A little leaven actually leavened the whole loaf in that family.

OUTER STEPS WILL COME EASILY

Of course, I do not mean to imply through all these people's experiences that you simply entertain and radiate the mental equivalent of the good desired, and then do nothing more. Often you have to take definite external steps as well. But you will discover that, by working out the mental concept of the desired good first, the outer steps will then unfold easily—almost automatically at times—without strained effort on your part. The more you turn your mind in rich directions, the less you seem to have to exert undue human effort to produce results. Work you will, but it will be work as satisfying self-expression rather than work just to survive. Your rich mind power and radiations seem to have a way of going forth and producing right opportunities, events and circumstances for prosperity and success, so that you almost seem to walk into them without conscious effort.

RELEASE YOUR PENT-UP SUBSTANCE

We are all filled with pent-up substance, energy and divine ability which wishes to work for us, through us and around about us. Psychologists declare that the average person uses only about 10 percent of his mind power. Medical authorities claim that the average person uses only about 25 percent of his physical power. Psychologists further state that man can release more result-getting power in one hour of concentrated use of his mind than in 24 hours of physical work; some psychologists even believe that man can release more result-getting power through one hour of concentrated thought than through a month of physical work.

Surely there is great power within and around each of us for our use. You can release this pent-up substance, energy and power within you for prosperous living through releasing deliberate thoughts, feelings and mental pictures of success, prosperity and riches. As you do so, your rich thoughts, feelings and mental pictures are radiated outward into the rich, powerful ethers of this universe, where they make contact with the rich, universal substance. This rich, universal substance is filled with divine intelligence and power that then moves among and works through people, conditions and opportunities to attract that which corresponds with the rich radiations that you have sent forth, and the prosperous results then appear. Indeed, this wonderful universe is rich and friendly to everyone. It wishes all mankind to be prosperous, well, and happy, and for the affairs of man and the world to be in divine order.

At this point, however, don't be too concerned about

the theory of radiation and attraction. Just begin accepting it and using it as a prosperity secret. All of the prosperity laws stated throughout this book are but various ways of invoking this basic law of radiation and attraction. You will find your use of them a delightful, exciting, fascinating and richly rewarding process!

I now invite you to begin soaring forth through the pages of this book, reminding yourself of these truths:

"I AM AN IRRESISTIBLE MAGNET, WITH THE POWER TO ATTRACT UNTO MYSELF EVERYTHING THAT I DIVINELY DESIRE, ACCORDING TO THE THOUGHTS, FEELINGS AND MENTAL PICTURES I CONSTANTLY ENTERTAIN AND RADIATE. I AM THE CENTER OF MY UNIVERSE! I HAVE THE POWER TO CREATE WHATEVER I WISH. I ATTRACT WHATEVER I RADIATE. I ATTRACT WHATEVER I MENTALLY CHOOSE AND ACCEPT. I BEGIN CHOOSING AND MENTALLY ACCEPTING THE HIGHEST AND BEST IN LIFE. I NOW CHOOSE AND ACCEPT HEALTH, SUCCESS AND HAPPINESS. I NOW CHOOSE LAVISH ABUNDANCE FOR MYSELF AND FOR ALL MANKIND. THIS IS A RICH, FRIENDLY UNIVERSE AND I DARE TO ACCEPT ITS RICHES, ITS HOSPITALITY, AND TO ENJOY THEM NOW!"

THE VACUUM LAW OF PROSPERITY

— Chapter 3 —

You have heard it said that Nature abhors a vacuum. It is particularly true in the realm of prosperity. The vacuum law of prosperity is one of the most powerful, though it takes bold, daring faith to set it into operation, as well as a sense of adventure and expectation to reap its full benefits. When a person is honestly trying to be prosperous, is thinking along prosperous lines and still fails, it is usually because he needs to invoke the vacuum law of prosperity.

Basically, the vacuum law of prosperity is this: if you want greater good, greater prosperity in your life, start forming a vacuum to receive it! In other words, *get rid of what you don't want to make room for what you do want.* If there are clothes in the closet or furniture in your home or office that no longer seem right for you;

41

if there are people among your acquaintances and friends that no longer seem congenial—begin moving the tangibles and intangibles out of your life, in the faith that you can have what you really want and desire. Often it is difficult to know what you do want until you get rid of what you do not want.

LET GO OF THE LESSER

Inevitably, in your life experiences you will find that, when the good you wish has not appeared, it is usually because you need to release and let go of something to make room for it. New substances do not flow easily into a cluttered situation.

If you want greater good in your life, what are you letting go of or getting rid of to make room for it? Nature does abhor a vacuum, and when you begin moving out of your life what you do not want, you automatically are making way for what you do want. By letting go of the lesser, you automatically make room for your greater good to come in.

Recently a couple used this vacuum law of prosperity in furnishing their new home. From their former home they brought only the furniture they really liked and felt appropriate for the new atmosphere. They fearlessly gave away a great deal of their old furniture and simply left bare spaces in their new home, visualizing those spaces filled with the kind of furniture they definitely wanted. For a while, nothing seemed to happen, but they remained steadfast to their vision of beautiful, appropriate new furniture.

Then one day the husband, who works for a large company, was placed on a merit point system. As he produced certain prosperous results for his company, his points of merit increased; these points could be applied toward a number of tangible rewards, one of which was furniture.

A businessman had been trying for a number of months to sell his home because he was being transferred to another state. He heard about the vacuum law of prosperity and realized that though he had earnestly desired to sell his home for a number of months, he had done nothing to form a vacuum of any kind through which his desired good could begin manifesting. So he sat down quietly in his study one day and mentally pictured each room of the house as empty, just as it would look after the house had been sold and he had moved out. He visualized a vacuum of emptiness everywhere. He then made notes concerning the furniture mover he desired to handle the moving and mentally worked out all the detailed plans of the move, just as though the house was already sold. Within a few days a buyer appeared who liked everything about the house and gave him a check for the thousands of dollars equity, as well as for the downpayment involved.

FORM A VACUUM FOR HEALTH

Whenever you dare to form a vacuum, the substance of the universe then rushes in to fill that empty space. This applies on the spiritual, mental and physical planes of life.

A businessman got very sick and for weeks was under his physician's care. Every possible thing was done for him medically by his doctor, a very fine physician. But it all seemed to no avail; this man just got weaker and weaker. His body was filled with poison and nothing seemed to dissolve it. Finally, one night, while suffering from a high fever and deep cough, this man remembered the vacuum law and realized that there must be something he needed to release. Since he knew what a powerful effect the mind and emotions have on the body, perhaps there was some mental attitude or emotional feeling that he needed to let go.

He became very quiet and silently asked Divine Intelligence to reveal to him what he needed to release. Suddenly he thought of a person against whom he had been holding a strong grudge. He had said a number of unkind things about this person and had gone to great lengths to hurt him. He mentally reviewed the events between them that had caused the grudge and his later desire to hurt that person. As he honestly thought about it, he realized that the other person may not have known that his feelings had been hurt from the events that took place; and that perhaps there was no reason for him to hold a grudge at all. (There never is!)

As he lay in bed with a high fever, he began to declare over and over: "I FULLY AND FREELY FORGIVE YOU. I LOOSE YOU AND LET YOU GO. SO FAR AS I AM CONCERNED, THAT INCIDENT BETWEEN US IS FINISHED FOREVER. I DO NOT WISH TO HURT YOU. I WISH YOU NO HARM. I AM FREE AND YOU ARE FREE AND ALL IS AGAIN WELL BETWEEN US." In a little while a feeling of peace, quietness, and release came over him. For the first time in many nights he slept peacefully. The next morning his fever was gone, and his physician declared that the poison had miraculously left his system overnight. At long last he was on the road to recovery. Through forgiveness, this man had formed the vacuum needed so that new life could restore his body to health and his mind to peace.

FORGIVENESS IS THE ANSWER

Most folks are afraid of the word "forgive," thinking that it means they must do something unpleasant and dramatic; but the word simply means to "give for" — to let go of old ideas, feelings or conditions and to give something better in their place. The "giving-for" process forms a vacuum and makes way for new good to rush in.

I have discovered from talking with hundreds of people about their problems and from corresponding with hundreds more that, inevitably, when a stubborn problem does not yield, it is because there is a need for forgiveness. I have further discovered that if only one person connected with the problem will start the action of forgiveness, all concerned will respond, be blessed and the solution will come.

For instance, a very wealthy woman became involved in a legal tangle over some of her deceased husband's business property. It was all very embarrassing to her because the defendant in the court case whom she was suing was a former family friend. In great distress she attended a prayer group one night and poured out her plight to those present. To her dismay, however, the prayer group members did not become upset about her problem at all; nor did anyone seem particularly sympathetic. In fact, they completely surprised her by saying that her problem would be solved if she would forgive the man whom she was suing. Aghast, she replied, "Forgive him? I only wanted you to pray that I would win against him in this court case. He has done such terrible things!" But the prayer group stood firm. She left in disgust but returned the next week and was again assured that forgiveness could solve everything. For many days after that she began to consider seriously the power of forgiveness. One day as she was driving along in her car thinking of this former family friend with whom she was now at law, she cried out, "Lord, I humanly cannot forgive that man. But if You can, please forgive him *through* me." Suddenly a feeling of great peace came, and she then gave thanks for it and dismissed the matter from her mind.

A few days later this man came into town and went to see her lawyer. He asked her lawyer if he might pay her a personal visit. Hesitantly, the lawyer replied, "I suppose so, but it will do you no good. If you want to settle this case, you will have to deal with me as her attorney." The defendant replied, "Oh, I do not wish to visit this lady to talk about the court case. I wish to visit her simply because we were once friends and I always greatly admired her husband. I would just like to see her as in former times and talk of old times." And so in a friendly way he paid his call, during the course of which, the subject of the court case finally arose. They amicably agreed to settle the matter quietly out of court to the mutual satisfaction of all concerned. Thus, the power of letting go of fixed ideas, attitudes, and opinions makes way for more pleasant experiences.

A FORGIVENESS TECHNIQUE

Here is a forgiveness technique that can form a vacuum for whatever good your life seems to need just now: Sit for half an hour every day and mentally forgive everyone that you are out of harmony with, feel badly toward or are concerned about. If you have accused anyone of injustice, if you have discussed anyone unkindly, if you have criticized or gossiped about anyone, if you are legally involved with anyone, mentally ask their forgiveness. Subconsciously, they will respond. In like manner, if you have accused yourself of failure or mistakes, forgive yourself. Forgiveness can form the vacuum that will undam your prosperity and success. Mentally declare to others: "GOD'S FORGIVING LOVE HAS SET US FREE. DIVINE LOVE NOW PRODUCES PERFECT RESULTS AND ALL IS AGAIN WELL BETWEEN US. I BEHOLD YOU WITH THE EYES OF LOVE AND I GLORY IN YOUR SUCCESS, PROSPERITY AND COMPLETE GOOD." It is good to declare for yourself: "I AM FORGIVEN AND GOVERNED BY GOD'S LOVE ALONE AND ALL IS WELL."

I once talked with a lady who was having great difficulty in her marriage. Her husband was on the brink of losing a very fine job because of his drinking and instability. When I suggested that she let go of those ideas about her husband and form a vacuum for greater good to come to them by forgiveness, she self-righteously declared, "There is no reason for me to try forgiveness. There is nothing to forgive. I love my husband!"

But I suggested that some kind of vacuum obviously needed to be formed; that there was much about their situation that she would like to be free of; and that perhaps it was not her husband she needed to forgive, but that all of us need to practice forgiveness every day because of many negative, subconscious attitudes stored in our emotions of which we are not even consciously aware.

Rather reluctantly, she finally agreed to sit for half

an hour every day and practice forgiveness. Later, she declared in amazement that the names of people she had long forgotten came to her during those times, and that unpleasant or unhappy experiences of the past floated up in her memory. To all of these she declared words and thoughts of freedom, release and forgiveness, as well as for and concerning her husband's recent behavior. As she began to feel relieved and freed of a lot of old, half-buried, hostile emotions and attitudes, her husband's drinking ceased. He began to work very hard in his job again, and success came in such a big way that she was even able to stop working and provide a beautiful home for her husband, which had long been their desire. Thus, the power of forgiveness.

RELEASING IS MAGNETIC

Are you clinging to the thought of how some troublesome situation in your life can be made right, what shape and form the solution *should* take? Then release, loose, let go. Declare to the situation or personalities involved: "I RELEASE, LOOSE, LET GO AND LET GOD." Do not be fearful of letting go. Nothing can ever be lost through spiritual release. Instead, your own good and the good of all concerned is much freer to move into your life. Through release, your power of attracting good is greatly increased.

One word of caution here about attitudes toward the tangible things you release. I once felt led to go through my closet and give away most of the clothes therein to my sister. These clothes were perfectly good but I had tired of them, and no new clothes had recently appeared, so I felt that by passing them on, I was making way for the new clothes.

After mailing these clothes to her, I felt happy and expectant about the new clothes I was so sure would manifest. But for a number of weeks nothing happened. Finally I realized that I was still mentally hanging on to the clothes I had sent her, thinking, "If I had that dress or suit I sent Sis, I would wear it today."

It was then necessary for me to re-release what I thought I had already released. In my mind I went over every item I had sent her and declared to each individual piece of clothing mentally: "I FULLY AND FREELY RELEASE YOU. I COMPLETELY LOOSE YOU AND LET YOU GO. SO FAR AS I AM CONCERNED YOU HAVE SERVED YOUR PURPOSE IN MY WARDROBE AND I NO LONGER NEED YOU. YOU ARE NOW IN YOUR PERFECT PLACE." Thereafter, new and more beautiful clothes appeared very fast in my closet!

It was as though a "magnetic influence" had gone to work for me. A friend who knew nothing of my empty closet, quietly came to me and said, "I have some money I wish to share with you. When I prayed about what to do with this particular amount, the only thought that kept coming to me was that I should give it to you, perhaps for some clothes. You appear well-supplied with clothes, but the thought persisted and so here it is with my blessing."

That started the flow of substance which then came to me from here, there and everywhere. Some magazine articles I had written had not been accepted and so in a doubtful but hopeful mind I had revised them, weeks earlier, and re-submitted them. *Now* they were accepted and I was paid. Several people saw items while shopping and thought, "That looks like Catherine." They purchased them for me as gifts. In each instance, it was items of clothing I had been mentally imaging as hanging in that closet! One friend back home went on a shopping trip there. We had not corresponded in some time, so she had no conscious way of knowing about the empty closet. Nevertheless, packages arrived with gifts of clothing for me resulting from her shopping trip. She wrote later, "I just kept 'getting the feeling' you could use those various items, and somehow I could not resist getting them for you. I shall be very happy if you can use them."

I learned quite a lesson from this experience. None of this happened until I freely released the clothes I had sent my sister. A gift that is not freely released after being given is not a gift at all. If you cannot give freely, don't bother. But if you do give, be sure you graciously release what you have given. Otherwise, no good has been done; no vacuum has been formed.

USE THE SUBSTANCE AT HAND

Another way of invoking the vacuum law of prosperity is by using your present visible substance without withholding it, thereby making way for new prosperity to flow to you. However, you have to do this in a certain attitude of mind in order to produce rich results.

When there does not seem enough prosperity on hand to meet present needs or when you seem blocked in attaining greater prosperity, take control of the situation; take control in your thoughts and feelings. Rather than feeling helpless, defenseless, or sorry for yourself, declare to those financial appearances: "PEACE, BE STILL."

Take your wallet, checkbook or other tangible evidences of financial supply in your hands and declare concerning them: "YOU ARE EVEN NOW FILLED WITH THE RICH BOUNTY OF GOD WHO SUPPLIES MY EVERY NEED."

Then is the time to fearlessly and boldly use the substance they contain as far as it will go in the present situation. If there are bills to be paid, do not wait until "enough money" comes in to pay all of them, but go right ahead in faith and pay those you can. That is breaking the substance on hand and sending it forth, so that it can multiply.

LOOK UP! TOWARD PROSPERITY

Establishing and maintaining a prosperous attitude just as though your bounty were already completely visible is important at this point. This is not the time to talk lack, to withhold, or to practice stringent economy. Instead, this is the time to use up to the last of your financial assets — to the last penny, if necessary. If you withhold, talk about financial lack at this point, it will cost you double. Instead, look up mentally and give thanks for the substance you already have to send out. Then boldly send it forth with a rich flourish and a rich blessing. Joyously declare: "THIS IS THE BOUNTY OF GOD AND I SEND IT FORTH WITH WISDOM AND JOY." When you "look up," regardless of appearances to the the contrary, you are always provided for!

Perhaps the person who taught me the most about this phase of the vacuum law of prosperity is a quiet, unassuming housewife who constantly "looks up," boldly sending forth the money in her pocketbook with a rich flourish. Unfailingly, she is provided for in opulent ways.

Several years ago she became interested in beautifying the church in which I was then serving. Quietly, she came to me and suggested various improvements she would like to make, assuring me that she had "private funds" to do this. It was months later that I learned the "private funds" she had were her own grocery money, which she generously used for some lovely items for the church.

In that way she began to send forth with a rich flourish the money she had. As she continued to "look up," her every private need was met. New channels of supply opened to her and her husband in most unexpected ways, so that for the first time in her life she employed a maid, received gifts of a new car and a monthly allowance.

As for the church redecoration, it "snow-balled" and many rich gifts then came, all because one housewife dared to quietly "look up" and use the substance at hand boldly, fearlessly, richly—even if that substance was her own grocery money. It overwhelms me even now to realize what faith she has had in the vacuum law of prosperity, and what rich results she continues to experience. She has often said that she has had no financial need that has not been met, since she began forming a vacuum.

PUT YOUR BEST FOOT FORWARD

Another way to "look up" regardless of financial appearances, is to put your best foot forward. Wear your best clothes; look your best. Live as richly as possible on what you already have. I recall once needing new clothes for a conference I was required to attend, but there seemed no money on hand for new clothes. When I prayed about the matter, I got the feeling that I should begin wearing my very best clothes in order to help me feel rich. Every day for almost a week I wore my best dress, over and over. One day a gift of money was sent to me for some services I had rendered in the past. Of course, I immediately shopped for the desired new clothes.

When you have released, let go, and formed a vacuum for new prosperity, that is the time to do whatever you can to effect the rich feeling, the rich atmosphere, the rich look with your present substance. Mention the apparent lack or vacuum to no one. Speaking of economic lack and limitation keeps many people in the poorhouse financially. Never think of yourself as poor or needy. Do not talk about hard times or the necessity for strict economy. Do not think how little you have, but how much you have. This is the time to use your best china and silver, and to eat by candlelight, even if your menu consists of only "pork and beans."

As you form a vacuum and let go of what you do not want; as you use your present visible supply to meet the immediate needs as best you can, not withholding it; and as you live as richly as possible in the face of appearances—the rich results will begin to come forth. Almost mysteriously, new channels of supply will appear to meet your needs. You will discover other financial assets in your midst, of which you were previously unaware. Other people will unknowingly do things to add to your supply, too.

In quietness and confidence is your strength when there is a need for greater prosperity, if you dare to "look up," bless, and break the substance at hand in whatever ways seem best. Always ask for divine guidance concerning the practical as well as the spiritual ways in which you may form a vacuum for new prosperity when these financial needs loom over you.

Don't get panicky; this is just further opportunity for you to prove that the invisible laws of prosperity can produce visible, satisfying results. This is just your initiation in the power of prosperous thinking.

If you learn how to form a vacuum for new good early in your conscious development of prosperous thinking, then you do not panic at financial challenges, but know that you can and shall meet them victoriously and be much richer in the long run for having learned how to use the invisible laws of supply to meet visible needs.

Often when you are forming a vacuum by using what you have, you find that the amount on hand is sufficient; that too much is wasted or spoiled; and that that amount which at first seems small or even insufficient, becomes adequate as you use it fearlessly. It even seems to supply you during that period when no more substance immediately appears, if you continue to use it fearlessly, and in the faith that every need *is* being met.[1]

MAKE ROOM FOR YOUR GOOD

We all want better financial conditions and we should have them. Here is the way to obtain them: Do not talk about financial lack, but begin thinking in terms of the rich, universal abundance that is everywhere. Then learn to let go, to give up, to make room for the things you have prayed for, worked for and so strongly desire. As you give up and cast away old ideas

---

1. See Chapter 4, "How to Gather Your Prosperous Manna" in the Ponder book, *The Millionaire Moses.*

and attitudes, old possessions, and put in their place new ideas of prosperity and progressive achievement, your conditions will steadily improve. You always want something better than you now have. It is the urge of progress. Just as children outgrow their clothes, you outgrow former ideals, broadening your horizons of life as you advance.

There *must* be constant elimination of the old to keep pace with this growth. When you cling to the old, you hinder your advance or stop it altogether.

Why not dare to form a vacuum now, and invite that complete prosperity and success which you have so yearned to experience and which is divinely meant for you?

THE CREATIVE LAW OF PROSPERITY

Let us get down to business about prosperity. Now that you have formed a vacuum, you are ready to fill that vacuum with rich, new good through the creative law of prosperity. Actually, the creative law of prosperity concerns the three basic steps given in this chapter and the next two: (1) Having a plan, writing out one's desires concerning that plan, and constantly expanding it; (2) Mentally imaging that plan as fulfilled; (3) Constantly affirming its perfect fulfillment.

However, the first part of the creative law, as discussed in this chapter, is all important, because without a plan and notes concerning it, the other two steps are ineffective.

STRONG DESIRE IS SUCCESS POWER

The first step in the creative law of prosperity is desire, and the ability to do something constructive about that desire. Recently a businessman told me he has discovered in his work that when a customer comes to him greatly desiring certain products, he has found it best always to sell that customer what he really wants. This businessman said that even though he personally may feel that there are other products that would better serve his customer, if his customer has already made up his mind and strongly desires certain products, he never tries to change that desire, because desire is so impelling. He stated that strong desire denotes faith in the product, which almost inevitably brings satisfaction.

There is nothing weak or lukewarm about true desire. It is intense and powerful. If properly developed and expressed, a strong desire always carries with it the power for success. The stronger your desires for good, the greater the power of your desires to produce that good for you.

In counseling people who have had various problems, I have discovered that the right kind of desire will dissolve anything that has stood in the way of fulfillment. Right desire is truly the first step in solving problems and getting on the road to prosperity.

How can you release your deep-seated desires for prosperity and success? By centering your attention on one big goal at a time. One big goal always includes a number of small desires that are automatically fulfilled when the big one is achieved. Psychologists agree that we influence people and events by having great desires and great goals. It is as though everything and everybody subconsciously tunes in on our big desires and goals, and gets busy helping us to achieve them.

The amazing thing is that, of the millions of people who think they want to be successful, few of them have any really strong, impelling desires. They have been content to idly drift in a stream of small events and small expectations. When you meet a person who is really going places in this world, usually it is a person of intense desire for the highest and best in life. One of the basic statements I have often asked people to use to help expand and intensify their constructive desires is "I DESIRE THE HIGHEST AND BEST IN LIFE, AND I NOW DRAW THE HIGHEST AND BEST TO ME."

WRITE DOWN YOUR DESIRES

The law of creative prosperity is to take your deep-seated desires and, instead of suppressing them as impossible dreams, begin expressing them constructively by deciding what they really are, and then doing something very simple but very powerful about them: *Write them down!* Make a list or draw up some kind of potential plan, which you should feel free to change, revise, reform and rearrange as your ideas about it unfold. This idea of writing out your desires and formulating a plan *on paper* clarifies the desires in your mind, and the mind produces definite results only when it has been given definite ideas through which to work.

Many people work hard at prosperity in external ways, but they miss the mark because they are afraid to get definite in their thoughts and desires. They want

to live better and to have more money, but they never
get definite in their desires about *how* they want to live
better or *how much more money* they need. In fact,
many people hesitate to get definite, fearing that they
are telling God what to do. But as Dr. Emilie Cady
once wrote: "Desire is God tapping at the door of your
mind, trying to give you greater good."[1] If you suppress those deep desires, they have no constructive
outlet and often turn into destructive channels expressed as neurotic tendencies, phobias, tension, or
perhaps as suppression that finds outlet through
alcoholism, mental illness, dope addition, sexual im-
balance, or other negative actions.

The power of writing out one's desires and plans was
first proved to me by the attorney for whom I worked a
number of years ago. One day, just after he had been
defeated in a Congressional race, instead of feeling
sorry for himself, he immediately got busy formulating
a new plan. He stated his desire for larger law offices;
his desire for the expansion from a two-man firm to a
five-or six-man firm; and the desire to increase the annual income he wished the firm to attain year by year
for the next five years.

At that time, I did not know that this was one of the
most powerful methods for attaining success. It seemed
so simple! Nevertheless, I watched his scribbled plan
come to life and fruition. The law firm gradually expanded into a five-man arrangement in which each
attorney specialized in certain phases of legal practice.
The firm moved from two small offices into spacious
new quarters that occupied the entire floor of a modern,
new bank building.

---

1. Emilie Cady, *Lessons in Truth* (Unity Village, MO: Unity
Books, 1894).

"Nothing succeeds like success" was surely manifested for that attorney after he formulated a plan, dared to put it in writing, and started moving toward it.

PROSPERITY IS A PLANNED RESULT

A stockbroker's story further proves the power of formulating plans for prosperity and success. A few years ago, the president of a large corporation died. At the time of his death, this corporation was in financial difficulties. The vice-president, who had been considered outstanding in a financial way, then took the helm. Immediately the corporation began to prosper, and today its stock is one of the best on the market. Its sales records during recent years have superseded those of all of its well-known competitors. The prosperity secret? Well, it seems that this vice-president had *for years* worked on a plan he felt wise for the growth and prosperity of this corporation. The day he became president, he took that plan out of his desk drawer and began executing it. Today his corporation is no longer a mediocre one with indebtness pulling it down. Instead, it is one of the most prosperous in the country! *He proved that prosperity is a planned result.*

Prosperity is the result of deliberate thought and action. There is nothing hit-and-miss about prosperous living. It is a planned result, just as a bridge or building is a planned result. Without deliberate, prosperous plans, there will be no prosperous results on a consistent, permanent basis.

This law of creative prosperity was one that surely "clicked" with the students in my prosperity classes. Many of the business people who attended told me that this one idea turned their previous faltering efforts tQward prosperity into amazingly successful results. They had worked long and hard, but not in definite or specific ways. Then they discovered there was no reason to be afraid to ask for what they really desired. The Bible promises, "Ask and it shall be given; seek and ye shall find; knock and the door shall be opened." (Matthew 7:7)

Perhaps you are thinking that you do not really know what you want; that your desires are not that definite as yet. In that case, simply begin thinking about and even making lists of those things now in your life that you don't want there. List things you wish to have cleared up and eradicated from your life. To that list declare, "THIS TOO SHALL PASS" or "BE THOU DISSOLVED."

I know of a man in the electrical business who did this. His business partner had died months earlier, leaving his share of the business in the hands of uncooperative heirs who would neither buy nor sell. It was almost in desperation that the surviving partner began applying prosperous thinking. His main desire was either to buy the other half of the business or sell his half. He simply wanted to dissolve the deadlock which was costing the business money; and he wanted to eradicate the unpleasantness, confusion and uncertainty of his business situation. Within a month after he wrote out notes about the unpleasantness and uncertainty being dissolved, he received word from a lawyer that his partner's heirs would sell! They did so immediately with no further ado.

A PROSPERITY FORMULA

One group of business people that experimented with me on prosperous thinking during a recession did this:

They first wrote out their desires for six months hence, and then wrote out their desired achievements for each of the six months. Each week they added to their list or changed their list of desired results, as they felt led. In some instances, they changed the list completely, expanding their desires or crossing off desires that no longer appealed to them.

Then each week the class members brought these listed desires to class. No one ever saw these individual lists except the students to whom they belonged. We began each class period by privately taking our lists in hand and verbally declaring together:

"I AM THE RICH CHILD OF A LOVING FATHER. ALL THAT THE FATHER HAS IS MINE TO SHARE AND TO EXPERIENCE. DIVINE INTELLIGENCE IS NOW SHOWING ME HOW TO CLAIM MY OWN GOD-GIVEN WEALTH, HEALTH AND HAPPINESS. DIVINE INTELLIGENCE IS EVEN NOW OPENING THE WAY FOR MY IMMEDIATE BLESSINGS. I HAVE FAITH THAT ALL THAT IS MINE BY DIVINE RIGHT NOW COMES TO ME IN RICH ABUNDANCE. MY RICH BLESSINGS DO NOT INTERFERE WITH ANYONE ELSE'S GOOD, SINCE GOD'S RICH SUBSTANCE IS UN-LIMITED AND EVERYWHERE FOR ALL TO USE. THERE IS NO DELAY! THAT WHICH IS NOT FOR MY HIGHEST GOOD NOW FADES FROM ME AND I NO LONGER DESIRE IT. MY GOD-GIVEN DESIRES ARE RICHLY FULFILLED NOW IN GOD'S OWN WONDERFUL WAY."

The students were also instructed to spend at least 15 minutes a day pouring their verbal prayers and blessings (which we will talk about in Chapter 6) upon their listed desires, and to work daily on their lists, revising, changing, expanding them. They were asked to do very definite things, such as listing the amount of money they wished to make for the day, week or month. They were also asked to place a time limit and definite dates by which they wished the fulfillment of their desires. They were further instructed not to wonder, doubt or question how their rich good was to be fulfilled, but they were to stay busy putting the creative laws of prosperity into action in these simple ways.

The results they attained were fabulous, and I have received letters from people all over the world who read of this creative method of prosperity, and who tried it, with similar prosperous results! As the group worked with their lists, revising and changing them, we often affirmed the words of Goethe, "What you can do or dream you can, begin it. Boldness has genius, power and magic in it." We often declared, "WHAT WE CAN CONCEIVE, WE CAN ACHIEVE WITH THE HELP OF GOD." And we often reminded ourselves of this truth: Every obstacle rushes to get out of the way of the man who knows where he is going; and all the world seems on the side of the man who tries to rise.

There seems to be almost magical power in thinking of one's desires, expressing them constructively by writing them down, stating the time by which one wishes their fulfillment, and then praying that God's good will be done in the matter. Does it sound too simple to work? Great truths and powerful secrets often appear simple. So simple, in fact, that the average person overlooks them in trying to find a more difficult way.

WRITE A LETTER TO GOD

One businesswoman invoked the creative method of prosperity in a slightly different way. At the first of the year, instead of making a lot of New Year's resolutions, she wrote a letter to God in which she honestly listed all of her desires for the new year. She then placed the sealed letter in her Bible. Toward the end of the year, she showed me that letter, which had specifically listed many things. All of the big desires she had expressed had been fulfilled: She was widowed and had expressed a desire to marry happily again. Toward the end of the year, I performed a private wedding ceremony for her and the bridegroom, whom she had met through friends after writing out that desire. She also had stated in the letter her desire for a better home. The bridegroom gave it to her! Her other big desire had been for a better job. In the middle of the year that, too, had come forth as a pleasant, satisfying, higher-paying position.

But I must caution you: Be honest with yourself when you write out your desires. Express, as did this woman, your really deep feelings. Don't write out what somebody else wants for you, or what you think you *should* desire. Be honest with yourself and your Maker, if you really want happy results.

I know of another businesswoman who wrote a similar letter to God at the first of the year, but instead of writing out her deep and big desires, she listed in a lukewarm, half-hearted way some of her surface and smaller desires. The things really gnawing at her heart were not even mentioned. And nothing happened.

Because she had kept her really deep desires locked within her, there had been no opened channel through which God's substance could pour forth its rich good for her. A loving Father always wants you to have better than the best that you are now experiencing. Because "the kingdom of heaven is at hand," if you wish God's help in experiencing it, the least you can do is to be honest with Him and with yourself. Otherwise, you block any possibility of fulfillment.

Perhaps you are thinking, "Yes . . . but what if my desires are not of the highest? Should I still be honest and list them?" Certainly, because by being honest, you are releasing them instead of suppressing them; as you release and face them, a loving Father can help you readjust them for good.

I have seen this principle work successfully in the lives of people whom I have encountered in my counseling sessions, people who wanted spiritual help, but perhaps felt that their problem was embarrassing or shocking. They would speak of their lesser problems, but would keep the thing which was really bothering them locked tight within them. It was only when they got at the heart of their problems that the answer and divine solution could come forth.

MAKE A DAILY LIST

The creative method of writing out one's desires proved so effective for a friend who has a modeling school that she recorded on tape specific instructions about making lists, revising them daily, etc. She plays that tape as a part of her modeling school course of instruction. The result? Scores of her students have obtained jobs of their choice in fashion modeling as well as in television and radio work, after faithfully making specific lists of the work they desired, the pay they desired, the hours they wanted to work, and the working conditions they hoped for.

Another simple but effective way of invoking the creative law of prosperity is by beginning and ending your day making notes and lists. In the morning I always sit quietly for a few minutes, often with a cup of coffee, while I think of my day and the many big and little things I wish to see accomplished by myself and others. I make lists of those desired accomplishments. It takes only a few minutes, which is time well spent, because I then feel in control of my day. I usually write a note of thanks to God at the end of that list for the "divine fulfillment and the divine achievements." It is amazing how many things are taken care of for me, without my doing anything more than listing them and giving thanks for their divine fulfillment.

In like manner, at the end of the day I take another few minutes, go back over the day and write "thank you" notes to God for the blessings received and the good accomplished. Usually, I also begin thinking of the following day and make some notes concerning its perfect fulfillment. It seems to assure me of a peaceful mind and a restful night. I have found this practice of making morning and evening lists so satisfying and enlightening — because there are always more blessings to list than expected — that I now feel something is amiss if I do not observe this daily ritual. When I stick to my list-making things rarely go wrong in my day.

MANY PEOPLE USE THIS METHOD

In case this list-making technique is beginning to sound slightly trivial to you, let me assure you that it is a success technique used by a number of successful people — more than most of us realize because successful people rarely advertise their success secrets.

Two prominent engineers have confidentially shown me little books that they keep in an inside coat pocket, which they take out when things become hectic during their business day, and in which they quickly make notations of the way they wish things to work out. No one suspects what they are doing, and so in the midst of people all around them, they quickly gain control of the various problems that confront them.

Recently a mother asked her son, who is a young business executive, about a special course of instruction that he was currently studying with his company. He explained that he had been instructed to use a new psychological technique in solving his executive problems. This course had taught him that the proper modern method for solving problems was to sit down quietly, write out the problem, write out what he considered the highest and best solution, then tear up his notes and relax, knowing that his solution or something better would work out, since he had been able to work out a possible solution in his mind and on paper! This executive seemed quite surprised when his mother informed him she had been using that method for many months, having learned it at a study class.

A doctor's financial income was boosted considerably within a few weeks after he began to write out the financial sum that he wished his practice to bring in each week. Previously, he had tried thinking in terms of boosted monthly income, but the figures had seemed too large for him to accept mentally. When he brought it down to a weekly level, it seemed easier for his mind to accept the idea of the weekly increase, and so it quickly manifested.

I agree with the writer of the Book of Proverbs when he instructed us, "Let not kindness and truth forsake thee; bind them about thy neck; write them upon the tablet of thy heart; so shalt thou find favor and good understanding, in the sight of God and man." (Proverbs 3:3,4) When you are trying to find favor and good understanding in the sight of God and man, the writing-out technique is indeed powerful.

WRITE TO THEIR ANGEL

If you seek understanding regarding financial matters, it is good to secretly write out notes to those involved, seal those notes and place them in your Bible for the time being. The mystics used to teach that everyone has an "angel" or higher self, and that when we cannot reach that angel in the usual ways, we should secretly write to it. In fact, the mystics even went so far as to describe seven types of people with whom it is easier to deal satisfactorily, by writing their "angel," than by trying to reason with them in the usual ways.[2]

Perhaps you are thinking, "I am sure that is fine mysticism, but how practical is this angel-writing method?" Well, you should realize that anyone you are having difficulty with, you have not been able to reach in the usual ways. So what have you to lose by secretly trying to reach them through their higher self or "angel"?

A businessman was having difficulty closing a business matter which had long been pending. Everyone involved was quite congenial and wished to conclude this matter, except one man who kept changing his mind and who seemed quite unsure about everything.

2. See Chapters 5 and 6 of *The Prospering Power of Love* (Marina del Rey, CA; DeVorss & Co., 1984).

This man kept things unsettled. In desperation the businessman decided to try the angel-writing method. It seems that the man giving the trouble was timid, apprehensive, always fearful about something. The businessman secretly wrote out just the opposite: "To the angel of (let us say) John Brown, I bless you and give thanks that you are bringing to a perfect conclusion this business matter, and that all concerned are satisfied and blessed by it." This businessman wrote out this statement fifteen times, because he had learned that the ancients believed in using the number fifteen to break up and dissolve hard conditions. Within a few days this businessman telephoned me long distance to report that the person causing the difficulty had visited his office and had said, "Come down to my office tomorrow morning and the papers will be ready for signatures. This situation has been delayed too long, and I am anxious to conclude it." The transaction was quickly completed.

NOTE-WRITING GETS THE BILLS PAID

Another note-writing technique that is particularly helpful in getting the bills paid is this: When those bills begin to arrive in the mail, instead of silently resenting them, write on the envelopes, "I GIVE THANKS FOR YOUR IMMEDIATE AND COMPLETE PAYMENT. YOU ARE IMMEDIATELY AND COMPLETELY PAID THROUGH THE RICH AVENUES OF DIVINE SUBSTANCE." When the bills have already piled up, it is also good to make a list of those owed and the amount owing, and beside or beneath each one write out this same statement concerning their immediate payment.

A businessman once brought a file folder full of bills

and said, "How can I possibly use the power of prosperous thinking to get these paid? Some of them are several months old." We then sat for an hour or so, making a list of the amounts owed and to whom, listing first those owed the longest and those which were the most urgent. We then wrote out the above statement about their immediate payment. Since it seemed humanly impossible to pay all these bills immediately, we then made a second list, showing the ones that should be absolutely paid within the next week, along with the statement, "I GIVE THANKS THAT YOU ARE IMMEDIATELY AND COMPLETELY PAID BY_____" and listed the date a week hence.

Once a week this businessman came with this file folder of bills and we watched them get paid step-by-step. It took about two months to completely bring his financial affairs up-to-date. When he did, it was agreed that he would use this same technique at the first of each month to get current bills paid on time. This method seemed to help him gain control in his thinking about his financial affairs. Once he gained mental dominion, he was able to meet his financial obligations on time.

WOE UNTO THEM THAT WRITE ABOUT THEIR TROUBLES

It was Isaiah who advised us, "Woe unto them that decree unrighteous decrees, and to the writers that write perverseness." (Isaiah 10:1) This surely applies to one's financial affairs. A man I know was having business difficulties. At the start, they were not too urgent, and with a change of attitudes could doubtless have been solved easily. But not realizing this, in his worried state of mind, this man began writing about his difficulties in detail to a number of his friends. As he magnified the difficulty in his mind and in the minds of others, it literally multiplied in his affairs. After he began to apply prosperous thinking to the situation, it took him several months to clear it up. He found it necessary to stop talking about his troubles to others and to stop putting anything negative in writing. When he started reversing the process and secretly writing out how he wished his business affairs to be, his difficulties began to diminish for the first time in months.

In like manner, it is good in the face of adverse appearances to secretly write out each day how you wish your affairs might be, in contrast to how they appear. Not only does that help your mind to accept the improvement you desire; but it is as though your written-out desire goes out into the ethers and is subconsciously tuned in on and everyone concerned begins to cooperate and help. Again, it may seem a mystical method, but if it produces practical, helpful results for you, why not dare to be a modern mystic?

GAIN CONTROL OF YOUR PAST AND FUTURE

It is also good to gain control of the past or future by writing out statements concerning them. I found in counseling that many people still live in the past and regret past mistakes. The backward look keeps you from going forward and making present and future progress. Also, many fine people are afraid of the future. In either event, write out how you wish things might have been concerning some past mistake; or how you wish your life to be now and in the future.

When you write out notes about how you wish past events might have been that have proved disappointing, it seems to take the "sting" out of the memory of those events. I have known of several instances where those involved in past unhappy experiences would write, telephone or appear to say the incident no longer mattered, and that all were forgiven concerning it. In some instances, better relationships than ever were happily re-established between those who had experienced past bitter grievances and misunderstandings.

In like manner, if there is some future event that seems to threaten you, take control of it in your thinking by making lists concerning the way you wish it to be. Write out the names of all involved and write out definite statements of harmony, understanding and perfect results that you desire to see come forth. Since there is no time factor in the mental realm, your mind can project itself into a future experience and can prepare harmony and right results ahead of time, so that everything will move easily, quickly and successfully. The mind is man's wonderful servant, when he realizes this and trains his mind to work for him.

One of the most successful younger executives I have ever met told me that, while he was still in his teens, he wrote out a twelve-year plan of progress for himself, which has amazingly manifested for him. Although he is still under thirty, he is considered wealthy, and it has been predicted that he will surely become a millionaire within the next few years.

THIS METHOD IS ALL-POWERFUL!

The creative law of prosperity can be all-powerful for producing success and happiness concerning your past, your present and even your future. There are desires that all of us wish to see come into visible expression and to grow into fine results.

Why not quietly begin joining countless others in producing greater good in your life through these creative methods for prosperity? Begin now by first asking yourself just what it is that you honestly desire most in your life. Be specific, be definite, and sincere with yourself. Then write down your dominant desires. Thereafter, declare in privacy, without telling anyone what you are doing, the divine fulfillment of your desires. Declare: "I GIVE THANKS FOR THE IMMEDIATE, COMPLETE, DIVINE FULFILLMENT OF THESE DESIRES. THIS OR SOMETHING BETTER COMES FORTH WITH PERFECT TIMING, ACCORDING TO GOD'S RICH GOOD FOR ME." Then daily change and revise your lists as you feel led.

Spend at least fifteen minutes a day on your list. Dare to persist in this simple procedure and then get ready for a landslide of happy results. More than you have dreamed possible will come your way because God's friendly universe wishes you to be prospered and blessed.

Again I wish to remind you of the promise of Goethe, "What you can do or dream you can, begin it; boldness has genius, power and magic in it." Why not prove it now? As one prosperous thinker has often said to me, I find the results really begin to come forth only after I start toward them." The creative methods I have presented here are simple but provable ways of helping you "start toward" your good. After you do start toward your good, however, don't be surprised if it rushes forth to meet you more than halfway!

THE IMAGING LAW
OF PROSPERITY

— Chapter 5 —

Once you have made your lists and worked with them daily in changing, expanding and revising them, there is another step you are ready to take. At this point, the imaging power of the mind, which has an almost magical power, should be invoked to work for you.

We are told in this modern age by authorities who are making a study of the mind that man can create anything he can imagine; that the mental image does make the conditions and experiences of man's life and affairs; that man's only limitation lies in the negative use of imagination. In other words, if there is failure and lack in your life, it is because you first imagined it in your mind. You first set up life's limitations in your mind and it is likewise in mind that you can begin dissolving those limitations and re-making your life into what you wish it to be.

It was the French doctor Emile Coué who first declared that the imagination is a much stronger force than will power; and that when the imagination and will are in conflict, the imagination always wins out.

We have seen this proved in hypnosis. Often when a mental picture is first suggested, the will does not want to accept that picture. But when the mental picture is repeated sufficiently, the imagination has no choice but to accept it and to bring it to pass, no matter how unlikely the mental picture appears to the reasoning power of the will. As we study these various laws of prosperous thinking, we are not being hypnotized, however. Instead, we are being de-hypnotized from the ignorant, superstitious, limited beliefs of centuries of poverty thinking.

Since you are hoping for greater good in your life, you should begin to form the mental image of it in your mind. Your reasoning power may tell you that it can never be, but that doesn't matter. Your will may say your dream is too big to come true; that it is impossible to fulfill. But if you just dare to continue imaging it anyway, then your imagination will go to work for you to produce the visible result you have been imaging, and in due time your will can work for you also. Whatever the mind is taught to expect, that it will build, produce, and bring forth for you.

HISTORY PROVES THE POWER OF IMAGING

History has proved this many times. Perhaps you recall the facts connected with the Peloponnesian War of ancient Greece. This war was significant because it lasted for 27 years. You will probably remember why it is believed to have lasted so long. Historians say that both sides lacked purpose or strategy. They had no particular plan for victory and so they just drifted along indefinitely, never quite losing, yet never quite winning the war—just fighting.

Finally, a Spartan of foresight and ability, obviously a man who knew how to image victory and success, appeared on the scene, went into action and led his side to victory. Historians write that in one single hour he brought the long war to an end. And how did he do it? Was it through battle and bloodshed? Absolutely not. Instead, he led the enemy to believe that they had his ships and men cornered at the entrance of the Dardanelles. There he waited patiently for four days until the enemy became sure of themselves, thinking that his silence signified weakness and inability to fight. On the fifth day, when they sent most of their crew ashore to get food, Admiral Lysander suddenly came to life, sailed out and captured almost the entire fleet of 180 ships without a single blow.

Often we have been like those ancient Greeks. We had no plan or image of victory and so we just went along never quite winning, never quite losing in life— just fighting. It was in 500 B.C. that Sun Tze wrote, "In all fighting the direct method may be used for joining battle, but indirect methods will be needed in order to secure victory."

When you use the all-powerful imaging power of the mind to envision your good, you are using the indirect method that will secure the victory over life's problems for you. Instead of battling with poverty, failure and financial lack, which often only multiplies your problems, begin using the indirect method — that of quietly, deliberately and persistently imaging your good.

SUCCESS IS CREATED MENTALLY FIRST

In the Book of Genesis, we are told how Joseph proved the power of the imagination for success and prosperity. From him we learn what to do and what not to do with our imagination. In Joseph's dreams at the age of 17, he had dominion over the situations about which he dreamed. In one dream his brothers' sheaves were bowing down to Joseph's sheaf. In another dream, the sun, moon and stars were honoring Joseph. These dreams were symbolic of the dominion Joseph was to have later as prime minister of Egypt.

Joseph dreamed of dominion, and so must you. Joseph dreamed of dominion when he seemed to have none, and so must you. Success is created mentally first. But Joseph made the mistake of telling his dreams to his jealous brothers, who resented his claims of dominion, so they sold him for 20 pieces of silver to some Ishmaelite merchants on their way to Egypt. Unlike Joseph, you should not tell your dreams and mental images of greater good to others, who will only try to tear down your pictures of grandeur with their doubt and unbelief.

After Joseph was sold into Egyptian slavery, he apparently continued to image better than the best he was then experiencing. He proved that vision is victory; he also proved that the victim can become the victor! When he arrived in Egypt, he had to meet a number of unjust experiences before the tide turned

for him. Only after years in prison and many tribula-
tions did Joseph become prime minister of all Egypt,
second in command of the most powerful empire of
that age.[1]

PERSIST IN PICTURING SUCCESS

Sometimes the imaging power of the mind produces
immediate results for you. But if (like Joseph) it takes
longer, you can be assured that the results will be even
bigger when they do come, provided you do not get
discouraged and give up. The longer it takes your
mental images to produce results, the bigger they will
be, if you hold on to them.

The truth of this was once brought to my attention
by a businessman who revealed to me how the imaging
law of prosperity took him from a truck driver's job to
wealthy retirement in ten years! In 1940 this man was a
truck driver. He lived in a rented house with his wife
and children; they did not even own a car. He was
making $25 a week and barely getting by. Then he
heard about the imaging power of the mind, and he
decided to find out if it really was as powerful as it was
reported to be.

He began mentally to image the standard of living
he wanted for himself and his family. He decided that
he wanted his own business; that he wanted to be
financially independent; that he wanted to own his
own spacious, comfortable home; that he wanted to
own at least two cars; that he wanted his wife to feel
completely free to shop any time she wished, without

---

1. See Chapter 7, *The Millionaires of Genesis.*

having to pinch pennies out of the grocery money or run up charge accounts all over town. In every possible way he mentally imaged a high standard of living and income for himself and his family. Within a year he had been made a sales manager instead of a truck driver for his company!

But he still did not have the house, cars, or his own business and financial independence. When Christmas came that year he said to his family, "I believe that by next year at this season we will have our own home and our own car sitting in the driveway." But at the next holiday season, a year later, they were still living in a rented house with no car of their own. His children then reminded him of his previous prediction and he replied, "Don't give up hope. Perhaps I made that prediction a little too soon, but we *will* have those blessings, and soon."

By the next holiday season they had moved into a new home and there was not one but two new cars in the driveway! This man stated that after he began imaging the prosperous standard of living he wished, while still a $25-a-week truck driver, it actually took him two years to convince his own thinking that it was possible, and to get his mind to accept those rich mental pictures. But he declared that, after his mind was fully convinced he could become prosperous, it was like breaking a hard shell; suddenly success began to come so fast he could hardly keep up with it. It was then that the house and two cars appeared. The man further stated that it took him six years from the time he began to image a high standard of living to completely achieve his goal. But within six years after he began imaging prosperity on a grand scale, he had attained it in the insurance business. Within ten years he had made so much money he retired!

In fact, he concluded his story on the imaging power of prosperity by saying:

> I went from a penniless truck driver to a fortune in insurance in ten years. But that was only my first fortune. I have now tired of retirement, and plan to make my second fortune during this next ten-year period through the same method—by imaging it!

THE POWER OF A MASTER PLAN

Charles Fillmore once described the terrific power of the imagination when he wrote, "Imagination gives man the ability to project himself through time and space and rise above all limitations."

One of Mr. Fillmore's sons, who was an architect and official of Unity School of Christianity, proved that this can be done. In 1926 Rickert Fillmore drew up a master plan for the growth of Unity Village. In this master plan he drew all of the buildings, walkways, fountains and even the shrubs that were to beautify Unity School. Finally, in 1929, two of the buildings, the Unity Tower and the Silent Unity building, were completed. Because of economic conditions during the depression era that followed, no more building was undertaken for eleven years. But Rickert Fillmore persisted in his vision by going right ahead and landscaping the grounds, even filling in shrubs around the future buildings.

I remember hearing him relate at a Ministers' Conference how he sat in his office located in the Unity Tower during those years of non-building, and how he would look out over the Unity grounds where the prospective buildings were to be erected. He would image them as already there, picturing how they would look in every detail. After years of his faithful imaging, beginning in 1940, a number of other beautiful buildings were constructed. The beauty of Unity Village is now enjoyed by visitors from all over the world, who can behold what the imaging power of the mind has accomplished there.

THEIR RESULTS FROM
A WHEEL OF FORTUNE

Truly, nothing is impossible for the imagination to accomplish. But perhaps you are thinking, "I am not yet well versed enough in the imaging power of the mind to get results as you have described. Isn't there some simple way I can begin training my imagination to produce such results for me?"

Yes, there is!

An engineer in my first prosperity class devised a practical method for training the imagination to produce rich results. He designed a "wheel of fortune" to help project his mind through time and space, thereby rising above present limitations and bringing forth happy results. After this engineer began to use the imaging power of the mind through his "wheel of fortune," he went into a multi-million dollar construction job.

This "wheel of fortune" he designed has fascinated and helped scores of people. For instance, some ministerial friends of mine told me that they used his wheel of fortune idea for a short period, and realized a lifetime dream by taking a trip to Europe. Another ministerial friend told me that after she made a vacation

wheel of fortune, she was able to take her sick mother
to Florida in the middle of winter for the warm sunshine which the doctors had prescribed for her.
Through a series of events that brought about that
Florida trip, they were offered a friend's house on the
beach at the height of the winter season, free of charge!
There they made friends with neighbors who invited
them into their homes for happy social events during
their stay. Another result was that later she was *given* a
beautiful fur coat by one of those new friends, just
before she returned home to the cold weather.

HOW TO MAKE A WHEEL OF FORTUNE

Actually, the wheel of fortune idea is a very simple
method for putting the imagination to work for you.
The engineer made his wheel of fortune in this way:

On a large piece of poster board, he drew a round
circle that encompassed most of the space. In the center of this circle he placed a picture of some religious
idea or scene that denotes a Higher Power. (This could
be a picture of the Bible, a picture of Christ, the
Lord's Prayer, or whatever religious symbol means
most to you.) Under this center circle he typed the
following words: "DIVINE INTELLIGENCE IS IN CHARGE OF
MY LIFE. I AM NOW OPEN, RECEPTIVE, AND OBEDIENT TO
ITS RICH INSTRUCTION AND GUIDANCE." This formed the
innermost part of his wheel of fortune. This idea was
its "hub."

From this innermost part, he drew four lines to the
circumference of the circle. After dividing his wheel
into four parts, he then labeled the four parts: *business, family, spiritual, social and recreational.* In each

of these four parts he then placed pictures of the results he desired to achieve in those four phases of his life.

For instance, in the *business* phase he placed pictures concerning the "perfect engineering job" he wished as a result of a job transfer which was pending. Under this picture, he placed these words: "I AM NOW ACTIVATED BY DIVINE LOVE AND GUIDED BY DIVINE POWER INTO MY RIGHT WORK, WHICH I PERFORM IN A PERFECT WAY FOR PERFECT PAY. THE DIVINE PLAN OF MY LIFE NOW TAKES SHAPE IN DEFINITE CONCRETE EXPERIENCES, LEADING TO PERFECT HEALTH, HAPPINESS, SUCCESS AND PROSPERITY."

In the *family* phase of his wheel of fortune, he placed a picture of his present home, and under it these words, since it would be necessary to sell that house because of his job transfer: "DIVINE INTELLIGENCE DIRECTS THE RIGHT BUYER TO THIS PROPERTY. EVERYONE CONCERNED IS BLESSED BY A JUST AND ORDERLY EXCHANGE OF VALUES." He also placed the picture of a new home and under it these words: "DIVINE INTELLIGENCE KNOWS OUR NEED, KNOWS WHERE THE RIGHT HOUSE IS AND KNOWS HOW TO MANIFEST IT TO US AT THE RIGHT TIME." To help his wife through the transition period of moving and readjustment that would come as the result of this job transfer, he placed her picture in this area, too, and under it these words: "MY WIFE IS NOW MOTIVATED BY DIVINE INTELLIGENCE AND DIVINE LOVE. SHE IS ALSO GUIDED BY DIVINE POWER WHICH NOW MANIFESTS IN HER EVERY EXPERIENCE AS PERFECT HEALTH, HAPPINESS, ABUNDANCE AND SUCCESS." For their ability to go forth to new experiences in faith, he placed on their wheel of fortune the picture of a door and under it these words: "AS ONE DOOR CLOSES, ANOTHER BIGGER AND BETTER DOOR OPENS."

In the *social* and *recreational* phase of his wheel of fortune, he placed the picture of a sandy beach with an ocean background, under which went the prayers: "WE GIVE THANKS FOR THE DIVINELY PLANNED VACATION, UNDER DIVINELY PLANNED CONDITIONS WITH THE DIVINELY PLANNED AND DIVINELY MANIFEST SUPPLY." For his general prosperity he added these words: "I AM NOW GUIDED BY DIVINE INTELLIGENCE, SO THAT DIVINE ORDER IS ESTABLISHED AND MAINTAINED IN ALL MY FINANCIAL AFFAIRS."

In the last part of his wheel of fortune, the *spiritual* phase, he placed the picture of a church under which he wrote: "I AM GRATEFUL THAT FAITH ABIDES IN MY HEART, AND THAT I AM DIVINELY GUIDED TO THE RIGHT CHURCH IN MY NEW SURROUNDINGS." Near these words he also placed the picture of a Bible.

He then placed this wheel of fortune with its pictures and words in a spot where he could privately view it and go over it every day. These simple words and pictures helped his imaging power of the mind to go to work for him. In a few weeks he was informed that his job transfer would be the biggest promotion he had ever received! For the first time in his engineering career, he would enjoy complete freedom of action, with responsibility only to the vice-president of the company.

As he continued to view his wheel of fortune, he became so confident that their present home would be sold on time that he and his wife went to the new job assignment in a distant state, and immediately found the perfect place to live. They then proceeded to set a date to come back and arranged to move their furniture, a date by which they confidently expected their house to be sold. They went so far in faith as to make plane reservations on that date to fly back, so as to be present for the sale of their house.

After they confidently set the dates and made their plans, everything they had expected began working out on time. Their house was sold on time, and their furniture was moved to their new home on the dates they had planned. After getting settled in their new location, they took a vacation in a lovely tropical area where there were sandy beaches along the ocean, as their wheel of fortune had indicated.

Later, they were guided to the perfect church for them in their new location, as pictured on their wheel of fortune. Thus did this engineer prove, in working with the imaging power of the mind, what he already knew to be true in his engineering profession from working with blueprints — results have to be planned and then visualized before they can become a living reality.

NAPOLEON USED THE IMAGING LAW

Before you can discount this as just one man's way of making his imagination work for him, let me assure you that one of the most powerful figures in history used the wheel of fortune idea to win many a battle and to achieve world fame. Napoleon kept a huge map before him with colored flags indicating the various moves he planned for his armies to take, months in advance. He even used the prosperity technique of writing down his desires and plans, so as to clarify them and start them into action from the invisible realm. In one instance, historians say that he dictated in detail the order and length of the marches, the meeting places of the two armies, the attack, the movement of the enemy and even the blunders he expected the enemy to make — all two months before it happened and at a distance of six or seven hundred miles away from the scene! But Napoleon met his Waterloo, because he in a great measure used destructively the very techniques that are so powerful for good when used in a positive, constructive manner.

THIS TURNS THE TIDE OF YOUR THINKING

Thus, if you want something very much that seems completely out of reach, make a wheel of fortune! They are powerful because they turn the current of your thought and expectation from "I can't have" to "I can have"; from despair to hope, from discouragement to encouragement; from failure to success. If you do not wish to make a wheel of fortune for all the departments of your life, make it for your main desire — perhaps for the one big thing you would like to experience in life, which so far has evaded you. A friend of mine makes what she calls "quickie" wheels of fortune for a period of one month, on which she places pictures and phrases concerning the things needed for that short period of time. She says that by expecting immediate results, her mind seems to go to work for her much faster to produce an immediate result; whereas, if she makes wheels of fortune for longer periods, somehow her imagination isn't sufficiently stimulated to do much about it.

MAKE A NOTEBOOK OF YOUR DESIRES

If you are not free to make a large wheel of fortune to help you change your mental images, perhaps you would like to do as did a schoolteacher I know, who made a notebook similar to the kind she constantly carries around in her work. Only this notebook contained pictures she had cut from magazines of the good she desired, along with catchy phrases she had clipped and pasted about them. When she had a lull in her day, she would browse through her notebook of desires, which kept her imaging power uplifted, expectant, and at work for her highest good. No one around her was aware of what she was doing, and in this simple way she was able to avoid becoming depressed, discouraged or doubtful.

IMAGE IN DETAIL

A housewife who has used the imaging power of the mind with amazing results has often told me that she has to work for a long time to get her mind to image *in detail* a desired result. But she declares that once she can picture the complete, detailed result she can then dismiss the matter from her mind completely, knowing it will soon manifest itself. She states that she has found it is worth the time and effort to daily picture as much of her desires as possible. Gradually her imagination is able to image the whole picture in detail. As it does so, she states that often she personally needs to take little or no physical action to produce that result. More often, it is accomplished for her, since her greatest work in the matter had already been done.

I am discovering that the imaging law of prosperity is one of the most fascinating. The more you develop it, the more it seems that the whole world rushes toward you in a friendly fashion, only too happy to grant your desires.

YOU CONSTANTLY IMAGE

A very "self-righteous" type of woman once indig- nantly said to me after a lecture I had given on the im- agination, "I don't believe in making mental images — that's nothing but mental force." I tried to explain that she was constantly making mental images whether she wanted to or not, because the mind thinks through mental pictures. It is the natural action of the mind. But this indignant woman just rushed out. Later, I began to receive reports of what a hard time she was having financially. Finally, she spoke to a church coun- selor about her financial difficulties, and the counselor said "You will continue to have financial problems un- til you change your mental images. You are thinking about, talking about, and picturing financial lack, and your mind is producing what you are imaging. Change your images and think, talk and picture plenty and you shall have it." This time the woman was des- perate, and so she began to image prosperous results. Soon she began to experience them. In due time her attitude had changed completely and she became a beautiful, harmonious, prosperous individual whom everyone loved; whereas, she previously had been

avoided on every hand because of her constant recita-
tion of financial woe.

I agree with that lady that we can use the imaging
law of prosperity as mental force, if we try to force
good to us that belongs to someone else. If we mentally
image what belongs to someone else as ours, we are
asking for trouble. We never need to image someone
else's good as being taken from them and coming to
us. What belongs to another is not ours by divine right.
If it were, it would have been given us in the first place.
And since it is not ours by divine right, it would do us
no good if we got it.

HOW TO IMAGE UNSELFISHLY

You need not covet another person's blessings because his blessings would not satisfy you even if you
had them. What belongs to another never quite fits
your needs. Instead, when you see something another
has that you would like to have, do not covet it or mentally try to image and force it to you. You should
realize that his good that appeals to you is simply an
indication that similar good is on the way to you and
that you *can* have it. To help bring it to pass, declare
to yourself: "I, TOO, AM IN CONTACT WITH THE SOURCE
OF THAT GOOD. THE DIVINE EQUIVALENT OF THAT GOOD IS
NOW ON ITS WAY TO ME, AND I GRATEFULLY ACCEPT IT.
MY OWN SIMILAR, GOD-APPOINTED BLESSINGS NOW AP-
PEAR. THEY ARE SATISFYING AND APPROPRIATE AND FOR
THIS I GIVE THANKS." Truly, there is no danger in using
the imaging power of the mind unselfishly. It is only
when you use it selfishly, to try to force from another
that which you desire, that you run into difficulties.

In like manner, you should never mentally image for another that which you would not want to experience yourself, since the mental image you send out inevitably comes back to you. Instead, you should image health, wealth and happiness for others, as well as for yourself.

IMAGE SUCCESS IN FAMILY PROBLEMS

A distraught mother, whose son's behavior had been especially disturbing, began sitting quietly every day and mentally imaging him as she wished him to be. She thought of him as standing in a pool of light and love, as being calm, peaceful, confident, harmonious, happy. She stopped trying to *make* him that way in any of her outer actions or words. Gradually, he began to express those qualities and became calm, peaceful, confident and harmonious, so that in a few months he hardly seemed the same child.

I have noted in talking with a number of women whose husbands would go astray and get interested in "other women," that almost inevitably it happened after the wife began to image her husband as "interested in another woman." One wife, whose husband had strayed early in their marriage, came to me feeling very sorry for herself because she was going through the third "other woman" experience. As I closely questioned her, I realized that, early in their marriage, she had begun to wonder what she would do if such a thing were to happen; and soon it did happen. The pattern repeated three times before she realized that she had imaged each experience for her husband, and thus had helped bring it forth. Be careful what you image for yourself or those who are receptive to your mental images, because it will surely happen!

You should always give others the benefit of only good mental images. Often life's results are the difference between constructive and destructive mental images that you entertain for yourself and others. The writer might have been describing the power of mental images when he wrote, "Two men looked out from prison bars; one saw the mud, the other saw the stars." What we see depends mainly on what we look for.

IMAGE SUCCESS IN FINANCIAL AFFAIRS

I would also suggest that you begin daily developing your imaging power for prosperity and success by taking a little time at the beginning or end of the day—perhaps when you are writing out your plans and notes—to image them in definite form mentally. In other words, if there are bills you are listing to be paid, after making your notes, sit quietly and image the checks already written to those owed in the specific amount. Mentally image yourself putting those checks in envelopes and dropping them in the mail box. If there is a definite need for some specific amount of money, mentally image a check written out to you, showing a current date, and showing the amount of money needed as received on that check. Your imagination loves to be given definite pictures to build and form, which the subconscious mind then gratefully accepts, and gets busy producing as definite results for you.

Actually, you have been using your imaging power all the time, and perhaps you used it to image lack of money, lack of success, and all the things you don't really want in life. Take your wallet and checkbook in your hands during your quiet time. Closing your eyes, mentally image bills of large denomination bulging from the wallet. Mentally image your deposit slips showing large amounts of money being deposited into your bank account. *Image, image, image,* all the good that you wish to experience.

I know of a businessman who had gone through a period of severe financial lack and who felt he could no longer endure the privations. Realizing the imaging power of the mind, he purchased some "play money" and placed the bills of large denomination in his wallet, so that every time he opened it, his eyes would first see those large amounts. He declared that soon his imaging power had accepted the picture of large amounts of money in his wallet, rather than the previous image of lack. He further stated that never again did he find himself without sufficient money in his wallet to meet his needs.

IMAGE FOR TRAVEL

A friend of mine remembered the imaging power of the mind when she wished to travel around the world. She purchased a dress, the pattern of which depicted a map of the world. She wore this dress often, thinking of the trips she would take. Very soon someone started a "travel fund" for her with a gift of money. As the fund gradually increased, she talked with a travel bureau, and tentatively decided upon a trip to Europe. Within six months from the time she began wearing her dress of the world, her trip to Europe came about. In the intervening years, she has often worn that "travel dress."

The result has been enjoyable trips to other parts of the world.

IMAGE BEAUTY AND WELL-BEING

Mentally image the way you personally wish to dress, look, act, react. Give other people a success and beauty treatment by picturing them as prosperous and successful. I often give people a private beauty treatment by mentally viewing them as wearing more beautiful clothes. It is amazing how often they appear soon in the very clothes I had pictured for them.

The more you use the imaging power of the mind, the more delightfully will it work for you. You are constantly imaging whether you have been aware of it or not. So why not take conscious control of your imaging power and produce the health, wealth and happiness that are yours by divine right?

IMAGE YOUR TRUE DESIRES

Let me remind you of something mentioned in the last chapter: Don't compromise in your mental images. Image what you really want, not just what you think you can probably have. Pay no attention to your will and reason, which will try to talk you out of mental images. Your active imagination will soon take control of your will and put it in its place, if you will first take control of the imagination by feeding it the mental pictures of what you deeply and sincerely want. If you feed your imagination half-hearted, lukewarm, mental pictures, that's the kind of results you will get.

Since they will not be satisfactory, then you will have to start all over again, imaging what you really want. So do it in the beginning and save yourself double work.

Truly the image does make the condition, but it is up to you to make the image. Realizing this, you can now know that there is no need to fight or force your good to you. Instead, just get busy and quietly image it *in detail* as you wish it to be, and then declare concerning those images: "THIS OR SOMETHING BETTER, FATHER; THY UNLIMITED GOOD WILL BE DONE!"

It is true that man becomes what he imagines, and that man's continuous imagination is sufficient to remold or create anything! But don't just take my word for it. Instead, join with me and many others who are discovering that the imaging power of prosperity is one of the most delightful and powerful of all.

THE PROSPERITY LAW
OF COMMAND

— Chapter 6 —

Shakespeare wrote, "There is a tide in the affairs of men which, taken at the flood, leads on to fortune." It is through the law of command that you release this floodtide of good which has been built up through your list-making and mental images.

The prosperity law of command is your key to dominion. The word *command* means "to have authority or control." Through an attitude of authority, you can take control of the good which you wish to experience in life. Many people look "up" at life, as though it were a mountain towering over their insignificance. The law of command helps you to move up to the summit and look out over your world with a feeling of authority and control which then produces like results.

The secret of the law of command is this: A positive assertion of the good you wish to experience is often all that is needed to turn the tide of events to produce good for you swiftly and easily. It's amazing how fast doors open to us when we dare to take control of a situation and command our high expectations to manifest themselves. But there's nothing new about the law of command. In Genesis we are told that Jehovah created the earth by commanding, "Let there be . . . and there was." (Genesis 1)

Actually the law of command is one of the easiest to use. After having made lists of your desires and after having mentally imaged them as fulfilled, it is then time to release the substance of them into words of decree and command which can move the ethers into action. What you decree you get, as the Bible promises "Thou shalt decree a thing and it shall be established unto thee and light shall shine upon thy ways." (Job 22:28)

YOU COMMAND THROUGH WORDS

You are now using the law of command because you are constantly making decrees, though often they are the wrong kind of decrees, producing what you do not desire. A businessman recently told me of an acquaintance who had been having trouble with his right arm. Doctors examined it and said there was nothing organically wrong with it. Finally, this man, who knew the power of words, realized that he had been exclaiming, "I'd give my right arm if I could _____." He stopped using this expression and his arm got well. It was Isaiah who warned us, "Woe unto them that decree unrighteous decrees." (Isaiah 10:1) Our woes can often be traced to our thoughtless remarks.

Once I prayed with a woman who was having trouble with her feet and legs. Her need for healing seemed acute. Her physician told her that he had done everything possible for her. After we began praying, her condition improved, but a complete healing did not seem to come. One day in our prayer time, I said to her, "Now just ask, 'Father, what is the truth about this situation? What do I need to do to be healed completely?'" And she did.

In a little while she quietly said:

> I have the answer! I recently went into a new business venture and I have not yet made a success of it. I have been foolishly saying, "If only I could get on my feet financially." I was on my feet physically when I began making that statement, but soon my feet began giving me trouble. My subconscious mind must have taken my words seriously and got me off my feet, which is what I was decreeing through my idle words.

She then declared, "I am going to change that statement and declare that I am financially secure; that I am *on* my feet financially." Soon she was, both physically and financially!

I know of a woman who is quite deaf in one ear. She constantly declares concerning anything she does not wish to hear about, "I'm going to turn a deaf ear to that."

Students of the mind have always been taught the power of words. The spiritual leaders of Egypt, India, Persia, China and Tibet all taught their students to speak only when they had something constructive to say. Knowing the danger of idle talk, they set up a standard to determine whether it was wise to say a thing: "Is it true? Is it kind? Is it needful?" Even if it is true, if it is not kind, then surely it is not needful!

From counseling hundreds of people with financial problems, I have found that 99 times out of 100 they do not solve their problems until they not only know, but fully use the law of command. When they begin daily, consciously, and deliberately to assert the good they want, their commands seem to call it forth.

AFFIRMATIONS ARE A FORM OF COMMAND

In modern times we hear about "affirmations," which are a form of command. Many are proving that the daily practice of verbal and silent affirmation is the simplest way of invoking the law of command to create good. In fact, the use of affirmations is such a simple way of bringing forth rich results that many people mistrust it, looking for a more complicated path to prosperity.

The word "affirm" means "to make firm." Through verbally affirming or declaring the good you want, rather than continuing to talk about what you don't want, you begin to make firm in the mind and in the invisible ethers the good you desire. As you continue to affirm the desired good, it rushes forth as a visible result.

YOU MAKE YOUR WORLD WITH WORDS

Never underestimate the power of words. You make your world with your words, as did Jehovah in the beginning. But if you do not like the world you have previously made with words of discord, lack, limitation and hard times, you can begin building a new world of limitless good and prosperity by changing your words of command and decree.

The people in my prosperity classes found the law of command one of the easiest and fastest to produce rich results for them. They took affirmative statements that met their needs and declared them over and over verbally for at least 15 minutes or perhaps for 5 minutes three times a day. If they were not in circumstances that gave them the privacy to speak aloud the statements, then they would write them out dozens of times. One of the statements of command they used often was: "I LOVE THE HIGHEST AND BEST IN ALL PEOPLE. I NOW DRAW TO MYSELF THE HIGHEST AND BEST PEOPLE" (customers, clients, patients, etc.).

A salesman discovered that by using this statement, he attracted into his department only people who really intended to buy his merchandise. Daily, consistent use of this commanding statement also helped him to make a number of sales that he previously thought he had lost.

In another instance, a saleslady used this statement for 15 minutes each day for several weeks with such success that she became the leading sales person in the entire store. She was honored by her employers for having sold $44,000 worth of merchandise within a short period. Only three other salespeople (all men) sold $30,000 worth of merchandise during the same period. This lady's department included mostly lower-priced merchandise, which required that she make many more sales by comparison with other department sales.

Another statement of command that people in my prosperity classes found especially powerful was: "EVERYTHING AND EVERYBODY PROSPERS ME NOW AND I

PROSPER EVERYTHING AND EVERYBODY NOW." By the daily, consistent verbal use of this statement, a government employee soon was informed of an inheritance that had been available, but unclaimed for several years. Another student, who used this statement of command, became one of eleven heirs to inherit a gravel pit. Because of the number of heirs, the amount to be realized from this inheritance was predicted to be quite small. But as this person continued to daily declare, "EVERYTHING AND EVERYBODY PROSPERS ME NOW AND I PROSPER EVERYTHING AND EVERYBODY NOW," the income checks received from this gravel pit began arriving monthly in substantial amounts. During the winter months when the gravel business was supposed to "slump," this student received the largest checks of all!

COMMAND YOUR GOOD TO APPEAR

There are hundreds of affirmative statements you can use that will command good to appear, but definite declarations of command should be used to meet definite needs. You should not hesitate to use them. For instance, if your money supply is low or if your purse seems empty, take it in your hands and declare aloud a number of times (in privacy, of course): "I BLESS YOU AND BLESS YOU FOR THE RICHES OF GOD THAT ARE NOW BEING DEMONSTRATED IN AND THROUGH YOU." As you enjoy your meals, it is good to think statements of blessing and and appreciation for them, along with the old-fashioned habit of table blessing. When you dress, it is good to think thoughts of appreciation and blessing for your clothing.

Once in a lecture I gave the following statements for definite uses, and was amazed at how many business people commented on them afterwards and asked for their exact wording. For the perfect clothes and wardrobe which every prosperous thinker should have: "I GIVE THANKS THAT I AM BEAUTIFULLY AND APPROPRIATELY CLOTHED WITH THE RICH SUBSTANCE OF GOD."

For the perfect, beautiful comfortable home, whether it be one room, an apartment or a house: "I GIVE THANKS THAT I AM BEAUTIFULLY AND APPROPRIATELY HOUSED WITH THE RICH SUBSTANCE OF GOD."

And for the perfect transportation, which every prosperous thinker should have: "I GIVE THANKS THAT I AM BEAUTIFULLY AND APPROPRIATELY TRANSPORTED WITH THE RICH SUBSTANCE OF GOD."

The ladies especially liked this statement of command: "I GIVE THANKS FOR EVER-INCREASING HEALTH, YOUTH AND BEAUTY." I suppose I might be considered an extremist on the subject of affirmative statements because I have them scotch-taped in various spots in my home. Some of the neighborhood children have been so fascinated with them, that they drop by occasionally just to see if I have changed the statements, and to ask for copies. The above statement about clothes is attached to my closet door. The one on health, youth and beauty is taped to my mirror. The one I keep taped on the pantry door is: "I REJOICE IN THE BOUNTY OF GOD, CONSTANTLY MANIFESTING AS OVERFLOWING SUPPLY HERE AND NOW." To keep down unnecessary telephone calls, which can be such a waste of time, near my telephone is this declaration of command: "DIVINE ORDER IS NOW ESTABLISHED AND MAINTAINED. HARMONY REIGNS SUPREME."

It is good to begin the day with affirmative statements which help you to gain control of your day. I suggest this one: "WITH PRAISE AND THANKSGIVING, I SET THE RICHES OF GOD BEFORE ME THIS DAY TO GUIDE, GOVERN, PROTECT, AND PROSPER ME. ALL THINGS NEEDFUL ARE NOW PROVIDED. MY RICH GOOD BECOMES VISIBLE THIS DAY!"

So that you will speak words of prosperity and success each day, which is a form of commanding it to come forth, I suggest this affirmation: "MY WORDS ARE CHARGED WITH PROSPERING POWER."

Other favorite statements of command in some of my prosperity classes have been: For increased income: "I GIVE THANKS THAT MY FINANCIAL INCOME NOW INCREASES MIGHTILY THROUGH THE DIRECT ACTION OF GOD'S RICH GOOD." For the payment of bills, indebtedness and financial obligations: "I GIVE THANKS FOR THE IMMEDIATE, COMPLETE PAYMENT OF ALL FINANCIAL OBLIGATIONS, IN GOD'S OWN WONDERFUL WAY." For increased success along all lines: "I GIVE THANKS THAT EVERY DAY IN EVERY WAY I AM GROWING RICHER AND RICHER."

A statement of command that the business people found helpful for harmony in their homes and businesses was this: "LET THERE BE PEACE WITHIN MY WALLS AND PROSPERITY WITHIN MY PALACES." (See Psalms 122:7)

AFFIRMATIONS ARE HELPFUL
TO YOUR WORK

A railroad employee told me how he used statements of command to help in his work. He was asked to repair a train engine that no one else had been able to adjust. When he heard that various mechanics had failed to repair this engine, he became apprehensive.

But then he remembered the prosperity law of command. Before beginning work on the train engine, he went aside to a quiet place. From his wallet he took this statement and went over it a number of times: "I AM A CHILD OF THE LIVING GOD, THEREFORE I AM ONE WITH HIS WISDOM. THAT WISDOM NOW LEADS ME IN PATHS OF RIGHTEOUSNESS, PEACE, AND TRUE SUCCESS." As he was thinking of these words and letting them fill his mind with peace and confidence, another railroad employee passed through the shop and asked what he was doing. He replied that he was going over "a plan" he intended to use in repairing the train engine. Shortly thereafter, he returned to his work and quickly repaired the troublesome train engine. Soon the other employee again approached him and asked for a copy of "that plan" he had used with such success!

A postal employee was required to take an efficiency test. He decided to take control of the experience rather than to fear it. He declared over and over, "DIVINE INTELLIGENCE NOW SHOWS ME ALL I NEED TO KNOW." His test proved that he was most efficient, and it was an easy experience for him.

Recently a man in New York City used a number of the foregoing statements of command. After reading an article that I had written on the subject, he reported these results:

At the time I read of the affirmative power of command, my business was in a state of great uncertainty. It soon developed that I was going to have to move out of the rent-free office I had been occupying. Through grace, I found a new and convenient office at a reasonable rate. But there was no new business in sight. It became clear to me that I must have absolute faith in God and go ahead with the radio production I had been planning, though I had not the faintest idea where the capital would come from to finance it. And there were personal and business debts to be paid as well.

Then, in the subway, on the way to work, I read your article containing a number of definite affirmative statements on prosperity and success. I began using all the affirmations in the article, and when I got to the office I copied them off and continued using them.

The next day I was led to call an acquaintance in the financial world who had suggested a year before (in what I had taken to be an offhand remark) that I come around and see him sometime. When I called him, he wanted to see me immediately. We had lunch, and I laid before him my plans and told him how much money I would need. He immediately agreed to all my proposals, except that he refused to take as large a share of the profits as I was ready to give him; and the loan I needed, he insisted, must be interest free.

Exactly a week later, our charter having been filed in Albany, and a check received for initial working capital, I was signing stock certificates as president of my new company!

Thus, one businessman's proof of the law of command.

AFFIRMATIONS PRODUCE
SATISFYING RESULTS

I have never known a person to conscientiously follow the method of daily affirmation and command for even a short time without producing satisfying results in his life. Nor have I ever known a student to really succeed if he omitted the daily use of verbal and silent declarations of command. Often I have met students who could tell me all about the theory of successful living, but they were demonstrating little of it. Upon questioning them, I invariably found that they did not use the law of command. Many of them thought it was "beneath their dignity" to say definite prosperous statements and definite words of success for 15 minutes each day, although they did not find it beneath their dignity to speak definite words of hard times, lack and financial difficulty the rest of the day; nor did they find it beneath their dignity to live in indebtedness and financial embarrassment.

You can take your choice and follow the high road or the low road of life. The law of prosperous command leads you to the high road, the royal road of success. A mind that has been steeped in poverty and failure thinking for years, needs daily help in rising into richer thoughts, attitudes and expectations. Often it takes special methods to bring results in the face of extreme circumstances. If saying definite words of success and prosperity seems an unusual method, then so be it. But go ahead and try it, if you wish to change the tide of your thinking from poverty and failure to prosperity and success.

In the midst of extraordinary experiences, you will often find it necessary to exert a little added effort to produce satisfactory results. Jacob found it necessary to wrestle with the angel until the break of day, or until the breaking forth of good in the situation, in order to obtain his blessing. Sometimes you will find it necessary to do likewise.

THIS LAW IS NOT NEW

Jesus often used the law of command, as did many of the great people of the Bible. He proved the power of command when he said to the fig tree, "Let there be no fruit from thee hence forward forever." And the passage further reads, "Immediately the fig tree withered away." (Matthew 21:19) When Jesus was tempted in the wilderness three times, He met the challenge through the law of positive assertion. Each time the devil tried to tempt Him, He used strong, positive statements from the Scriptures until He finally put the devil in his place by declaring, "Get thee hence, Satan." (Matthew 4:10) That is a powerful statement of command to use upon a worrisome situation.

You will sometimes find that, when you have used the law of command and have not yet gotten the desired results, perhaps you have been too gentle in your use of words. When Jesus raised Lazarus from the dead, he did not use gentle methods. The passage reads, "He cried out with a loud voice, 'Lazarus, come forth.'" (John 11:43) In like manner, to try to use gentle methods on glaring, ungentle appearances of poverty and failure is as ineffective as trying to speak English to a Frenchman who does not understand English. There is no communication or contact made.

AFFIRMATIONS CAN SOLVE YOUR PROBLEMS

Dr. Emilie Cady, formerly a physician in New York City, has written that when she faced extreme situations, she always struck out and used the boldest, most daring statements of command she could think of. Only after she took command did she find relief from her problems.

In one instance the statement of command which she used to be freed of the strong personality of another who had tormented her was: "THERE IS NO PERSONALITY SUCH AS THIS IN THE UNIVERSE. THERE IS NOTHING BUT GOD." In another instance, she had a sprained ankle that was badly swollen and painful. Finally she shut herself up in the privacy of her own room and affirmed over and over: "THERE IS ONLY GOD. ALL SEEMING ELSE IS A LIE." Immediately the pain and swelling subsided, and her healing came quickly.

At one point, she had been trying for two years to prove that God was the source of her supply, regardless of her patients' financial responses to her treatment. In prayer it was finally revealed to her that she had not used the law of command; she had not made the positive assertion of prosperity. She then began affirming, "IT IS DONE. GOD IS NOW MANIFESTED AS MY SUPPLY." She writes that this thought proved to be her deliverance from poverty, and that never again did she have a financial need that was not met.[1]

Mere knowing about the power of prosperous thinking isn't enough. You must put it into action. The daily, verbal use of positive statements helps you to do that.

AFFIRMATIONS CAN WORK WONDERS

Recently a prospective mother asked for a positive statement of command to use when she went into the

---

1. Cady, *How I Used Truth* (Unity Village, MO: Unity Books, 1916.)

delivery room. Though she did not anticipate difficulties in giving birth to her child, it was possible, since she was 40 years old and had not had a baby in several years. The statement of command given to her was this: "GOD IN THE MIDST OF ME IS MIGHTY IN LIFE, HEALTH AND STRENGTH. IN JOY AND WITH EASE I BRING FORTH MY PERFECT CHILD." Over and over she declared these words when the activity of birth began. She was pleased to discover that though there was the usual activity which accompanies childbirth, there was practically no pain.

Then a little later the doctor declared that she would not give birth in the usual way, but that the position of the baby made it necessary for a breech birth. Instead of becoming fearful, this mother continued to affirm over and over: "GOD IN THE MIDST OF ME IS MIGHTY IN LIFE, HEALTH AND STRENGTH. IN JOY AND WITH EASE I BRING FORTH MY PERFECT CHILD." A little later the doctor declared, "We must wait a few minutes. It seems that the baby is changing its position and that perhaps you will give birth in the normal way, after all." And she did, normally and almost painlessly.

Most of us have been human pygmies when we might have been spiritual giants, had we dared to command God's good to manifest as He empowered us to do, as stated in the first book of the Bible. A Methodist minister once described the law of command as the "great affirmations that work such wonders in human lives." He told how he discovered some years ago that *the most poised, integrated and well-balanced people in his congregation were those who were using the affirmative approach to life.* He related that many in his congregation were convinced that they received more concrete help from the use of great affirmations of faith than from any other technique. Learning of their success, he too investigated the power of affirmation and began using it. He said that after he began applying the technique of affirmation consistently, his congregation grew from 400 to more than 2,000. I can readily understand why this would happen because I discovered, while in the business world and later as a minister, that the masses today are lonely—lonely for a spiritual way of life that isn't just theory and doctrine, but one that works to produce health, harmony and abundance in their lives.

JOIN IN AFFIRMING WITH ANOTHER

It is good to have at least one other person use the power of affirmative command with you, especially when situations do not seem to respond immediately to your own commands. Be sure, of course, that it is someone that is in agreement with you, with what you are trying to accomplish, and that that person also believes in this success technique. I often asked members of the church staff to use the law of command with me about various situations. My secretary and I affirmed often for the perfect results of our work day: "THIS IS A TIME OF DIVINE COMPLETION. THE FINISHED WORKS OF DIVINE LOVE AND WISDOM APPEAR THIS DAY." The bookkeeper and I affirmed for the financial ministry: "THIS IS A TIME OF DIVINE COMPLETION. THE FINISHED RESULTS OF DIVINE SUBSTANCE AND SUPPLY NOW APPEAR." Often the church board members united with me in affirming for the entire ministry: "GOD'S KINGDOM IS COME AND GOD'S SUPREME GOOD WILL IS NOW DONE IN EVERY PHASE OF THIS MINISTRY." Always our periods of affirmative command brought satisfying results.

WRITE OUT YOUR AFFIRMATIONS

Perhaps you are in a situation where there seems little privacy for verbal use of the law of command. In that event, write out your affirmations over and over again. A successful businessman, lecturer and writer once told me how he had handled such a situation years ago after he learned of the law of command. He was doing work that greatly dissatisfied him. He wished to expand into other fields to receive greater compensation, and to be free to write, lecture and travel in connection with his work. Furthermore, at the time he was very thin and in poor health. His home life was inharmonious and dissatisfying, too. Indeed, every phase of this man's world needed uplifting. He was convinced that the law of command could change all this, but because his family was not interested in trying such a "new fangled idea," he realized it would be necessary to make his affirmations silently.

Since he felt that this would not be completely successful, he hit on the idea of writing them out. Quietly each night he would retire to his room with sharpened pencils and sheets of paper. There he would write out one statement, with which he wished to impress his mind, hundreds of times. He wrote statements concerning his health, wealth and happiness. At the conclusion of one day that had seemed unusually hectic, he wrote an affirmation hundreds of times concerning the perfect solution to a business disagreement that had arisen between him and his business

partner. Over and over he wrote: "THIS SITUATION DOES
NOT DISMAY ME. GOD IS WITH ME TO UPHOLD AND SUSTAIN
ME, AND TO MAKE ALL THINGS RIGHT. I TRUST EVERY-
THING IN MY LIFE TO THE TENDER CARE OF THE FATHER. I
KNOW HIS WILL FOR ME IS HEALTH, HAPPINESS, PROSPER-
ITY, SPIRITUAL UNFOLDMENT AND ALL THAT IS GOOD."

As he went to sleep that night, he silently affirmed
over and over "NOTHING BUT GOOD CAN COME INTO MY
LIFE, FOR GOD IS IN CHARGE." The next morning, very
early, his business partner telephoned to say that he
wished to buy out this man's portion of the business.
They then amicably agreed upon a sale price and the
transaction was quickly concluded. The man was then
free to begin building a better life for himself and his
family. His health soon improved, as he began to gain
weight, and later he even had to diet. His wife found
work similar to that which she once had done, and the
new activity led to a sense of freedom, fulfillment and
harmony between them. Through his writing, lectures
and financial transactions, many others are being
blessed with health, wealth and happiness. It all began
when he dared to write out hundreds of times how he
wished things to be, rather than fretting about how
they appeared at the moment.

AFFIRM YOUR WAY TO HEALTH

A friend once related to me how the power of affirmative commands had helped her to regain her health.
It seems that she had undergone a very serious operation, after which her doctor informed her and her husband that she would probably live only about three
months. Her husband, however, knew how sensitive the

body is to the power of thought, and how it responds positively or negatively to one's attitudes about it.

When she returned home, he said to her, "You heard the three-month diagnosis. You can accept it and die, or you can reject it and live. But if you want to live, you must do two things: First, you must stop talking about your operation and hospital experience. It is over; forget it. Second, you must think about life, affirm life, and expect to live." He then suggested that she affirm daily: "LET DIVINE HEALTH MANIFEST FOR ME AND IN ME NOW." She began using these simple words of command until it became a subconscious habit with her to think them many times a day. When friends or neighbors came to call, her husband always said, "We are not discussing her operation or hospital experience. That is over. She is enjoying good health now." That was 22 years ago. That lady told me she has never had another sick day since that time!

Perhaps you wonder why I write about healing in a book on prosperity. The word "prosper" means to thrive or succeed in any given goal or desired objective. When I write about prosperity, I write of the desire for wholeness and balance in one's life and affairs. Truly, life is worth little without health or the ability to produce it. Psychosomatic medicine, as well as psychology and psychiatry, all agree on the remarkable power which the mind has over the body for illness or for health.

AFFIRMATIONS FASCINATE AND INSPIRE

The whole world desires and is fascinated by the prosperity law of command. Once when I spoke to a group of college students, I showed them the various types of printed statements of command which spiritual counselors give to people who come for spiritual help in solving their problems. I showed this college group perhaps a dozen different affirmative statements, explaining that each statement applied to specific types of situations and problems.

At the close of my lecture, I left the affirmative statements on the lecture table and invited the students to inspect them more carefully, and to take them with them if they wished. I was astonished how fast those students rushed forth after the lecture and picked up every affirmation! When one student mentioned how concerned she was about a quiz that afternoon, I offered her an affirmation to use. All of the other students who had attended the lecture remained and wrote out the affirmation, too. It was: "I AM LETTING DIVINE INTELLIGENCE THINK THROUGH ME. I KNOW. I REMEMBER. I UNDERSTAND. I EXPRESS MYSELF PERFECTLY."

Paul might have been thinking of the prosperity law of command when he advised, "Be ye transformed by the renewing of your mind." (Romans 12:2) Truly affirmations are filled with uplifting and renewing power.

A businessman once came to me to discuss the various ways that affirmations have helped in his life and affairs. He declared:

I think the power of affirmation has literally saved my life. Six months ago I was contemplating suicide when I found my way to one of your lectures and first heard of the power of command. It sounded too good to be true, but being in desperate circumstances financially as well as in my marriage, I decided to try the affirmative way—after all, what could I lose? Today, I am on top of the world again, thanks to affirmations. It really works!

Only a few weeks ago I met an old friend who seemed as low as I had felt six months ago. He said, "You know, I don't see how I can go on. Suicide seems the only way out for me. Now if I had your happy, optimistic, victorious outlook on life, how happy I would be."

I replied: "A few months ago I almost did what you're talking about, but I learned about the affirmative way of thinking and acting. It pulled me up by my bootstraps and now I am on the road to success again." I then gave my depressed friend some printed affirmations that had helped me to achieve success. Though they were slightly frayed around the edges from much use, the friend seemed grateful for them. Recently I again met my friend who said, "Thanks for those statements. They pulled me up by the bootstraps, too. I don't see how a few words can change a fellow's whole life, but they certainly have changed mine."

You can have any of God's rich good for which you are willing to pay the price of daily affirmation and command. There is no easier or more delightful way of changing your thinking and getting on the royal road to success. You, indeed, become what you want to be by affirming that you already are!

I suggest that you make this the last phase of a three-step formula for prosperity: First, daily write out your notes of desired good. Second, mentally image the successful results. Third, boldly and deliberately affirm and command those successful results to appear. If you persist daily in following these three simple steps, you will not be able to stop the floodtide of good from overflowing into your life!

THE PROSPERITY LAW
OF INCREASE

— Chapter 7 —

The time has now come to relax and enjoy what you have already learned in the previous chapters. Indeed, the time has come to act as though you are a full-fledged "prosperous thinker," because by the time you have gotten to this chapter, you are truly beginning to be! And you are now ready for the prosperity law of increase.

The use of the law of increase is easy and pleasant. It consists first in establishing and maintaining an attitude of rich increase toward everything and everybody. In other words, let your main thought, when thinking of yourself and others, be the thought of riches, prosperity, success and victorious good.

Just by thinking of yourself and others as rich, successful, prosperous and victorious, you help make it so.

As you contact others by mail, telephone and in person, let your thought about them be one of increased good. Giving them the benefit of your rich thoughts is a giant step in helping them to become that way. They may not be consciously aware of your prosperous thinking about them, but they will subconsciously receive and be richly blessed. Often they will respond to you in some rich and happy way!

THOUGHT OF INCREASE TURNS THE TIDE

I do not believe that jail is quite the proper place for a prosperous thinker but, nevertheless, a man who once found himself imprisoned decided to make the best of the situation. After he was made a "trusty" in the jail, he was allowed to make occasional telephone calls and sometimes he would telephone me, reporting his progress. Once he called, very excited, declaring that for some time the main office of the jail had needed to be air-conditioned. He had visualized, affirmed and given thanks that it would be, since the people working there had been kind to him and he wished to see them comfortable and happy. He said that at last the office had received air-conditioning; and that if no other good came out of his jail experience, at least he felt that this increased good for the office force was an indication of how prosperous thinking could bring happy results.

How quickly affairs change for people after they begin thinking prosperously about themselves and others! A woman who had been married 18 years began to apply the prosperity law of increase in her world. She received a letter from a man she had worked for prior to her marriage. He declared that when she married, he had been in financial straits and had not been able to give her a decent wedding gift. Now that he was successful he decided the time had come to do something about the matter, and had mailed a nice wedding gift to her and her bridegroom of 18 years!

A woman in a poor section of the city heard about prosperous thinking, and began to give her neighbors the benefit of the thought of increase as well as herself. In a few days a check came in the mail for $125, which seemed a tremendous sum to her. It was from an insurance company, which explained that it was a balance due her from the estate of her sister who had died eight years previously.

A businessman who knows the law of increase uses it constantly in his work as a credit manager to collect accounts owed his company. Little wonder that last year he led in collections for the entire company, which has offices all over the South. One customer owed his company thousands of dollars, which no one had been able to collect. The account was so large that one of the company's officials came from the home office in another state to investigate the collection of this account.

The credit manager stated to the company official before they visited the customer, "The only way we will ever collect all this money is by being kind, courteous and positive in talking with him. We've got to restore his faith in himself; we've got to show him that we believe he will soon be able to pay this amount in full. We've got to use the thought of increase on him. Criticism will get us nowhere." Thus, when they talked with this customer, they spoke of their faith in him and their belief that he could and would pay the debt he had contracted in good faith. Several days later, this customer rushed into the credit manager's office with his first payment on his account, after months of non-payment. He declared, "The other morning when you walked into my office, I was feeling so low and such a failure in my business affairs, that if you had criticized me, I would have immediately given up and gone to my lawyer's office and declared bankruptcy. But you were so kind to me and so positive in your faith that my business could be saved, it gave me the courage to believe it, too. And already, the turning point has come!"

YOU ALWAYS USE THE LAW OF
INCREASE OR DECREASE

All normal people are seeking an increase in food, clothes, better homes, more beauty, knowledge, leisure, pleasure, luxury, more satisfaction in their work, more increase of good in everything. And rightly so, for it is a divine desire. Thus, the normal desire for increased good should not be condemned or suppressed. It is divine, and can be lifted to divine levels of expression through the spiritual laws of prosperous thinking.

How wonderful to use the law of increase rather than the negative law of decrease. When people criticize, condemn and belittle others, they do not realize that through the law of mind action, they are asking for the same things to happen to them. Never waste your time giving yourself or others the thought of decrease. Like bread cast upon the water, what you send out comes back to you multiplied, and it will produce corresponding experiences in your own life.

During a steel strike, two professional men proved the power of the law of increase. One, a chiropractor, refused to talk hard times or listen to such talk from his patients. Even though his office and much of his practice was located in the strike area not far from the steel mills, he constantly talked increase, prosperity and success. One night he attended a monthly meeting of the local chiropractors' association, and most of the men present described what a tough time they were having in their practice "because of the strike." Finally, someone asked him about his practice and he amazed the group by replying, "My practice has never been better. I refuse to talk hard times during a steel strike or at any other time. I have found that the power of prosperous thinking can change all that."

A lawyer in the strike area also used the law of increase during this same period. His associates in the legal profession were constantly declaring how bad business was and that their practice was off. This man decided that to avoid falling into that limited state of thought, he had better be firm in his thinking.

One night in his prayer session he said, "Lord, I believe that You are my shepherd and that I need not want. I know those steel mills have been my main clients, but I also know that You have many equally prosperous clients who need my legal help. I am trusting You to provide new prosperous clients whom I may serve."

At this time he had four big corporation clients who were his largest channels of income. Soon three of these corporation clients were giving him more business than the steel mills ever had! Thus, he was richly provided for during a period when almost everyone was talking the law of decrease and getting that result.

INVOKE THE LAW OF INCREASE IN SIMPLE WAYS

You can invoke the law of increase in a number of simple ways. You should speak the law of increase about yourself and others boldly and positively. You should look and act out the law of increase. You should write out notes of increase and image and affirm rich increase. It was Nehemiah of the Old Testament who used the law of increase to get the walls of Jerusalem rebuilt after the Jews returned from Babylonia. As cup-bearer to the King of Persia, Nehemiah secured from the King the materials and manpower to rebuild the walls of Jerusalem, but he soon discovered that hostile tribes had occupied Jerusalem while the Jews were in exile. It was necessary for Nehemiah to organize two crews of workmen, one to build the walls of Jerusalem and one to fight off the enemy tribes. The walls were rebuilt in 52 days, after Nehemiah affirmed, "The God of heaven, He will prosper us." (Nehemiah 2:20)

Often we have used the law of decrease rather than the law of increase, and have only delayed our prosperity. We have been like the Children of Israel who remained on the border of the Promised Land for 40 years, when they might have gone forth into the land reportedly "flowing with milk and honey."

Perhaps Joshua and Caleb are two of the most prosperous thinkers of the Old Testament. Of the twelve messengers whom Moses sent in to inspect the Promised Land, they were the only two who returned with proof of its riches, in the form of an enormous bunch of grapes. When the other messengers reported that the land was rich, but inhabited by warlike tribes, Joshua and Caleb confidently added the law of increase to the situation by declaring, "Let us go up at once and possess it; for we are well able to overcome it." (Numbers 13:30)

But the majority were against this plan, and the Hebrews remained in the wilderness. Years later, when they finally did go into the Promised Land, they discovered those warlike tribes were not as big as giants, as previously reported, and they discovered that the people of Jericho had been as afraid of them as they had been of the people of Jericho.

These people had seen the smoke from their campfires across the Jordan River, and had feared there must be hundreds of thousands of them, rather than only about forty thousand. Thus, the Hebrews discovered that the people they feared were afraid of them. Because of their hesitation to go in and claim their good, they had only prolonged their stay in the wilderness. Eventually they had to face the situation and master it anyway.[1]

The same applies to each of us. If you use the law of decrease and limit your good, you are never satisfied with the limited result. Eventually you have to begin applying the law of increase anyway. So why not do it in the the beginning, and get on into your Promised Land of greater good, rather than remaining in the wilderness of want, lack and privation?

GIVE OTHERS THOUGHT OF INCREASE

You should convey the impression of increase with everything you do, so that all people will receive that rich impression. When writing, telephoning, thinking

---

1. See Chapter 4 of the Ponder book, *The Millionaire Joshua* (Marina del Rey, CA: DeVorss & Co., 1978).

about or meeting others, give your family, social acquaintances, business acquaintances, friends, world leaders — all people — the thought of increased good. Declare for them: "I BLESS YOU WITH A RICH INCREASE OF GOD'S ALMIGHTY GOOD." Speak bold words of faith, confidence and increase to them directly as well. Just a few words can work wonders for another.

A retired Army officer recently said to me, "You'll never know how much you helped me several years ago when I was feeling low and was actually on the brink of suicide. Your words turned the tide of my thinking and of my life." When I thought back, I realized that the only thing I had said to that man was, "You aren't too old to begin life anew. You've been a success in the past and you can be a success again. Take a new lease on life, because you have what it takes to succeed." Speak words of increased good to others often. You may never know how much it means, but the results will show forth.

When speaking of someone, speak in terms of their success only. If you know of someone who has been making a comeback from past mistakes, contribute to his unfolding success by ignoring his past and emphasizing only his present good. Not only will you add to his increased good, but you can be assured the skeletons in your own closet will be rattled less.

GIVE YOURSELF THOUGHT OF INCREASE

Give yourself an equal thought of increase. You can do it just by feeling that you *are* becoming more successful and that you *are* helping others to do so. Your every act, tone and look should express a quiet, rich assurance of success. Words to convince others of your success are not necessary when you get the feeling of richness implanted in your mental atmosphere. It is then radiated from you and subconsciously communicated to others. They will want to be associated with you in business transactions and otherwise, for they are subconsciously and consciously benefited by the feeling of richness, success and prosperity that you radiate.

Just by quietly working to get the feeling of richness, success and prosperity, you will draw to you prosperous-minded people you have never seen before, who will become your customers, business associates and friends. People unconsciously go where there is an atmosphere of increase. It is thus that business expands rapidly, and many rich blessings flow forth. As you give the thought of increase to others and entertain it quietly in the deep recesses of your own mind, others are attracted to you and automatically prosper you.

Dare to invoke the law of increase in every way it reveals itself to you, both large and small. A housewife recently spoke of how she helped to pull her husband out of a financial slump by saying to him every day when he returned home from work, "Now, tell me, dear, every *good* thing that happened today." They were both surprised to see how much good came to pass and how much they had to be thankful for. The whole tide of their thinking turned from failure to success. Anything you can say to help yourself or others get the feeling of prosperity is worth the time and effort.

AVOID HARD-TIMES TALK

Do not think, talk or act any way but prosperously. Do not allow others to talk to you in any way but prosperously. Do not read anything or take seriously anything that is printed or said that seems contrary to prosperous thinking. If you mix up your trend of thought, you set up cross-currents that neutralize your efforts of prosperity. In order to be permanently prosperous, dare to be different!

You should not become upset when people talk hard times. Neither should you join their sad chorus unless you want to experience hard times yourself. Instead, declare in the face of apparent hard times: "DIVINE RESTORATION IS TAKING PLACE. THE GOOD WHICH THE LOCUSTS OF LACK HAVE EATEN IS BEING DIVINELY RESTORED. THE DIVINE LAW OF BALANCE AND EQUILIBRIUM IS DOING ITS PERFECT WORK." The law of divine adjustment and balance is a universal law, and you can help that balancing factor work for good through your prosperous state of mind. This can be a time of rich blessings and great prosperity for you, because, as the salesman declared, "There's gold dust in the air!"

A saleswoman recently pointed out what hard-times talk can do. She spoke of a fellow employee who constantly talked lack, recession, hard times. Understandably, this employee was not making her quota of sales. Instead of thinking of prosperity, she was spending her lunch hour roaming about town, talking with other failure-minded people. When she returned to her sales job after lunch each day, she always said the same thing, "I've been in stores all over town. Business is terrible. Nobody is selling a thing!" The result? Well, the woman to whom she so often said these things refused to accept these ideas of hard times, for she knew the power of prosperous thinking. As she invoked it, her sales remained high and her commission checks appeared regularly. But the woman doing all the "hard-

times" talk got an unwanted result: One day the manager of store called her in and placed her on part-time
work, although she wanted to work full-time. You can
and do produce tangible results with your attitudes.
This lady proved it, but in the wrong direction.

THINK UPON "PLENTY" IDEAS

Charles Fillmore showed us how to use the law of increase when those about us may be using the law of
decrease:

> The spiritual substance from which comes all visible
> wealth is never depleted. It is right with you all the
> time and responds to your faith in it and your
> demands upon it. It is not affected by your ignorant
> talk of hard times, though we are affected because our
> thoughts and words govern our demonstration. The
> unfailing resource is always ready to give. Pour your
> living words of faith into the omnipresent ethers and
> you will be prospered though all the banks in the world
> close their doors. Turn the great energy of your think-
> ing upon "plenty" ideas and you will have plenty re-
> gardless of what men about you are saying or doing.[1]

A businessman recently said to a banker, who was
trying to talk hard times to him, "There's plenty of
money in the world; there's plenty of wealth; and there
are plenty of wealthy resources to be developed and
tapped. I refuse to believe in anything but wealth and
prosperity for myself, for you, for all mankind." The

---

1. Charles Fillmore, *Prosperity* (Unity Village, MO: Unity
Books, 1936) p. 13.

banker shook his head and said, "You are the most optimistic person I know." He then proceeded to lend this
businessman a sizable amount of money, with which
this man proved that there is wealth and prosperity for
anyone who thinks prosperously, and who uses words
expecting prosperity.

Conserve and rightly use the substance of your being
for prosperity by concentrating your thoughts, feelings, relationships and activities on prosperity, not
failure or lack. Expect to become prosperous; start
thinking and speaking in those terms and no other. Remind yourself often that scattered, idle thoughts,
words and expectations bring scattered, idle, poverty-
striken results. Hitch your mental image of prosperity
to the rich star of success and keep it there.

OVERCOME DISCOURAGEMENT
AND DISAPPOINTMENT

When you become discouraged in your efforts
toward greater prosperity, remind yourself that to
think according to the general beliefs of the human
race is easy—and useless. But to think prosperously in
spite of appearances to the contrary is worth every
effort, because it produces rich results. One editor has
often said to me, "Remember, Catherine, the majority
is often *wrong!*"

Another way to invoke the law of increase, and thus
to avoid the pettiness and destructiveness of the law of
decrease, is by training your mind never to be disappointed. If certain things do not come at certain
expected times in the way you wished, do not consider
it a failure. Since you have not received that thing, you

can instead stand firm in the faith that something much better is on the way and will appear at the right time. When you seem to fail, remind yourself that it is because you have not asked big enough. Expand your viewpoint and expectation, and a larger answer than you orginally anticipated will surely come. Failure is nothing but success trying to be born in a bigger way. Most seeming failures are just installments toward victory!

AVOID HURRY

As you invoke the law of increase, remember that there is no hurry, force or push on the prosperous plane of life, and there is no lack of opportunity. Do all that you can do in a successful manner every day, but do it as calmly as possible without undue haste, worry or fear. Go as fast as you can, but do not hurry. The moment you begin to hurry, you cease to be prosperous in your thinking and become fearful, which is the prologue to failure.

Whenever you find yourself hurrying along trying to force a result, call a halt. Fix your attention on the mental image of the thing you are working toward, and then begin to give thanks you are receiving it and accomplishing it in God's own wonderful way.

A saleslady I know says that when she gets the feeling that she has "so much to do," she does nothing. Instead, she goes off for a little while to relax, have a cup of coffee and regain her equillibrium, after which she can usually accomplish twice as much in half the time.

"But," you may object, "how can I do this when I am living in the midst of people who do not know these laws of prosperous thinking, and who are constantly trying to rush me?" When I worked as a secretary in the business world, I knew what was it was like to be in such a situation. But I also discovered that one person who uses the power of prosperous thinking has more control of a situation than a whole army of hurried, harried people who scatter their power in futile rushing around. At such times mentally declare, "PEACE, BE STILL," and observe the atmosphere around you calm down to a reasonable pace.

FREE YOURSELF FROM PETTY THINKING

Do not waste time holding grudges, even toward those who have treated you unjustly. You will meet such people along the way, as you rise toward success. Others who are not making the grade will try to hold you down to their mediocre level, but they can't if you refuse to be bothered by what they say or do. Nobody can keep your success and prosperity from you but yourself.

If some people seem to try and even to succeed to dissuade you for a time, remember that success has endless doors ready to open to you, endless ways and means of providing your good. If one door closes, just know there are bigger and better doors trying to open. Don't get jammed in the half-closed door. Let it close. Be ready for the new doors that wish to open all the way for you.

You can also free yourself of petty thinking in regard to others' success and free yourself from their petty thinking by declaring: "REFUSING TO CRITICIZE AN-OTHER'S PROSPERITY, I TURN TO GOD, ASK HIS DIRECTION

AND I AM PROSPERED. IN LIKE MANNER, OTHERS REFUSE
TO CRITICIZE MY PROSPERITY. INSTEAD, THEY TURN TO
GOD, ASK HIS DIRECTION AND THEY, TOO, ARE PROSPERED.
THERE IS PLENTY OF SUCCESS AND PROSPERITY FOR ALL."

Never become disappointed, discouraged or upset
by what others say or do in an effort to hold you down
or take your good from you as you begin to rise
through prosperous thinking. It's a sure sign that at
last you are succeeding and that others realize it. In
the long run, they cannot hurt you, only themselves.
At such times, take a deep breath, give thanks that
your success is now manifesting, and consider it a compliment that others bother to criticize or try to pull
you down. There is doubtless something about you
they secretly admire and feel is lacking in themselves;
otherwise they would not feel the lack keenly enough to
resent finding its opposite in you.

MAKE THE LAW OF INCREASE
YOUR NEW FRONTIER

All of these methods and attitudes are a part of the
prosperity law of increase. As you think boldly about
this fascinating law, it will reveal its own "ways and
means" of expression to you further, in regard to your
own individual circumstances.

I suggest you begin invoking the law of increase fully
with these ideas: "I AM NOW EXPERIENCING PERFECT
HEALTH, ABUNDANT PROSPERITY AND COMPLETE AND
UTTER HAPPINESS. THIS IS TRUE BECAUSE THE WORLD IS
FULL OF CHARMING PEOPLE WHO NOW LOVINGLY HELP
ME IN EVERY WAY. I AM NOW COMING INTO AN IN-
NUMERABLE COMPANY OF ANGELS. I AM NOW LIVING A

DELIGHTFUL, INTERESTING AND SATISFYING LIFE OF THE MOST WIDELY USEFUL KIND. BECAUSE OF MY OWN IN-CREASED HEALTH, WEALTH AND HAPPINESS, I AM NOW ABLE TO HELP OTHERS LIVE A DELIGHTFUL, INTERESTING AND SATISFYING LIFE OF THE MOST WIDELY USEFUL KIND. MY GOOD — OUR GOOD — IS UNIVERSAL."

Your good is created as fast as your good words are uttered! Dare to begin invoking the law of increase in the practical ways mentioned. As you do, your thoughts, prayers, words and expectations of increased good shall circle the globe and may even reach into "outer space." Indeed, you shall become a part of the "new frontier" for universal good that is now spanning this planet!

PROSPEROUS ATTITUDES TOWARD MONEY

— Chapter 8 —

Recently a friend sent me a comic postcard which read, "Rich or poor, it's good to have money!" I'm sure most of us would agree.

All sorts of wonderful things are being written about money, and of our potential for having and enjoying more of it. It has been pointed out that more fortunes have been made since World War II than in any comparable period. One writer has declared, "You can still make millions!" Another boldly stated, "Your chances of becoming a millionaire are better than you think."

As you study the lives and experiences of prosperous-minded people, you will find that they have a friendly attitude toward money. On the other hand, you will discover that a more general attitude is that there's something wrong with having money and being prosperous.

131

Once I was guest speaker at a club luncheon at which a hospital executive was given a check to aid in furnishing a new wing of his hospital. In response to receiving the check, this executive declared, "It isn't the money that is so important. It is the club members' love and interest in this new hospital wing that really counts."

Somehow I wonder if he realized what he was really saying, because my first reaction (which I suspect was the silent reaction of a number of others) was, "If the money isn't important, why is this man here? He is a very fine and busy executive, and I wonder if he would have come to lunch with these ladies had they merely sent him word that they were impressed with his hospital expansion program." Surely this man was taught as a child what many of us were erroneously taught— to dislike money.

If you listen closely to the conversations of people about you, you will discover that this is a general attitude. People often discount the importance of money in one breath, and yet they admit that they are working very hard to get it in the next. They do not realize the cross-current they are setting up in their thinking, which in turn voids most of their efforts. Through such crossed-up thinking about money, they are working at cross-purposes, and often they will experience a crossed-up result.

MONEY IS DIVINE

I shall never forget the first time that, as a minister, I lectured on the importance of money for successful living. When I declared that money is wonderful because it is divine substance; that money is good when rightly used, a lady sitting in the front row gasped and almost fell out of her chair. When I stated, "money is divine, because money is God's good in expression," she almost passed out. She had come to this lecture because she was interested in having greater prosperity in her life. Yet when I mentioned money as a legitimate form of prosperity, it shocked her completely.

After the lecture, one of the members of the church board cornered me and said, "Don't you think you put it a little too strongly about money being good because it is a symbol of divine substance?" And I found myself replying, "I hope I put it strongly; I surely meant to." The board member then said, "Yes, but you shocked that lady on the front row so much that she may never come back." And my reply was, "If I shocked her, it was doubtless because she needed to have some old, erroneous ideas about money shocked out of her thinking, as we all do."

I then pointed out that my whole purpose in teaching the spiritual and mental principles of prosperity was to help people to learn God's good truth about prosperity being their divine heritage, so that they might be freed from failure, poverty and all the other sins of lack. I realized that sometimes the process *was* a shock.

At the next lecture that lady was back, sitting in a front seat. The only difference I could detect in her attitude was that she had pulled her chair up a little closer toward the lecture platform, happily awaiting further shocking truths about prosperity!

After she attended a number of lectures, she calmed down considerably in her strong attitudes regarding the pros and cons of prosperity. In due time she came to see me and confessed that, when she first began attending the prosperity lectures, her life and affairs were in dire shape, financially and otherwise. Her husband had left her; her children seemed to have turned against her; her physician predicted that she was nearing a nervous collapse; she had a good job, but her money never seemed to go very far, and she could not get along with her fellow workers; she was even involved in a lawsuit concerning her previous job.

But week by week as she began to entertain new ideas about prosperity and successful living, her whole attitude changed, as did her way of life. Before long her husband returned; she gradually was able to establish a more harmonious relationship with her children; she did not have a nervous collapse; the lawsuit regarding her former job was quietly and amicably settled out of court; and she began to find joy and satisfaction in her work. Indeed, before long she seemed a transformed individual, and it all began the night she dared to change her thinking about money.

Most people are sensitive about their capacity to earn money. In most instances, a person's capacity to earn money would increase if his attitudes toward money were positive and friendly. It was the late Mike Todd who has been quoted as saying, "I've never been poor, only broke. Being poor is a frame of mind. Being broke is a temporary situation."

THE GOOD NEWS ABOUT MONEY

Many people seem confused about the correct spiritual attitude toward money because of some things Paul wrote on the subject. Perhaps one of the most

misunderstood biblical passages about money is found
in his warning to Timothy, that the "love of money is a
root of all kinds of evil." (I Timothy 6:10) However, a
closer study of this passage reveals why Paul spoke as
he did.

Paul had put Timothy in charge of the early Christians' work at Ephesus, a city in Asia Minor that had
been a center of learning and commerce. It was noted
for its temple that had been built for worship of the
goddess, Diana. In other words, at the time Paul wrote
his first epistle to Timothy, the city of Ephesus was a
city of idolatry and heathen worship, a city of superstitious and pagan beliefs; a city of general materialism,
that placed no emphasis upon God as the source of its
supply.

Thus, it is easy to see why Paul wrote to Timothy,
warning him of these people's materialistic view of
money. However, Paul also instructed Timothy in the
same letter to preach to these material-minded people
in this way: "Charge them that are rich in this present
world, that they be not high-minded, nor have their
hopes set on the uncertainty of riches, but on God who
gives us richly all things to enjoy." (I Timothy 6:17) In
modern language, Paul was simply reminding Timothy
that God is the source of man's supply, and that Timothy was to instruct the rich among his followers about
this eternal prosperity secret. Our American government knows this great truth, for on our coins we find
this motto: "In God we trust." That is a fine prosperity
prayer.

So let's get the record straight: There's nothing
wrong with money, or in our wanting money. It is a
God-given medium of exchange, and there's nothing
evil about that. The moment we let go of those false

ideas that someone ignorantly taught us years ago—that money is evil—we will find that money circulates in our financial affairs much more easily and more satisfyingly.

APPRECIATING MONEY CAN PROSPER YOU

One lady recently told me that since she had released the vague notion that she was supposed to think of money as evil, she had much more of it to enjoy. She said that previously all her money was gone within three days after payday, but now there seemed enough to share and to spare regularly. Truly she is one of the most generous people I know. Another lady declared, "One of the things I have learned so vividly is to stop saying, "Oh, it's *just* money." She then went on to say that since she had been appreciating rather than depreciating money, she had gotten a wonderful new job at a much higher rate of pay. She is now enjoying both her new work *and* her new pay.

Perhaps you wonder why it is important to cultivate a sincerely favorable attitude about money, in order to attract happier financial situations. Well, money is filled with the intelligence of the universe, from which it was created. Money reacts to your attitudes about it. Since it is the law of mind action that you attract whatever you appreciate, and repel whatever you depreciate, money responds accordingly. If you think favorably about money, you multiply and increase it in your midst; whereas, if you criticize and condemn it in any form, either your own money or another's, you dissipate and repel it from you.

Perhaps you have noticed how this law works in regard to your moods. Notice how much more you are able to purchase for your money when you are in a good mood. But if you shop in haste or while in low spirits, everything seems to go wrong, including the purchasing power of your money.

Since your thoughts make your world, your thoughts about money have to be appreciative in order for money to appreciate you and be attracted to you. In talking with hundreds of people about their financial affairs, I have discovered that often when they do not have enough money to meet life's demands, it is because they have been scoffing and condemning money in financial matters, their own or another's.

I once talked with a man who was "down and out" in every way. He was in ill health, out of work, and extremely lonely and unhappy. As he talked I tried to discover what attitude of mind had brought him into such pathetic circumstances. He told me how hard life had been for him and how difficult people, situations and events had been along the way. As his conversation progressed, he began talking about "the politicians in Washington and the terrible way they were spending the country's money." As gently as I knew how, I suggested that he try reworking his attitudes toward people in general and toward the Washington politicians in particular, if he wished health, prosperity and happiness to come to him. After giving me a penetrating look which seemed to imply that he doubted my sanity, he finally agreed to try the prosperous thinking approach.

Months later when he returned, he had to remind me who he was, because his appearance had improved so much. He then radiantly described that previous cold winter afternoon, when he left my study and walked all the way back to his boarding house because of lack of funds for busfare. By the time he got home he discovered that, in his absorption of some of the ideas we had discussed, all pain had left his body. That night he slept peacefully for the first time in months.

As he began to use prosperous thinking every day, wonderful things began to happen. He fully regained his health and soon a new field of work opened to him. At the boarding house he met a lady who was also in ill health and financial despair, and he passed on to her some ideas about prosperous thinking that had meant much to him. Her whole outlook toward life changed. When they both began to appreciate rather than depreciate, in due time their appreciation involved each other. On his second visit to see me, this man said that he now wished to marry this fine little lady. He brought her to see me and she was as radiant as any bride-to-be half her age!

This man then declared that all his life he had been scoffing at money and financial matters, and at people who had wealth. He now realized how much destruction he had doubtless caused in his own life as a result. This man had learned at last that, when we do not have enough money to meet life's demands, it is often because of our depreciation of money, our own or another's.

THE GOLDEN RULE OF PROSPERITY

People sometimes bring financial hardship upon themselves by declaring that they personally are prosperous and blessed, but that Mr. and Mrs. So-and-So haven't a cent to their name. Such people often triumphantly discuss the difficulties of others at length. If you think of yourself as prosperous but of others as living in lack, through the law of action and reaction you are inviting the same thing to happen to you. The golden rule of prosperous thinking is that you should not think or say anything concerning another's financial affairs that you would want to experience in your own.

An unusual example of this truth was demonstrated in a court case where two partners were dissolving their business. One partner kept declaring that she would get everything; that the court and judge would doubtless favor her completely; and she triumphantly declared that the other partner would be left with nothing. But the other partner was a praying, positive, fair-minded individual who put the matter in Higher Hands, affirming that the Divine Law of love, justice and perfect equity would manifest for the highest good of all concerned in the situation. The accusing partner went so far as to take her lawyer to look over all the property and financial assets that she was convinced the court would give her. She constantly thought of herself as prosperous, but declared that the other partner would be left in utter financial ruin.

However, when the judge heard the facts in court, he decided that the accusing partner was entitled to only one small piece of property. He awarded the rest of the financial assets, which included a housing project, a cleaning plant, and several other pieces of real estate, to the partner who had prayed for divine justice. Thus, this woman proved that if you think of yourself as prosperous but of others as in financial lack, you are unconsciously inviting the same thing to happen to you.

HOW TO MAKE MONEY YOUR SERVANT

On the other hand, to envy another's money indicates a belief in lack of sufficient supply for everyone. Remember that you will experience what you most strongly give your attention to. When you hear of another's good fortune, rich inheritance or wealthy possessions, you should do so with great joy and appreciation. Another's demonstration of riches is but further proof of a loving Father's divine bounty, which is available to all mankind. You should rejoice in its every rich evidence.

Money is so charged with divine intelligence that it seems to tune in on what you say or think about it, and it responds accordingly. A friend has related at various times how the appreciative attitude toward money helped to keep food on her table during the depression years. Her young son seemed to know how to get the most for their money at the grocery store. When the money supply was low, she would send him grocery shopping with the substance on hand. Regularly he would come home with much more than anyone else in the family could have purchased for the same amount. Perhaps it was because any amount of money seemed to work overtime for him!

Through positive, appreciative attitudes toward money, you can make money your servant, instead of becoming its slave. You should master money rather than be enslaved by it, because you were placed in this universe to achieve mastery and dominion of substance in its every form, as is pointed out in the first chapter of Genesis.[1] Deliberately cultivate the habit of appreci-

---

1. See Chapter 3, "The Seven Secret Attitudes for Success," in the Ponder book, *The Prosperity Secrets of the Ages.*

ating money, and make no excuses about your appreciation.

If you do make excuses and depreciate money, it seems to know it and to be repelled by your depreciation. I shall never forget the first time I made this statement in a lecture: "Appreciate money as the rich substance of God and make no excuse for your appreciation of it, for if you do, money will be repelled from you by your foolish excuse-making." A lady carrying a big purse was sitting in the audience. Suddenly her purse flew open and money fell out all over the floor, making a lot of noise. We all had a good laugh while others helped her to collect her money. Of course, we passed the experience off as a joke for the sake of this woman's feelings. But later when I met her personally, I gave her some rich statements with which to charge her mind, because she seemed to radiate a deep feeling of financial limitation. It was as though her money had heard what she had been saying about it, and was trying to get away from her!

Charles Fillmore has written:

> Watch your thoughts when you are handling your money, because your money is attached through your mind to the one source of all substance and all money. When you think of your money, which is visible, as something directly attached to an invisible source that is giving or withholding according to your thought, you have the key to all riches and the reason for all lack.[2]

Perhaps you have heard the story about the careless Scot who tossed a crown, thinking it a penny, into the

---

2. *Keep a True Lent* (Unity Village, MO: Unity Books, 1953) p. 102.

collection plate. When he saw his mistake, he asked to have it back, but the deacon taking the offering refused. The Scot grunted, "Aweel, aweel, I'll get credit for the crown in heaven." "Na, na," replied the deacon, "ye'll get credit for the penny."

GIVE UP MIXED ATTITUDES

Let's give up our mixed attitudes about money which can only bring mixed results. John D. Rockefeller, Jr. once described the wonder and glory of money by saying that man could use money to feed the hungry, cure the diseased, make desert places bloom, and bring beauty into life. And how right he is! As Solomon once declared, "The rich man's wealth is his strong city; the destruction of the poor is their poverty." (Proverbs 10:15) Indeed, money is good, and we should have more of it than ever in this rich era we have now entered.

An editorial once pointed out the power of money for world peace, in suggesting that the president of the World Bank be nominated for the Nobel Peace Prize because of the excellent work he had done in producing financial peace in several countries. The editorial concluded: "Wouldn't it be timely to recognize that the proper use of cash can be a big factor for peace in the world?"

Just as you should not turn up your nose at money, neither should you make a god of it. Money is filled with the desire for life, movement, expansion and activity. It does not like to be grasped, clutched or restrained in idleness. Indeed, it is the active circulation of money that brings prosperity, whereas depressions and recessions are caused by the miserly hoarding of money. Even as our national economy depends upon the active circulation of money, so your individual prosperity depends upon the active circulation of money. This does not mean that you should not save money, but you should not abuse money by misuse.

Several other attitudes toward money are especially helpful, too. For instance, never declare, "I can't afford this" or "put on a poor mouth" (as we say down South) about things. Such statements sow seeds of poverty and limitation which will produce after their kind. Instead, it is better to declare that it is not "wisdom's way" to undertake certain financial matters; or at least it is better to phrase your financial "no" in a more positive and prosperous manner. Affirm often: "I USE THE POSITIVE POWER OF GOD'S RICH SUBSTANCE IN WISDOM, LOVE AND GOOD JUDGMENT IN ALL MY FINANCIAL AFFAIRS, AND I AM PROSPERED IN ALL MY WAYS."

It is also unwise to magnify financial difficulties. If you brag about your financial troubles (and some people actually do so to gain sympathy and attention), then you will always have financial troubles to brag about. A businessman who has achieved independent wealth through his stock market transactions said that early in his stock market ventures he invested heavily and lost heavily. In one transaction alone he lost $20,000. But never once did he mention his financial losses to anyone, not even to his wife. Instead, they continued to live prosperously, and soon the situation changed so that he was able to compensate in rich gains for the lessons he learned through previous heavy losses. To this day he has never openly discussed those early losses, and he is now enjoying financial independence. In difficult financial periods, it is good to affirm: "I HAVE FAITH THAT THIS TOO SHALL PASS," and then continue holding to the high financial vision of success toward which you are working.

Another attitude toward money to beware of is this: When you give money to another person or to an organization, do not give it with the thought of need or obligation. Such thoughts only attract more needs and obligations to be financially met. Instead, give to "add to their prosperity." This applies to the money you pass out to your husband, wife, children, employees, club, church, to the grocer, the banker and the candlestick maker, as well as to the government and everyone else. This attitude makes the giver and the receiver feel richer.

Your thinking concerning the receipt of money or other financial supply is also important. The prosperous way is to graciously receive your good in all forms, and make no excuse for your acceptance. It is an offense to both the gift and the giver for the recipient to declare, "Oh, you shouldn't have done it." Welcome money and divine supply from all directions, if it is being freely given and incurs no sense of obligation. Declare often: "ALL FINANCIAL DOORS ARE OPEN; ALL FINANCIAL CHANNELS ARE FREE, AND ENDLESS BOUNTY NOW COMES TO ME." And then joyously let it come!

I know of a woman who desperately prayed for greater prosperity, yet she constantly refused gifts or favors that were lovingly extended to her, thus closing many channels of her prosperity. If you cannot use the gifts that are bestowed upon you, do not say so; simply accept them for the generous thought they represent, and then pass them gladly along to someone who can use them.

The only time this attitude does not apply is when someone is trying to bribe you or buy your friendship with his favors, so that a sense of obligation is being incurred. True generosity has no strings attached. There are no bribes, unspoken favors or obligations involved in true giving. If you sense such a purpose behind a gift, you should feel free to say "no" to false generosity.

PRAY ABOUT YOUR FINANCIAL AFFAIRS

Another attitude toward money that needs to be clarified is this: Don't be afraid to pray about money or to get specific about your financial affairs. The ancient Hebrews did not hesitate to pray to God for exactly what they wanted. They had seven sacred names for Jehovah, each one of which represented some specific idea of God. They used the name "Jehovah-jireh" when they wished to concentrate on the aspect of substance. It means "Jehovah will provide," "the Mighty One Whose Presence and Power provides, regardless of opposing circumstances."

Many of the great leaders of the Bible prayed specifically for prosperity when it was needed. Jesus prayed that the 5,000 would be fed, by looking up to heaven and giving thanks for the few loaves and fishes, which were then multiplied to meet every need. Elijah prayed persistently for rain to end a three-year drought, so that the Hebrews could again have crops, food and prosperity.

A rich Father never intended men to suffer along in this lavish universe, and we are fooling only ourselves if we think that we must live in lack. If you have a financial need, dare to pray about it specifically and ask your loving Father to help you meet that need richly and completely. The promise, "Ask, and it shall be given you" (Matthew 7:7) contains no hidden clauses. Nor does this promise from the Book of Job, "If they obey and serve Him, they shall spend their days in prosperity and their years in pleasure." (Job 36:11) We have national days of thanksgiving, and we say grace daily at our tables, to help remind ourselves that God is the source of our supply in every form.

In regard to prayer for riches, you have probably read of the late George Muller of Bristol, England, who established orphanages for children many years ago through his belief in the prospering power of prayer. He has been described as a man of faith to whom God gave millions. He has also been called a prince of prayer, because of his habit of asking God directly for whatever was needed, rather than speaking of his needs to people.

Mr. Muller once said that the great fault of most of us is that we do not ask big enough, and we do not continue in prayer until it comes. He also advised, "Expect great things of God and great things you will have." He once told a friend, "I have praised God many times when He sent me ten cents and I have praised Him when He sent me $60,000." Solely in answer to prayers for prosperity, $7,500,000 was given to him for the building and maintenance of his orphanages.

The story has often been related of how Charles Fillmore, the co-founder of Unity School of Christianity in Unity Village, Missouri, often prayed concerning Unity's financial affairs in the early years of the movement. One time a payment was overdue on the printing presses, and the sheriff came to repossess the machines. But when Mr. Fillmore confidently declared, "I have a rich Father Who is going to take care of this," the sheriff believed him literally and replied, "Well, in that case we will give you a little more time."

Mr. Fillmore then continued to pray for prosperity and the money came in. Those printing presses were never repossessed. Later, during the depression years, the love offerings that came in from all over the world to support Unity School were much less than usual. Again, the founders of Unity prayed specifically, boldly and deliberately for money, financial supply and rich prosperity. One day as the workers on Unity Farm were drilling for water, they struck oil! That oil well proved an adequate answer to their financial needs throughout the depression.

Of course, the Unity movement is now worldwide in its scope. In recent years appraisers have stated that the financial value of Unity Village, which is now incorporated, is so rich that its true value can scarcely be estimated, but that it would run into the millions.

HOW TO DEMONSTRATE MONEY

One of the secret teachings of the occult religions of the past was knowledge of how to demonstrate money. Those privileged to learn this secret were taught to make a concrete mental picture of the amount they wanted, the denomination of money, and how it looked. After making a picture of a definite amount, they were then taught to hold it distinctly in mind as though it were already visible, and they could mentally see it very plainly. They were then taught to command the rich substance of the universe to give it to them. They were instructed to affirm: "Give me this," and to repeat this demand many times, day after day, until it manifested.

Since the mind is all powerful, you have the same right and privilege of mentally claiming money, financial assets and rich supply if you wish to use a strictly mental method. Many successful people have either consciously or unconsciously used this method. A powerful statement with which to charge the mind, along with charging it with the mental picture of the specific amount desired, is: "ALL FINANCIAL DOORS ARE OPEN, ALL FINANCIAL CHANNELS ARE FREE AND (then name the specific amount) _____ NOW COMES TO ME." It is also wise to affirm that it manifests through divine channels in God's own wonderful way.

Along with mentally visualizing and mentally claiming specific amounts of money; and along with praying definitely about money, it is also good to speak specific words of riches for yourself and your possessions. For yourself declare often, "I GIVE THANKS THAT I AM NOW RICH, WELL AND HAPPY AND THAT MY FINANCIAL AFFAIRS ARE IN DIVINE ORDER. EVERY DAY IN EVERY WAY I AM GROWING RICHER AND RICHER." For your wallet, checkbook or other channels of financial supply, it is well to affirm: "MONEY, MONEY, MONEY, MANIFEST THYSELF HERE AND NOW IN RICH ABUNDANCE." Don't be afraid to declare that "large sums of money," "rich pleasant financial surprises," and "rich appropriate gifts," are manifesting for you. Do not be vague about money, unless you want money to be vague in its response to you.

A woman on the West Coast, who had read some of my ideas about money, once wrote me in appreciation. She said, "I am glad to find at last a minister who isn't afraid to speak plainly of money as a blessing. A minister I know has often spoken to me in terms of 'plenty to share and spare,' and I found out what this minister meant last Christmas, when I received four fruitcakes. I had been affirming 'plenty to share and to spare' for Christmas. I had so many fruitcakes to share and to spare that I gave three of them away. How nice it would have been to have received something for Christmas beside fruitcakes! That experience taught me to be definite about what I wanted, if I expected to get definite and satisfying results."

Thinking in definite terms opens the way for definite results. Don't limit your income by decreeing "just enough to get by." This is a pauper's prayer. Instead, remember the words of Paul, "It is God who giveth us richly all things to enjoy." (I Timothy 6:17)

At one period in my life when my financial income was inadequate, I cut these words out of a magazine, pasted them on a card and placed them on my bedside table where I viewed them daily. "YOUR MONEY STARTS GROWING NOW. YOUR EARNINGS DOUBLE!" I was astounded when my financial income did start growing immediately through a remarkable series of events that occurred. Within a few months I suddenly realized that my income *had* doubled! Money adores the prosperous attitude and richly responds to it.

SUBSTANCE, THE SOURCE OF MONEY

Along with an appreciation of money, you should also understand and fully appreciate substance, out of which money and all tangible objects are formed. Times of depression bring out the fact that in days of prosperity, man either forgot the prayers and struggles that brought him to success and apparent safety, or else he failed to build his fortune on a firm financial foundation. If he had thought more about the source of life and substance, he would have escaped the needless grind of poverty he has endured right in the midst of abundance.

The scientists say that substance is that which stands under and supports every visible and tangible object. If you do not have money and if it does not seem to manifest as you think prosperously about it, then perhaps the divine equivalent of money wishes to come to you. As you appreciate substance and know that it is everywhere universally present in the ethers about you; as you realize that it is passive, and waits to be formed and brought into visibility by your thoughts and words, you will realize that you have control of the invisible world of rich substance and rich supply, as well as the visible world of riches.

It was Einstein who first stirred up the scientific world when he claimed that substance and matter (which includes money and all visible objects) are convertible. He declared that the formed and unformed worlds are made out of the same energy, ether, or substance. He said that the visible and invisible realms are relative, convertible, and interchangeable.

From a financial standpoint, we can use his theory of relativity. If the formed and unformed worlds are relative, then what have you to worry about if your finances get low? You can use the law of relativity to produce either money or its financial equivalent to meet your needs! If substance hasn't manifested as money, don't get panicky. Instead, declare that, "DIVINE SUBSTANCE IS THE ONE AND ONLY REALITY IN THIS SITUA-

TION. DIVINE SUBSTANCE DOES NOT FAIL TO MANIFEST IN RICH APPROPRIATE FORM HERE AND NOW." Then let substance come forth to you in manifest form, as it deems best.

The scientists declare that substance is filled with life, intelligence and the ability to take visible form. As you affirm that divine substance is doing whatever is best in the situation, you release its universal intelligence and its ability to take visible form. Your financial good may come forth to you in completely unforeseen ways; perhaps from halfway around the world, or through strangers that you have never met. But it will come when you give it your attention, and free it to work in its own wise way.

If the usual channels of supply have not opened, then invite unusual channels of supply to open by recognizing that divine substance stands under every visible form of supply, with endless ways in which to manifest its riches for you. Substance is friendly to you and wishes to supply you richly. Give it your attention and appreciation; place your faith in it, though it seems invisible; and then let it prove its power to prosper and care for you.

Never underestimate the power of affirming substance as the one and only reality, which never fails. It will then manifest as money or in the most appropriate financial form, perhaps through people you've never seen.

As you invoke the various prosperous attitudes about money and substance contained in this chapter, confidently do so with these words of Emerson ringing in your financial ear: "Man was born to be rich, or inevitably to grow rich, through the use of his faculties."

And then get ready for rich results! As those rich

results appear, perhaps you would like to be reminded of this truth a young man in the armed forces recently wrote his mother: "Yesterday is a cancelled check. Tomorrow is a promissory note. Today is the only cash you have. Spend it wisely." Whether in terms of time or money, it still applies, doesn't it?

WORK—A MIGHTY CHANNEL FOR PROSPERITY

— Chapter 9 —

Perhaps you wonder why this chapter on work did not come earlier in the book, since work is considered a mighty channel for prosperity.

The answer becomes more apparent, when we look about us and realize that the world is filled with people who are working hard to become more prosperous every day; yet many of them are not becoming prosperous at all. Why? Often because they are not thinking about prosperity and success, along with working at it. Their attitude is not right. For all the hard work they do that should produce prosperity, they neutralize it by their failure talk, by their association with failure-minded people and perhaps by their criticism and condemnation of others who are moving up the ladder of success. They have not realized that there must be an inworking of prosperous ideas before there can be an outworking of prosperous results. Thus, the preceding chapters were necessary to condition your attitudes for the rich good, the expanding prosperity, and the enduring satisfaction that should be yours in the process of work.

ATTITUDES CAN MAKE THE DIFFERENCE

Once a secretary was working vigorously to attain prosperity. She was heavily in debt, had been fired from several jobs, and was in dire need of steady employment. She was adequately educated, since she held two college degrees, along with business school training. At first glance, she seemed easy enough to work with. But as others became better acquainted with her, they realized that she secretly held grudges against the whole world, and all her past employees in particular. It became apparent that she constantly sought sympathy for her "hopeless financial affairs."

When it was suggested that a change of emphasis from failure to prosperous thinking might be the answer, she became furious. She wanted to keep her prejudices, grudges, and failure attitudes, which filled the atmosphere around her with such heavy pessimism that people were repelled by her. With her mind so cluttered with hostility, it is little wonder her work was unsatisfactory, her inefficiency at an all-time-high, and that she disliked her various jobs and employers.

Conversely, another working lady seemed to realize that the prosperous, victorious attitude paves the way for satisfying, productive work. To all appearances, this lady had no reason to feel victorious or positive.

She was past the half-century mark. Many people in her age group would say that they were getting too old, which alone was reason enough for their lack and unhappiness. Furthermore, she was a widow and very much alone in the world, having no children or other close relatives. But she did not use this as an excuse for failure. Instead, she was a very happy and successful person.

Even more challenging, her sales product was one that most of us would not care to attempt selling—she sold cemetery burial lots! Yet she sold them in large numbers and seemed very happy about her product. She also seemed to convey her enthusiasm to those who purchased them, though most of us like to put off thinking of this particular item as long as possible. The result was that she enjoyed most of life's comforts: a lovely, comfortable, spacious home in which she often entertained her host of friends; financial security such as rental property, stocks, bonds, and other investments, as well as a high, steady income from her sales work. She had time for social, church, and cultural activities, as well as for vacations and travel. To her, work was divine, even though she sold a product that most of us would least want to buy.

WORK IS DIVINE

The word "work" means different things to people. In the dictionary I found a half-page of definitions. A prosperous thinker might think of work as divine or sublime; or as the creative activity of good in some satisfying form which is balanced with play, rest, and harmonious surroundings. Kahlil Gibran has written that "work is love made visible."[1]

Perhaps you do not agree that work is divine, sublime or even a satisfying inner expression of your talents and abilities. The work you are doing at the moment may not seem divine; if not, there is a reason and that reason is good. But let us go back of the result to the cause. William James once stated that 90 percent of us are using only 10 percent of our mind power. Psychologists believe that every human being is a dynamo of concentrated, creative energy which is ever seeking new avenues of expressions.

The desire for prosperity and for beneficial self-expression in work is but a part of that creative energy trying to express in our lives. When the right avenues are found for the constructive outlet of that creative energy, and the right attitudes are established, man is happy, well-adjusted, and considers his work divine. But when right avenues of expression have not been found, and the right attitudes are not established, that same creative energy is restricted to expression in mediocre ways. Then man is unhappy and considers work a curse, instead of the divine blessing it is intended to be.

Many people find themselves in work that they consider unpleasant while they are still near the bottom of the ladder of success. It is their attitude and reaction to their work at this point which determines whether they remain at the bottom and go on cursing their work, or whether they go on up the success ladder, step

---

1. Gibran, *The Prophet* (New York: Alfred A. Knopf Publishers. Copyright 1923 by Kahlil Gibran; renewal copyright 1951 by Administrators C.T.A. of Kahlil Gibran Estate, and Mary G. Gibran).

by step. Dissatisfaction can be good because it often prods one to aim higher, and then to do whatever is necessary to get there.

YOUR PRESENT CIRCUMSTANCES
ARE FOR A PURPOSE

Let us face the issue squarely! You may discover that you are where you are now for the purpose of redeeming certain character traits or certain attitudes of mind which have impeded your progress in the past. If you are in uncongenial work, realize that you are there for a purpose, which may be to develop divine qualities that will eventually add to your general progress, and advance you further up the ladder of success. After entering the ministry I realized that every job, big and little, that I had held along the way was a part of my training for the lecture platform, for the counseling room, and for my writing ministry.

Jesus might have been explaining it when He said "To whomsoever much is given, of him shall much be required; and to whom they commit much, of him will they ask the more." (Luke 12:48) Your immediate need is therefore to discipline your attitudes and reactions, so as to glean the good from your present experiences, and to pass beyond them to higher phases of self-expression in satisfying work as soon as possible. In other words, when the pressure of desiring more good is upon you, when dissatisfaction with your present way of life assails you, or when the pressure of financial strain disturbs you, it is then that you are feeling the actual pressure of your talents and abilities, which are straining to express or pass forth through you as richer degrees of success and prosperity.

PERFECT YOUR ATTITUDES TOWARD WORK

Concerning how to discipline or perfect your attitudes and reactions, here are a few suggestions: Your entire outlook may be wrong. Like that unfortunate secretary, you may resent everything and thereby poison yourself with the thought of bitter injustice. Folks who are still at the bottom of the success ladder can usually explain how others have kept them from succeeding. They often go into detail about things that happened years ago, which they still claim are the cause of their troubles. James Allen has written that a man only begins to be a man when he ceases to whine and revile, and commences to search for the "hidden justice" which regulates his life.[2] In like manner, you may be going around in a negative rut because you do not make sufficient mental effort to be free from it, or to rise above it.

At such times, you can paraphrase the words of Jesus and declare often, "ALL THAT WHICH THE FATHER HAS GIVEN ME NOW COMES TO ME." (John 6:37) Remind yourself that there is a divine plan for every life, a plan that will make man healthier, happier and more successful than he has ever been. Know that your present experiences can lead you into the divine plan, and then open the door by declaring often: "THE DIVINE PLAN OF MY LIFE NOW UNFOLDS, STEP BY STEP. I HAPPILY RECOGNIZE EACH PHASE OF IT, ACCEPT IT IN MY PRESENT

---

2. *As a Man Thinketh*, (Marina del Rey, CA: DeVorss & Co.).

AND FUTURE AND LET IT SHOW ME HOW TO MAKE THE
MOST OF MY LIFE." Concerning your present experi-
ences, it is good to affirm the words of the Psalmist
"I DELIGHT TO DO THY WILL, O MY GOD." (Psalms 40:8)
You can know that God's will for you is supreme good
in your present and in your future.

WHAT ARE YOU DOING ABOUT
DISSATISFACTION?

If you are not satisfied with your present lot, what
are you doing to prepare yourself for better circumstances? Do you have a concrete goal in mind? Are you
willing to spend your leisure time taking night courses
or attending special lectures or reading particular
books or engaging in constructive activities that would
prepare you for greater success? Most folks aren't. Are
you the exception?

Instead of doing these things, many people prefer to
spend their leisure hours speaking in critical terms of
their work, their associates, the boss, and the world in
general. They believe that by tearing down the other
fellow, their own failures and dissatisfaction won't
show quite so much. When you find yourself tempted
to do likewise, change your thinking. To help do that,
affirm: "NEITHER DO I CONDEMN THEE. THE DIVINE LAW
OF JUSTICE AND FREEDOM IS AT WORK FOR ALL, IN ALL,
THROUGH ALL, AND I REJOICE IN THIS. NOBODY OR NO SET
OF CIRCUMSTANCES CAN KEEP MY GOD-GIVEN GOOD AWAY
FROM ME AND I REJOICE IN THIS KNOWLEDGE."

A secretary, whose boss has a political job, recently
described the injustice she faced in her office. Another
employee with much less seniority was given an assignment with regard to the boss's campaign work, which

this secretary felt she alone was entitled to do. It was interesting, exciting work, whereas her own duties were heavier and more technical. When she began using the above prayer statements to recondition her attitudes from condemnation and injustice to freedom and divine justice, the whole picture changed. The other worker was transferred out of the office, and the secretary then gained the seniority and job which she felt were hers!

In another instance, a woman who was working part-time told of all the injustices that were evident in her life. Her health was not good; she felt burdened with her mother who did not trust her and who even steamed open her mail; she was dissatisfied with her work, but felt she was not qualified for anything better. She was in debt; she had property she had been unable to rent and one piece of real estate she had not been able to sell. This woman was a spinster who felt that it was unjust that she had never married. Every phase of her life was beclouded by her attitude of bitter injustice. As she began to declare divine justice, freedom and satisfaction for all phases of her world, her whole way of life improved remarkably. She came to realize she had been her own worst enemy through her limited ideas.

DIRECT YOUR ENERGIES TOWARD A GOAL

When your energies are constructively directed to a specific end, non-essentials have a way of falling aside. Petty thoughts, useless relationships, ill tempers, destructive emotions that often result in ill health, discouragement and failure need find no place in your life when you begin thinking of how you want your life to really be.

Things cannot improve in an outer way until things change in an inner way, because the inner processes of the mind control all the outer experiences of our lives. If you are in the midst of apparent failure, financial difficulties, or restlessness and dissatisfaction with your work, none of these conditions need prevent you from entertaining ideas of abundance, plans for riches, and mental images of the success which you seek. Nothing can stop you from moving toward your goals mentally, as you ask Divine Intelligence what next steps you are to take to bring forth your desires.

We live in a sea of energy and intelligence, according to the scientists, and we have constant access to its benefits, if we ask for them. Your ships come in only after you have sent them out.

THERE IS AN ANSWER

Many folks "suffer along" in the midst of confusion and dissatisfaction because they do not realize that this is a friendly universe, filled with supreme intelligence that will lovingly answer their call for guidance, if they only ask for it. Concerning your present work and how to improve it, you should seek wisdom: "DIVINE INTELLIGENCE, WHAT POSITIVE, CONSTRUCTIVE, CREATIVE THOUGHT, WORD, ATTITUDE OR ACTION IS MY NEXT STEP TO IMPROVE MY PRESENT WORK? WHAT IS THE NEXT STEP INTO THE ABUNDANCE, SATISFACTION AND FREEDOM THAT IS MINE BY DIVINE RIGHT?"

A seeking mind is a healthy mind that gets answers to its inquiries which lead to healthy, progressive, satisfying results. It is much easier to entertain and work with rich, expanded ideas and to experience vital, valuable results than it is to compromise with failure by dwelling upon small ideas and expectations.

Recently an engineer explained to me how thinking big and expecting big results had helped him to find that his work was truly divine, sublime and most satisfying, as well as financially remunerative. In the past he had been assigned to much smaller engineering jobs, but when, through the application of prosperous thinking, his really big dream job came along, he was ready to handle it. He had prepared for it mentally and emotionally for a long time, and so it did not startle or unbalance him.

The method which this man had used to get out of a job that no longer satisfied him, and to be able to handle the really big dream job was this: He bought a little black book and began putting into it the biggest, richest, most successful ideas and statements he could find. This helped expand his thinking and helped him remain peaceful, poised and inspired in the face of job dissatisfaction. It was thereafter that the biggest job of his life opened to him.

For instance, he began his day by opening his little black book and meditating on these ideas he found there: "THIS IS GOD'S DAY, A GOOD DAY. I PRONOUNCE THIS DAY AND ALL OF ITS ACTIVITIES GOOD!" As he thought of the various activities of the day, he affirmed, "MY OWN RIGHT AND PERFECT WORK AWAITS ME THIS DAY." For the long-range work picture, he often affirmed, "I DEMONSTRATE MY RIGHT WORK NOW." For new ideas in handling various work problems, he affirmed, "I AM NOW

OPEN AND RECEPTIVE TO THE RICH, DIVINE IDEAS THAT NOW PERFECTLY INITIATE AND SUSTAIN MY BUSINESS AFFAIRS." When discouragement or some upsetting experience arose he affirmed, "NOTHING CAN DEFEAT ME. I GIVE THANKS FOR THE PERFECT, IMMEDIATE RIGHT RESULTS. I REJOICE THAT I AM NOW SUCCESSFUL IN ALL MY WAYS." When the feeling of pressure or uncertainty tried to appear, he affirmed, "MY YOKE IS EASY AND MY BURDEN IS LIGHT. MY ACCOMPLISHMENTS ARE MANY. I AM DIVINELY EQUIPPED TO ACCOMPLISH GREAT THINGS WITH EASE." For business conferences, he affirmed, "I PRONOUNCE THIS BUSINESS CONFERENCE AND EVERYTHING CONNECTED WITH IT GOOD. SATISFYING RESULTS QUICKLY APPEAR." At the end of the day, instead of rehashing its events, he affirmed, "THIS IS A TIME OF SATISFYING COMPLETION. I LOOSE AND LET GO THIS DAY. DIVINE INTELLIGENCE ESTABLISHES ONLY GOOD FROM IT. ALL ELSE FADES AWAY." For a night of rest and in preparation for a successful tomorrow, he affirmed: "AS I LIE DOWN TO PEACEFUL SLEEP, I THANK GOD FOR MY SUCCESSFUL DAY. I REST EASILY, KNOWING THAT DIVINE INTELLIGENCE IS RENEWING MY MIND AND BODY, AND PREPARING ME FOR AN EVEN MORE SUCCESSFUL DAY TOMORROW."

YOUR REAL WORK LIES BEFORE YOU

Your real work lies in a straight line before you. A new opportunity will open whenever you have gained all the discipline and knowledge that the old work has to offer you. Meanwhile, remind yourself that there is no work that is high or low, so long as it is essential to the welfare of anyone. So perform it as efficiently as you can, as long as you are active in it. When asking for guidance while holding expanded ideas, it helps to face your present experiences, reminding yourself, "THIS TOO SHALL PASS."

You should endeavor to live normally in the midst of present job dissatisfaction, at the same time making the most of your present work. This helps you to remain steady in working toward greater good. Of course, everyone who tries to be true to the highest, especially in his work, has periods of intense discouragement. There is no disgrace in becoming discouraged, but do not let discouragement overwhelm you, possess you and rob your mind of its wonderful visions of the success toward which you are striving.

In the face of discouragement, your function is to concentrate on your higher ideals of more satisfying work, and then to declare a divine solution for the experiences of the moment. James Allen explains, "Your circumstances may be uncongenial, but they shall not long remain so if you perceive an ideal and strive to reach it. *You cannot travel within and stand still without.*"[3]

When you seem downcast, it is helpful to remember that it is darkest just before the dawn of new good. Despair is usually an emotional indication that the tide is turning, and that the dawn is coming sooner than you think. As you continue to travel within, the without will take care of itself.

If necessary, use the mental law of reversal on the situation. Someone has said that in the mental realm, thought can conceive of opposites and produce them more easily than thought can accept a gradual degree of good and produce it. A radical change of view often

---

3. Ibid.

clears the mind of cluttered, limited ideas, so that the mental swing to the opposite can produce an opposite result quickly.

Dare to be a spiritual architect and to build pictures of larger good; dare to enjoy these pictures of increased good mentally as you go about your daily tasks. Feel and visualize success right in the midst of dissatisfaction. Dare to affirm rich, unlimited success for yourself, no matter what is happening to you or around you at the moment. Declare: "THIS OR SOMETHING BETTER, FATHER; THY SUPREME GOOD WILL BE DONE."

EXPECT CHANGES FOR THE BETTER

Then remind yourself that you do not make things better by fighting present unhappy working conditions. You do not make things better by blaming others for your disappointments and failure experiences. Take a non-resistant attitude toward existing conditions, and know that they already are changing for the better! When things appear at a stand-still, remember the principle of physics which states that the entire universe is in constant motion; that we live, move and have our being in an "ocean of motion," though with our five outer senses we do not fully realize it. Nothing stands still, everything is constantly changing, whether it seems to be or not. If you expect such changes to be for the better, they will surely come.

In periods when you know changes are working but are not yet apparent, don't be misled by fear thoughts which try to convince you that your higher ideas are too good to be true, too wonderful to happen, or too good to last. When fear or doubt arise, put your best foot foward and do something definite to effect the successful feeling and the successful look, so as to convince not only yourself but others that you *are* succeeding! One who conquers doubt and fear conquers failure. It helps tremendously for others to think that you are succeeding, whether your success seems evident to you at the moment or not. You reap the real benefits of others' thoughts and expectancies for your success; coupled with your own, they can expedite the results of success in your life.

THE SATURATION TECHNIQUE

Saturate yourself in atmospheres of plenty and in associations with successful people. When there seems no evidence that greater success and prosperity can be yours, take time to walk through the banks of your city, observing all the successful people who have plenty of money. This is the time to visit lovely surroundings in beautiful new buildings and stores. Move through the richest sections of your city and countryside where the abundance of God and man are in evidence.

Associate with creative individuals of rich talent, such as artists and intellectuals, if that brings you an enriched feeling. If attending operas and concerts or visiting art galleries makes you feel rich, do so. It might be that listening to music recordings or hearing lectures on cultural subjects will inspire you. I find it helpful to read the success stories and autobiographies of famous people. When we realize the challenges which celebrated people have met and overcome, our own slack periods seem slight by comparison, and we are renewed in the feeling that we definitely can and shall achieve our own goals.

During one difficult period in my life, I found that, by taking art lessons and doing some painting, my discouragement was soon transformed into hope for a better future. I know of a lady who conquered despondency by working daily in her lovely rose garden.

If it is the out-of-doors that gives you a feeling of richness, then enjoy more sunshine, fresh air and the peacefulness of Mother Nature. Attendance at sports events can recharge your mental batteries. Active participation in sports such as golf, horseback riding, fishing or swimming can help to relieve mental sluggishness. At other times a long walk or ride in the country gives the lift you need.

The beauty of antiques, interior decorating, preparation of exotic foods or the creation of special clothes can add to your feeling of richness. At still another tense period in my life, I found great joy in working with a dressmaker toward the design and creation of my clothes. It turned my attention away from my present job dissatisfaction long enough for the problem to work out, and a change in jobs came.

Perhaps reading the classics or the Bible, or participation in certain quiet games, will uplift you. Having quiet times to absorb new ideas is helpful. I like to read Sunday papers from all over the nation. Just by browsing through them, studying the ads showing beautiful clothes, far away places and reports of new books, art and music, I derive a heightened sense of freedom and richness.

It is never a waste of time to saturate your mind, body and affairs in rich ideas, rich associations, rich atmospheres, and in any activity, inner or outer, which brings a feeling of richness to your inner being, especially during those periods when it seems that success is slow in manifesting. Especially, make good use of your free time. In the course of your daily activities, you may not be free to saturate yourself with those things that make you feel rich. But in your off hours, you can surely find uplift in new diversions, although some free time should be devoted to additional study and self-improvement so that you can uncover greater job satisfaction.

Years ago, when my life was burdened by limitation, the only way I could gain a sense of freedom and the vision of possible success was to slip away for a quiet, leisurely walk around the block toward the end of each day. Yet that simple act enabled me to "hold on" to my higher visions of good so that they were later able to manifest. This is a rich universe with countless ways to shower its blessings upon us when we keep our expectancy high. Daily remind yourself that your cup is really half-full, rather than half-empty.

MAKE THE MOST OF YOUR
PRESENT SITUATION

Whether it is more satisfaction in your present work, or another step up the ladder in your work; or whether it is a whole new career you desire, or financial freedom from all organized work—in any event, your goal *can* be attained. You need not feel "trapped" by present conditions. There is always something you can do about it. A good statement to use in calling forth the right result, whether it would mean remaining in your present place or going on to other work, is this: "DIVINE INTELLIGENCE NOW WORKS IN ME AND MY LIFE AND AFFAIRS, TO WILL AND TO DO WHATEVER IS FOR MY HIGHEST GOOD, AND DIVINE INTELLIGENCE CANNOT FAIL!"

If you are convinced that your present work is not satisfying and cannot become so, set about changing the situation by declaring: "I AM NOW SHOWN NEW WAYS OF LIVING AND NEW METHODS OF WORK. I AM NOT CONFINED TO THE WAYS AND METHODS OF THE PAST. I EXPERIENCE MY PERFECT WORK IN THE PERFECT WAY, WHICH NOW RENDERS ME PERFECT SATISFACTION AND PERFECT PAY."

Follow through on whatever ideas or events that present themselves to you for change. Stop thinking about or talking about present dissatisfaction. Forget it; let it go.

Then begin bringing about order, harmony and beauty into your present job. If you are dissatisfied, set about doing everything possible to make your job more pleasant and orderly. Clean out file drawers, straighten up your desk. Add a plant or something of beauty, which you and others can view often for a "quick lift." Give fellow workers the benefit of your spoken praise, sincere appreciation, words of kindness, as well as your silent prayers and blessings. Above all, remind yourself that you are a mental part of any situation in which you now find yourself. As you give that situation the benefit of your highest thoughts and actions, you help to establish order, harmony and satisfaction for all concerned. When you make the best of your present situation, you can be assured that greater good will reveal itself. Meanwhile, as is written in the Book of Ecclesiastes, "Whatsoever thy hand findeth to do, do it with all thy might." (Ecclesiastes 9:10)

In other words, as a friend of mine has often said, "When you go through hell, make it pay—with greater understanding than you previously had, and the result of good from that experience will be lasting."

FREE YOURSELF OF CRITICISM

Dare to think, act, and react differently from those who are poverty-prone, unless you want to remain with them at the bottom of the ladder. There is plenty of room at the top in any line of work or profession for those who dare to free themselves of the usual thoughts of bickering, jealousies, and petty criticisms entertained by many people. When you are tempted to join in the chorus of such mass negative thought, declare instead: "THERE IS NO CRITICISM IN ME, FOR ME OR AGAINST ME. THE SUPREME LAW OF GOOD IS NOW IN CHARGE OF MY LIFE, AND DIVINE HARMONY NOW REIGNS SUPREME IN ME AND IN MY WORLD." This realization protects you from the negative thoughts of others. Give them in turn the blessing and protection of your constructive attitudes.

Are you thinking, "But is this worthwhile?" Listen! The greatest knowledge which you can gain about yourself and your fellow beings is that one person thinking and acting constructively in any situation, cannot fail to produce good results. All mankind is hungry for constructive attitudes, actions, and reactions and quickly reponds to them.

I once saw this happen in a situation involving two junior members of a large law firm. Known for its belief in hard work and productive results, their firm was very prosperous, as were all of its members. One of the junior law firm members was a happy, optimistic, joyous individual. He did not hesitate to pay a compliment when it was due, or to show kindness and courtesy to everyone he met. No one was too insignificant to receive kind attention from him. This young man apparently did not know what it was to criticize, condemn or complain. The other lawyer was actually better qualified for the work they were both doing.

Because he held one more college degree than the first man, the law firm was paying him several hundred dollars more per month. Thus, he had every advantage over the first man, or so one would suppose. But this high-paid lawyer was a "quiet complainer" and nothing could please him. Details upset him; people upset him; an unexpected assignment upset him; everything upset him. Within a year he was no longer employed by this firm. Within that same year, the other attorney had been promoted into his position and salary. Later this junior partner became a full-fledged member of the firm. Never in the history of that firm had any lawyer been advanced so rapidly into responsibility or in financial compensation.

TAKE A NEW LEASE ON LIFE

It has been said that work is the highest form of play. Whether work is pleasant activity or laborious toil depends upon your attitudes about yourself, others, and about the world in general. Be assured that work is divine, and that your true work and your true compensation seek you as much as you seek them! Man's true work is that which he does best, and from which he derives deep satisfaction.

Take a new lease on life right now, no matter what your life situation. Begin by boldly declaring, as did Charles Fillmore at the age of ninety-three: "I FAIRLY SIZZLE WITH ZEAL AND ENTHUSIASM, AND SPRING FORTH WITH A MIGHTY FAITH TO DO THE THINGS THAT OUGHT TO BE DONE BY ME."

Join countless others in getting into work or self-expression in some form that satisfies you by using this success formula:

1. As nearly as you can, form a mental picture of what you want your life to be like.

2. After forming a picture of what you desire, begin developing and living your desire mentally. Begin thinking of the desired results as though they were already obtained. You thereby take mental possession of your desired good and quicken its manifestation.

3. Ask divine intelligence to show you the next step toward attaining your desired picture of good. You will be shown whether it means going to night school for more courses of study, making drastic changes in your work and way of life, or developing a more constructive attitude about your present job and its potential. As you are shown the next step, boldly follow it in faith, knowing that it can lead only to richer satisfaction.

4. Persist and persevere in knowing that congenial work can and shall be yours. Emerson said that everything has a price and if that price is not paid, then not that thing but something else is obtained. So persist in paying the price in inner and outer ways, and you shall gain from life what you truly desire.

5. Continue giving your best in your present situation, even though you may be mentally living beyond it. And above all, keep your spirits high through the law of saturation.

Truly, as you travel within in these various ways, you cannot stand still without!

THE ANCIENT LAW
OF PROSPERITY

— Chapter 10 —

In ancient times, "ten" was considered "the magic number of increase," so it seems appropriate that this Chapter Ten should describe the ancient law of prosperity.

A Texas businessman once became irate when I talked about this particular prosperity law. He got so upset that he jumped up and interrupted my lecture, heatedly declaring, "Why are you talking about *that* subject? There's nothing about it in your book, *The Dynamic Laws of Prosperity.* Had I known you were going to talk in these terms, I would not have come!"

I explained to him that there *had been* a chapter on the ancient law of prosperity in my original manuscript of this book, but that a cautious editor had removed it, considering it perhaps too controversial a subject for a

173

new author to tackle. Since it was my first book with that publisher, I had reluctantly conceded to my editor's wishes, but I had regretted doing so ever since.

Instead of storming out of the lecture hall—as I had expected—that businessman remained and listened patiently. Some time later I returned to lecture there again. When I saw that same man approaching I thought, "What am I in for now?" But this time he said, "You were right. Your book *should* carry a chapter on prosperity's ancient law. I've tried it and it has helped me more than all the other prosperity laws combined!" He seemed to be enjoying his "conversion."

My desire of several decades has finally been realized, and I am now free to share with you in this chapter one of prosperity's most fascinating methods. I hasten to add that almost every book I have written since contains a chapter on this subject—whether the book is based on the subject of prosperity, love, prayer, healing or Bible interpretation. Why? Because this ancient success law affects every phase of our lives—not just the pocketbook.

Furthermore, I find that people are so fascinated with this ancient law of prosperity, that I receive more mail on this subject than on all the other subjects on which I've written combined! So much for that well-meaning, but overly-cautious editor of long ago. . .

THE ANCIENT LAW OF PROSPERITY
AND HOW IT WORKS

The importance of the ancient law of prosperity is shown in the fact that there has never been a nation, however remote or old, in which the practice of this particular success principle has not prevailed. The early Egyptians, Babylonians, Persians, Arabians, Greeks, Romans, and Chinese were among those who used this special prosperity method. Even primitive man, through the financial "sacrifices" he offered his gods, practiced this age-old prosperity method.

The ancient prosperity law is this: True prosperity has a spiritual basis. God is the Source of your supply. Your mind, body, abilities, talents, education, experience, job or profession are all instruments and channels of your prosperity, but God is the Source. Therefore, you must do something definite and consistent to keep in touch with that rich Source, if you want to be consistently prospered.

Sharing is the beginning of financial increase. Systematic giving opens the way to systematic receiving. However that giving must be done in a certain way: through the consistent sharing of your tithes with God's work and workers at the point or points where you are receiving spiritual help and inspiraton. The word "tithe" means "tenth" and the ancient people felt that "ten" was "the magic number of increase."

Jacob, at a low point in his life, made a tithe covenant with God, in which he asked for prosperity, guidance, peace of mind, and reconciliation with his family. In turn, he promised, "Of all that thou shalt give me, I will surely give the tenth unto thee." (Genesis 28:20-22) It is little wonder that Jacob became one of the Bible's early millionaires.[1] Those who tithe, taking God as their financial partner today, realize that this

---

1. See *The Millionaires of Genesis*, Chapter 6: "The Prospering Power of a Success Covenant."

holy alliance will help them to prosper in just and orderly ways, just as it did Jacob.

Various schemes have been suggested for getting-
rich-quick. Many of them fail because they are based
solely on "getting"—not on "giving." They have no
spiritual foundation. As related in my book, *Open
Your Mind to Receive*:[2] Two Chicago businessmen once
told me they had held the local franchise on one of the
most famous success courses in America, one that cost
thousands of dollars to take. Though they prospered
for a time, they eventually went broke—while teaching
success principles. It was embarrassing.

Only after these two businessmen found their way
into one of the local New Thought churches and began
to put God first financially through tithing, did their
affairs stabilize and prosper. It was then that they
realized their mistake. Their course had only emphasized "getting"— not "giving." They had not taught
the spiritual side of prosperity: that their students
could tithe their way to prosperity.

You may be thinking, "Yes, but I know people who
do not recognize God as the Source of their supply,
and do not tithe. Yet they are prosperous; some are
even exceedingly wealthy." We all know such people.
However, true prosperity includes peace of mind and
health of body, as well as financial peace and plenty.
Remember that the word "wealth" means "well-being"
and "wholeness." Perhaps those people are prosperous
in a financial sense. But what about their peace of
mind, health of body, the state of their relationships,
and their over-all well-being?

---

2. Published by DeVorss & Co., Marina del Rey, CA, 1983.

THE MOST EXCITING PROSPERITY
STORY OF ALL TIMES!

The Hebrews of the Old Testament became one of the richest groups of people the world has ever known through their use of the prosperity law of tithing. Abraham learned this success secret from the Babylonians, who were among the most prosperous people of the past, and he "tithed a tenth of all" (Genesis 14:20) to the High Priest of Salem. Abraham passed along the tithing law of prosperity to his grandson, Jacob, who included it in his success covenant. (Genesis 28:20-22) Jehovah later gave Moses specific instructions about tithing for the Hebrews, "The tenth shall be holy unto Jehovah." (Leviticus 27:32) The Hebrews developed such a consciousness of opulence that, at one point, they even had to be restrained from giving! "The people were restrained from bringing, for the stuff they had was sufficient for all the work, and it was too much." (Exodus 36:6, 7) Nevertheless, they continued to give. "The tithe of all things brought they in abundantly . . . and laid them by heaps" at the altar. (II Chronicles 31:5, 6) In the New Testament era, tithing was a required Temple practice, so both Jesus and Paul were taught to tithe.

The ancients intuitively knew that giving, sharing and putting God first financially was the first step to permanent, enduring prosperity. So tithing was a household word in Bible times, and over and over their sharing of the tenth brought them peace, power and plenty. They gave not the last and the least, but the first and the best, and their giving made them rich! They felt their tithing practices not only prospered them, but protected them from the negative experiences of life; so their acts of giving were occasions of

celebration and holy joy. No wonder theirs is among
the most exciting prosperity stories of all times![3]

PROSPERED, HEALED AND PROTECTED

Miracles Wrought in Her Life in Oklahoma: When I
began to tithe a year ago, my income started to grow.
I no longer worry about money. Neither do I experience sudden financial strains or unwanted surprises. Instead, the only financial surprises I have had
since tithing have been good ones: like having money
come to me "out of the blue." I am also surprised at
how much further my income now goes. Tithing seems
to have stretched it.

When I began to tithe in faith the small amount
I had, the first thing I noticed was that chronic car
repair bills ceased. Money not only began to flow in
unexpectedly, but new business opportunities also
prospered me. Also, the quality of my life improved so
that I now enjoy a harmonious lifestyle. Another surprise has been that a longstanding health problem no
longer plagues me. It simply disappeared. Putting God
first financially has wrought miracles in my life!

Just as the farmer returns one-tenth of his seed for
soil enrichment, so does impersonal giving and sharing
open the way to enriched living on all levels of life to
those who faithfully practice it. If the farmer refused
to give back to the soil a percentage of the crops which
the soil had given to him, he would have no crops.

---

3. See the author's books, *The Prosperity Secrets of the Ages,*
The Millionaires of Genesis, The Millionaire Moses, The Million-
aire Joshua, and *The Millionaire from Nazareth.*

The Difference Between Those Who Do and Those Who Don't in Missouri: I am grateful to have learned of the power of tithing. I have friends who have studied along inspirational and/or metaphysical lines for years. Yet they continue to struggle financially because they refuse to tithe. I have other friends who are studying along these same lines whom I've been able to introduce to the practice of tithing, and they no longer "strain and strive." Instead, they "tithe and thrive."

It has been said that the person who takes up the practice of tithing will have at least six surprises: (1) He will be surprised at the amount of money he has to give the Lord's work. (2) He will be surprised at the wisdom and good judgment tithing gives him in using the remaining nine-tenths of his income. (3) He will be surprised at the ease with which he can meet his financial obligations. (4) He will be surprised at the deepening of his prosperity consciousness, as well as his spiritual life. (5) He will be surprised at how easily he can go from one tenth to larger giving. (6) He will be surprised at himself for not having adopted the tithing plan sooner!

WHY THIS PRACTICE IS A PROTECTION FROM NEGATIVE EXPERIENCES

Why does the practice of sharing one-tenth of your income with God's work and workers help to protect you from the negative experiences of life? Why can it even produce for you the benefits described in the foregoing "tither's surprises"? Because when you put God first financially, you open your mind, body and affairs to the goodness of the universe; to its infinite life, love, wisdom, power and substance. You also tend to look to a loving Father for guidance, healing and supply. Since tithing is businesslike, orderly, scientific and practical, you open the way to receive similar results in your life.

Some of the most prominent millionaires of the twentieth century attributed their phenomenal success to tithing. These included the Colgate, Heinz, Kraft and Rockefeller families. In 1855, as a young man, John D. Rockefeller began tithing. His total income for that year was $95.00, from which he tithed $9.50 to his church. Between 1855 and 1934, he gave away $531 million dollars. When people tried to criticize the Rockefeller wealth, he had a standard reply, "God gave me my money."

Because your are a spiritual being, made in the image and likeness of God, a loving Father and a rich universe are happy to multiply your good as an expression of universal affection, appreciation and esteem. A loving Father always wants you to be happier and more prosperous than you have ever been before. Such blessings are yours by divine right.

Thus, through your acts of impersonal, unselfish giving you attune your consciousness to that of universal abundance, and you put yourself in line to receive its rich gifts. Moses, the great "law giver," put it bluntly, "Thou shalt remember Jehovah thy God, for it is He that giveth thee power to get wealth." (Deuteronomy 8:18)

It is only as we let go of our littleness that we can expand into a larger life. "There is that scattereth, and increaseth yet more. And there is that withholdeth more than is meet, but it tendeth only to want. The liberal soul shall be blessed, and he that watereth shall be watered himself." (Proverbs 11:24, 25)

Tithing is an act of faith, and faith moves on universal substance to enhance and bless the tither. So it is only natural that the faithful tither should prosper, and that problems should fall away from his life.

PROSPEROUS RESULTS THROUGH OVERCOMING RESISTANCE TO TITHING

Traditionally, the act of giving has always been a vital part of spiritual worship. In many cultures, it was a required practice. However, in modern times, people have sometimes had a psychological block against tithing, because theologians have tended to stress what tithing would do for the church, instead of what it could do for the tither. Yet when you look up the great tithing promises in the Bible (such as Malachi 3:10), you discover that the Bible assures you that it is the individual that will be prospered, protected and blessed through tithing. Naturally, the recipient of those tithes will be blessed, too.

Why She Resisted Tithing in Colorado: Reading about the spiritual and monetary benefits of tithing has made me realize how much resistance I had had toward organized religion in general, and the subject of tithing in particular. Upon reflection I realize that it was because I had always heard about what tithing would do for the church — not how it could help me.

The enclosed tithe check represents the beginning of my release of that resistance, so that I may become open to the universal love and abundance that are mine by divine right. I now realize that putting God first financially is crucial to my inner growth and well-being, as well as to my economic progress.

From Last Dollar to Over a Million in Texas: Having been raised in traditional religious beliefs, my wife and I both had heard about tithing as children. However, we had been taught what it would do for the church, so the use of tithing as a dynamic personal prosperity method was a new idea to us. At the time we learned of this success principle, I was out of work, with several children and a wife to care for. Although we had only $50 left, we decided as an act of faith to write out a tithe check for $5. Almost immediately, I found a position with an engineering firm.

In the next few years, as we continued to tithe, my career turned to the oil business. New opportunities presented themselves in abundance. In less than ten years we went from our "last dollar" to a net worth of well over one million dollars! I became a full partner in an oil company. We bought a ranch in the country, and a comfortable house with a pool in town. We acquired a fine thoroughbred horse. We drive the best cars, and travel where we please. We've gone from wondering where our next meal would come from to where our next "dining" experience would be. Both personal and professional acclaim came to us through putting God first financially.

Sharing the Whole Tithe Brought Increased Business In Montana: I had been practicing all the laws of prosperity—except total tithing. I had felt I could not spare that much. But from my recent studies, I realized I could not afford *not* to give God His full tenth of everything I received, if I wished to permanently prosper. Since I have done this, I have been blessed far more than I could ever have thought possible!

TITHING BRINGS DEFINITE
FINANCIAL INCREASE

It has often been said that tithers prosper ten times quicker and ten times easier. In any event, thousands have grown out of life-long poverty into financial affluence and comfort through practicing "ten, the magic number of increase." Hundreds of thousands more are doing so today. "You will never find a tither in the poorhouse" is still a powerful adage, as evidenced by the following reports from my readers:

Loosens Grip on Money in Maine: I have been tithing for two years. Not only has it done wonders for my prosperity consciousness, but it has loosened my grip on money so that it could flow and grow.

Instant Increase in Ohio: This morning I put my tithe check of $59 in the mail. The postman later brought me two checks totalling $669.54. How's that for fast action from tithing?

Receives $2000 in Oregon: On the same day I released my tithe check, I received $2000! Tithing *does* prosper.

It Works for a Teenager in North Dakota: I started tithing three months ago. Before that I had little income. Since my first tithes, money has come to me from every direction: First, came a babysitting job. Then some friends gave me clothing. Next, my grandfather gave me almost double the amount of money he usually sends for my birthday. Also, other lovely gifts I can use were given me. I now have a complete new wardrobe. If this can happen at sixteen, I may be a millionaire by the time I am twenty-one!

A New Business Prospers in Europe: When I founded my business just over a year ago, I could not have imagined that within the first year I would be writing an invoice for $60,000 worth of business from just one client! I attribute my success to tithing from my business income, as well as from my personal income.

Good Job in New Mexico: I had recently felt that life was passing me by; that I was not in the best job for me. Yet I could not see, humanly, how anything better

could come, nor how I could last until it did. Nevertheless, I began to tithe in faith. After writing my first
tithe check, I had only $48 left until payday.

Almost immediately I was offered a job of reporter
for the local newspaper. My starting salary is $12,000
per year — far more than I was previously making.
Within 90 days my annual salary is due to go to
$15,000, with a possibility of another raise within an-
other six months. I would suggest to people in a similar
"no win" situation that they begin to put God first
financially, then relax and watch what happens.

Sale of Land in California: I released my first tithe,
and three days later I sold fifteen acres in the beautiful
California "high desert." That land had been for sale
for more than two years. The sale came when I released
those tithes for universal good.

How $5600 Came in Idaho: Because of business and
personal stresses, I began to drink to relax. My daughter had died, and there were other wounded areas in
my life. I finally had to declare bankruptcy. When I
began to study along inspirational lines, I realized my
value as a human being was not tied to possessions or
prideful accomplishments. I joined Alcoholics Anonymous and found more loving friends than I could have
dreamed possible.

With no job or income, I started to tithe my time in
volunteer work, yet financial benefits started coming
to me immediately. $20 here, $50 there, gifts of food
and gas. It was amazing. Then I realized I must begin
tithing financially, even from those casual gifts, if
I wished to permanently prosper. So I began writing
checks to those people and organizations in spiritual
work who have made a significant contribution to my
growth and well-being. The result was that I immediately received two commission checks totalling $5600!
A friend who has owed me money for four years sent
$200 and a note saying the balance would soon be dis-
patched. I am now grateful that your writings on tith-

ing jumped off the pages at me, and showed me what to do when I needed it most.

Raises, Promotion in Alaska: My husband had not had a raise in two years. Company policy said no raises perhaps for another year or so. Yet within a few months from the time we began tithing, not only did he get a raise, so did everyone else in the company. Then he got a second raise. A few months later, he was given a promotion. Then I received a pay raise in my job. Next, some people who had owed us money for a long time — which we never expected to collect — started paying us back. Oh, the wonders of tithing!

Why Her Tithing Had Not Worked in Ohio: In the past I tithed in a haphazard manner so I received haphazard results. I became bitter and decided tithing was not working for me. I now see it was the manner in which I tithed, and the limited state of my thinking. More recently I have begun to tithe faithfully with love and appreciation for what I have to share.

Even though I began tithing only from net income, the results were tremendous. This prompted me to begin to tithe from gross income, and from savings. I now plan to begin tithing from an annuity, tax returns, and interest earned. I am delighted with the expanded life I am now leading. This practice has enlarged my spiritual understanding as well.

TITHING BRINGS HARMONIOUS PROGRESS
IN RELATIONSHIPS

Showers of Blessings in New Jersey: Three years ago I had two teenage children on drugs, I was a mental and physical wreck, and my marriage was on the rocks. I began to study inspirational books, to use affirmative prayers, and to tithe from my own personal income.

Things began to happen. Our children (twins) turned eighteen, left home, got an apartment and jobs. Both are now working their way through college. This is something I never thought they would do. I began to read books on natural and spiritual healing, and two major health problems were cured. My husband became more loving, understanding, helpful, and agreeable. Best of all he was offered a wonderful new job in the newspaper industry. This allows him to travel—something he has always wanted.

We are moving to a new location where I look forward to making new friends and getting a new job. Our 14-year-old son has dreamed of going to a military academy. My husband's new job will now make this possible. Due to circumstances beyond my control, I had not seen my mother or sister for ten years. The way opened for me to recently visit them, and our time together was enjoyable. God has truly showered me with His blessings, since I began to put Him first in my time and money.

From Death to a New Life in Mississippi: Two years ago, I was at an all-time low. My husband of twenty years had died suddenly at the early age of 42. I spent what insurance money there was on debts, the funeral and living expenses. I had no job nor prospects of one. I got into a miserable affair with a man in an "off-again, on-again" marriage.

At this terrible point in my life, I found one of the Ponder books and was intrigued with the tithing chapter. Although I had previously scoffed at the idea, I decided to make a tithe covenant with God. I also made a prayer wheel and started using prayers of forgiveness and release. My life had not instantly gotten into a mess, and it did not instantly get straightened out.

However, now as I look back, I hardly recognize the person I was then. My attitude is totally different. I am now financially secure with a great job. I have excellent health, a beautiful grandchild, and a kind, lov-

ing man with whom to share my blessings. I also have
sanity and peace of mind.

TITHING BRINGS PEACE OF MIND

Life on the Upswing in North Carolina: My life has
been on the upswing since I began tithing. I feel good
when I tithe. Most of all, I feel good *because* I tithe.

A Weight Lifted in Georgia: Every time I put a tithe
check in the mail, I feel as if a weight has been removed from my shoulders. I feel blessed, enriched and
at peace about my financial affairs, which are prospering accordingly.

Good Changes Occur in Virginia: Through the practice
of tithing, my life is continuously changing for the better. Putting God first financially has brought blessings
I would never have dreamed I could have into my life,
including the life-long desire for peace of mind.

THE HEBREWS' BITTER PROSPERITY LESSON

There is basically one problem in life: congestion.
There is basically one solution: circulation. Systematic
giving is, therefore, a powerful practice that blesses
every phase of our lives, as it keeps us attuned to the
wealth of the universe. Otherwise, through lack of circulation, and the resulting congestion, our lives can be
thrown out of balance. It is then that problems result.

The Hebrews' incredible prosperity story continued
until the billionaire, Solomon, eventually forgot that
God was the Source of his vast blessings. Instead, in an
effort to gain further wealth and prestige, he began to
play politics through making heathen alliances. At

that point, the Hebrews became lax in their tithing practices, and soon went into Babylonian exile. Later, when the poverty-stricken "remnant" of Jews returned from exile, the wise prophet, Malachi, pointed out the cause and cure of their problems:

First, he described the cause of the non-tither's problems:

"From the days of your father ye have turned aside from mine ordinances, and have not kept them. Return unto me, and I will return unto you, said Jehovah of Hosts. But ye say, Wherein shall we return? Will a man rob God? Yet ye rob me. But ye say, Wherein have we robbed thee? In tithes and offerings. Ye are cursed with the curse; for ye rob me, even this whole nation."

Second, he described the lavish blessings due the tither:

"Bring ye the whole tithe into the storehouse, that there may be food in my house, and prove me now herewith, said Jehovah of Hosts, if I will not open you the windows of heaven, and pour you out a blessing, that there shall not be room enough to receive it."

Third, he promised divine protection to the tither:

"And I will rebuke the devourer for your sakes, and he shall not destroy the fruits of your ground; neither shall your vine cast its fruit before the time in the field, saith Jehovah of Hosts."

Fourth, he promised personal happiness and universal prestige to the tither:

"And all the nations shall call you happy; for ye shall be a delightsome land, said Jehovah of Hosts." (Malachi 3:7-12)

Through their earlier tithing and non-tithing practices, the Hebrews had experienced both the bitter problems of congestion, and the abundant blessings caused by circulation. Thanks to Malachi, tithing as a spiritual discipline and prosperity principle, was again established as a required Temple practice. It continued through the New Testament era. And the collective prosperity consciousness it generated for the Hebrews of old has continued until this day for those people who tithe.

<h2 style="text-align:center">WHAT HAPPENED WHEN THEY
STOPPED TITHING</h2>

Many of us can identify with both the bitter and sweet prosperity lessons the Hebrews learned. A minister recently wrote in his church bulletin:

> One of the questions I am often asked is why people have health problems, since God is a loving Father. I have found that the most common denominator among the people who raise this question to me is that they are not systematic, accurate tithers. They want God to heal them, yet they have unwittingly caused the congestion in their bodies. It was caused by their own lack of circulation, through their lack of consistent giving. These people have unbalanced their contact with the rhythm of God's good, so they are getting an unbalanced result in the form of ill health.[4]

In Biblical times, tithes were believed to purge one of sin, illness, and even to deliver from death. No one

---

4. See the chapter titled "Your Giving Can Heal You" in the author's book, *The Dynamic Laws of Healing*. (Marina del Rey, CA: DeVorss & Co., 1966).

appeared empty-handed before God. In some eras of
the Old and New Testament periods, to break the tithing law of prosperity was considered so serious that it
was punishable by death.[5] Having evolved in our soul
growth into the power of individual choice, we no
longer have such stringent ideas on the subject. Yet
there are those people who have witnessed the "death"
of their good through similar laxness.

> **Learned Her Lesson** in Massachusetts: Last year when I
> faithfully tithed, I prospered in totally unforeseen
> ways. Then I married and stopped tithing because my
> husband didn't believe in it. I tithed again briefly, and
> won a $17,000 per year scholarship to Harvard Univer-
> sity. Then I stopped tithing again. I practiced the
> other prosperity principles, but without tithing, the
> effect was limited.
>
> I finally realized that tithing was the missing link—
> the only thing standing between me and permanent
> prosperity. My husband, who has seen this prosperity
> principle work for us on these occasions, has slowly
> become a convert, and I am again tithing. I feel I have
> now set my feet firmly on the high road to prosperous
> living.
>
> **Neglect Leads to Unemployment** in California: I am in
> the entertainment business, and I neglected my tithing
> during part of this year. The result was that I suddenly
> found myself unemployed. I've made my choice: God
> or money? I'll take God first! Then the money will
> follow.
>
> **Cause and Cure of Indebtedness** in Illinois: I practiced
> the tithing law for years and prospered. Then I got so
> busy being prosperous that I neglected my tithes.

---

5. See Chapter 6, "When Your Prosperity is Withheld" in the
author's book, *The Millionaire Joshua* (Marina del Rey, CA: De-
Vorss & Co., 1979).

When finances became complicated I realized why and began tithing again. Within one month from the time I resumed tithing—in the face of numerous financial challenges—here's what happened:

Insurance money was returned to us. My husband got extra jobs that brought us more than we would have believed he could possibly earn. We found $100 cash previously set aside. A new dental insurance plan, that we were unaware of due to his early retirement, paid us a large cash amount. The arrival of other unexpected funds made it possible for me to join my husband on a business trip, and also to visit relatives. When I paid the bills, I even had enough to pay some bills double—a great step toward paying off old debts completely. I have learned a valuable lesson by getting careless. I shall never neglect to put God first financially again.

TITHING GROSS OR NET

Strictly speaking, biblical tithing consisted of "a tenth of all." (Genesis 14:20) If you are not yet ready in your thinking to tithe from your gross income, you may want to consider tithing from your net income. But you will surely want to invoke "ten, the magic number of increase" to some degree. Tithing is an act of faith that moves on the rich substance of the universe to prosper you mightily, and to expand your world within and without in ways you would not have dreamed possible. Do not try to reason through the mysterious power of tithing. Instead, simply accept the fact that tithing releases a mystical power to prosper you.

When you systematically tithe *first*, before paying bills or meeting other financial obligations, you will find that the remaining 90 percent of your income goes much further. You will be helped in many unforeseen ways. Once you make a habit of tithing, you will never miss those tithes. The very act of tithing will provide you with a sense of security, protection and guidance in a way that nothing else can.

WHERE YOU GIVE IS VERY IMPORTANT

If you wish to be truly prospered by the act of tithing, it is wise to give at the point or points where you are receiving spiritual help and inspiration—whether that be the church of your choice, or a minister, spiritual counselor, teacher or practitioner. Your tithes will enrich the recipient, allowing that organization or individual freedom from financial strain. This enables them to fulfill their high mission of uplifting mankind, unhindered by the material cares which can be so burdensome.

Perhaps this was why Jehovah instructed Moses that the priestly tribe of Israel, known as the Levites, was to receive none of the Promised Land. Instead, they received *all* of the tithes of *all* of the Promised Land. (Joshua 13:33; Numbers 18:21-24; Deuteronomy 14:27) The priests of Israel became millionaires through the tithes bestowed upon them by the other eleven tribes, as proclaimed by Mosaic Law. In turn, they shared "a tithe of the tithes" known as a "heave offering" with the place of worship. (Numbers 18:26-29) In this way, both God's workers and the places of worship were abundantly provided for.

In turn, their freedom from material care helped the spiritual leaders of Israel to develop and generate a prosperity consciousness that was to bless those whom they served for many centuries to come. It has been said that "a Jew can make more accidentally than a Gentile can make on purpose." If so, it all began with the group prosperity consciousness developed by the Hebrews centuries ago through their practice of tithing.

WHY OFFERINGS CAN PAUPERIZE, WHILE TITHES PROSPER

One of the best kept financial secrets of the ages is this: While it is better to give meager or spasmodic "love offerings" and voluntary pledges to God's work, than to give nothing at all, the voluntary offering plan has so often unintentionally pauperized millions of people. It has pauperized their churches and ministers as well. Why? Because lack of systematic giving leads to lack of systematic receiving for all concerned. This is probably why freewill offerings, given over and above the tithes, were considered incidental in Biblical times.

One minister recently wrote in his church bulletin:

A "just-getting-by" church acts as a negative role-model for its congregation. Poverty-conscious churches breed poverty-conscious congregations. Another "fund-raiser" or "increased-pledge drive" is only a temporary measure, a "bandaid" approach to financial solvency for the church. Also, it does not provide the church members with a valid personal reason for consistent giving, which should be to also benefit them individually, as biblically promised.

Just as in ancient times, it would be wise for tithing to be a requirement for church membership. If so, the minister would be a tither. Every member of his board of trustees would be a tither, thus qualifying them to handle more wisely church business. All other church leaders such as counselors, practitioners, Sunday School teachers and ushers would be tithers. And the church would tithe regularly from its overall income, giving a "heave offering" to the other churches or organizations with which it is connected, or through which it was being helped and inspired.

A church with such a giving consciousness would naturally attract a loving, giving congregation, because *people unconsciously go where there is a consciousness of increase*. Such churches are never problem-prone, but are places of peace, harmony and inspiration because spiritual teachings, rather than constant fund-raising, are emphasized. This spiritual method of giving, developed in ancient times, still produces vast benefits for all who use it today, both individually and collectively.

As Kahlil Gibran wrote in *The Prophet*, "It is good to give when asked, but it is better to give unasked, through understanding."[6]

WHAT ABOUT CHARITY GIVING?

Is giving to charity or community events the same as tithing? No. For enlightened and spiritually-evolving individuals, the highest form of philanthrophy is that of giving to spiritually-enlightened causes, organizations, and individuals. The Hebrews of the Old Testament became wealthy when they gave the *first* tithe impersonally to their priests and places of worship. (Leviticus 27:30-32; Numbers 18:21-24; Deuteronomy 14:22-27) Their *second* tithe was a festival or

6. Gibran, *The Prophet*.

retreat tithe. (Deuteronomy 12:6, 7) Their *third* tithe was a charity tithe. (Deuteronomy 14:28-29) They also shared "the first fruits" of their crops, and many other offerings, totaling about one-fourth of their gross income.

If you are giving more than one-tenth, then you should feel freer to share your second- or third-tenth with charity or other humanitarian causes. But the first-tenth should go to spiritual work or workers whose philosophy is uplifting and helpful to mankind, and one with which you agree. If sufficient numbers of people did this, many of the lesser humanitarian causes in the world would not be necessary. Those being helped by charity handouts would, instead, be learning through spiritual methods how to help themselves. "Give a man a fish and you feed him for a day. Teach him *how* to fish and you feed him for a lifetime."

Of course, for those individuals who have no spiritual inclinations or interest, to give to various charitable, cultural, educational or humanitarian causes is most commendable, and a great step forward in the development of their prosperity consciousness of sharing, as well as beneficial to their soul growth. The recipient of their gifts is likewise assisted and benefited at the present level of their understanding. However, according to the ancient laws of tithing, this is a secondary form of giving, rather than the highest.

THE PROSPERING POWER OF SECRECY, RELEASE AND FOCUSED GIVING

The words "sacred" and "secret" have the same root meaning. Your giving is sacred and therefore it should be kept secret. It is wise to give quietly with no strings attached, regardless of the amounts involved, not referring to them again. If large tithes are involved, it is sometimes necessary to emotionally release and re-release them until one has a sense of freedom from them. There should be no sense of possessiveness about the tithes one shares, regardless of their size, since all we receive comes from God and is not ours to permanently own. In tithe-giving, we are only returning to God a portion of all He has already given us. So if one resents one's giving, then the practice of release is in order.

Also, it is wiser to give the tenth systematically and freely than to give much larger amounts spasmodically. Tithing is not a "get-rich-quick" scheme by which you can force your good. "There is no rush in spirit." Instead, the act of tithing is a process of growth by which one evolves into larger giving (and larger receiving).

To give and then to make demands upon the recipient of one's gifts amounts to a "bribe," not a tithe. The conscientious tither does not give for "show" or publicity. The recipient of one's tithes should be equally as quiet about such gifts. Otherwise it is easy to dissipate and "talk away one's good." As the ancient people knew, there is prospering power both in secrecy and in release.

One of the sins of many tithers is that they tend to scatter their tithes, giving to many causes. Scattered tithes tend to bring scattered, ineffectual results, both for the giver and for the recipient of those tithes. Scattered giving to many causes does little to help any of them; whereas, your generous, concentrated tithes can be "manna from heaven" that assure financial stability to a single or so worthy cause. Never be afraid of giving big tithes to one or two causes, if you wish to reap big results in your own life. Nor should you be afraid of giving "too much" for the benefit of the recipient of your gifts. That's hardly ever a danger! And it is a limiting thought for all concerned, as experienced by a businessman in the Southwest who said, "I became a millionaire after I first heard you lecture on tithing fifteen years ago. Later, when I decided I was giving 'too much' I stopped tithing, and I soon went broke! I learned an expensive lesson, so I am again tithing my way to wealth."

THE BEST INVESTMENT YOU CAN MAKE IN PEACE, HEALTH AND PLENTY

Pray about your giving. Ask a loving Father to reveal to you *where* to share your tithes, and you will be guided in your giving so that all involved in your gift — you the giver, as well as the recipient — will be prospered, uplifted and blessed. As you evolve, grow and change, your tithing practices may, too. You will probably go from one-tenth to larger giving — thus opening the way to receive even greater peace, health and plenty in your life. In any event, you will find that tithing is the best investment you can make in successful living, and also the most soul-satisfying.

In closing, I wish to share with you some favorite tithing prayer statements which were given to me by a powerful prosperity teacher several decades ago. My daily use of those prayers over the years helped me to grow out of long-lasting poverty — just as did the tithing promises of Malachi help the returnees from Babylonian exile to prosper. If you, too, have felt exiled

from your good, may your use of these prayers continually prosper you as they have so many others:

"I DO NOT DEPEND UPON PERSONS OR CONDITIONS FOR
MY PROSPERITY. GOD IS THE SOURCE OF MY SUPPLY, SO I
NOW PUT GOD FIRST FINANCIALLY. I TITHE MY WAY TO
PROSPERITY. THE VOLUNTARY, FAITHFUL TITHING OF MY
WHOLE INCOME NOW OPERATES THE LAW OF EVER-
INCREASING PROSPERITY FOR ME. YES, I NOW TITHE MY
WAY TO PEACE, HEALTH AND PLENTY!"

A SPECIAL NOTE FROM THE AUTHOR

Through the generous outpouring of their tithes
over the years, the readers of my books have helped me
to financially establish three new ministries—the most
recent being a global ministry, the nondenominational
Unity Worldwide, with headquarters in Palm Desert,
Califorinia. Many thanks for your help in the past, and
for all that you continue to share.

You are also invited to share your tithes with the
churches of your choice—especially those which teach
the truths stressed in this book. Such churches would
include the metaphysical churches of Unity, Religious
Science, Divine Science, Science of Mind, and other
related churches, many of which are members of The

International New Thought Movement. (For a list of such churches write The International New Thought Alliance, 7314 E. Stetson Drive, Scottsdale, Arizona 85251.) Your support of such churches can help spread the prosperous Truth that mankind is now seeking in this New Age of metaphysical enlightenment.

NOTE: For additional information on the success power of tithing, see additional material in the author's other books, specifically: *The Prosperity Secrets of the Ages, Open Your Mind to Prosperity, Open Your Mind to Receive,* and the "Millionaires of the Bible" series.

The Vision

that you glorify in your mind,
the Ideal that you enthrone in your heart:
this you will build your life by,
this you will become. — James Allen, As A Man Thinketh

Please fill out this card and send it to us if you would like a complete
catalog of DeVorss books on Metaphysical, Spiritual, Inspirational,
Self-Help, New Thought, Body Mind Spirit, and related subjects.

PLEASE PRINT

_____

Book in which this card was found

_____

NAME

_____

ADDRESS

_____

CITY STATE ZIP

_____

PHONE

_____

EMAIL

DeVorss Publications
800-843-5743 / www.devorss.com

DeVorss & Company
P.O. Box 1389
Camarillo CA 93011-1389

PART II

OTHER PROSPERITY LAWS THAT CAN BRING RICHES TO YOU

Introduction . . . .

MORE GOLD DUST FOR YOU!

Two "little ol' ladies" were having a conversation about money.

"What would you do if you found a million dollars?" asked one.

"That's simple," came the reply. "If I found a million dollars and I could find out who it belonged to, I would give it back—*if they were poor.*"

We used to think of a "millionaire" as one who was worth a million dollars or more. But some economists now claim that one must be worth at least ten million dollars to qualify, because of the times in which we live.

Regardless, prosperity is relative. It is a matter of perception, as it always has been.

A PROSPEROUS MYSTICISM THAT
LEADS TO WHOLENESS

One friend said, "When I took up the study of *The Dynamic Laws of Prosperity*, I expected it to be another 'get-rich-quick' primer. Instead, I found it to be filled with a practical, prosperous mysticism."

If that is so, the reason might be this: The word "dynamic" in its root means "spiritual." The word "law" signifies those ideas or methods that work if we apply them. And the word "prosperity" in its root means "wholeness." That's what this study is all about: the spiritual laws of wholeness, which when practiced, bring peace, health and plenty into our lives.

PROSPERITY CAME TO ALL WHO HELPED
WITH THIS BOOK

This was brought to my attention by those around me while I was writing this book in the early 1960's. After typing the first half of the manuscript, my secretary resigned. She explained that as she had typed the manuscript she had used the ideas in it, and her husband had been prospered so much in his sales work that she no longer needed the job!

A second secretary was then employed to type the last half of the book. Before completing it, she also resigned. She explained that her husband had been out of work when she took the job, but that he now had the finest engineering job of his life — one which would take them to another state. She felt the ideas in the book had turned the tide.

Finally, my housekeeper resigned. She had not seen the manuscript, but I had innocently explained the laws of prosperity to her while writing about them, chapter by chapter. As she began using them, she decided to do something she had long wished to do but never quite had the courage—become a dressmaker. She said, "I am resigning as your housekeeper. Now would you like to hire me as your dressmaker?" She has since prospered in that field of work.

On the day the book came from the printer and was handed to my New York editor, he was sitting at his desk carefully perusing it, when another editor walked into his office and handed him some money. He was startled to hear that editor explain, "Some time ago you loaned me lunch money. Until a few moments ago, I had forgotten about it." My editor wrote me in triumph, "How's that for fast action from *The Dynamic Laws of Prosperity?*"

"Gold dust results" came to me, too, while I wrote this book. I had first begun developing this prosperity philosophy while living in one room in Alabama— what appropriate circumstances in which to start! Through use of these ideas, we later demonstrated a church manse where I lived while beginning this book. As I immersed myself in the dynamic ideas contained in this manuscript, a dream came true. I married a long-time friend, who taught English at the University of Texas in Austin. I then completed the book from an apartment overlooking that multimillion dollar complex in that prosperous state. My husband did the final editing on the book, which I have always felt helped to make it a best-seller. So, rather dramatic results came to all of us who were associated with the creation of this book.

FROM MUNDANE TO MIRACULOUS RESULTS
FOR OTHERS

Since this book was first published in 1962, the letters I have received from readers everywhere, have described results ranging from the mundane to the miraculous. The following reports are just a sampling of how prosperous thinking has worked in every segment of society, both near and far, during these past decades:

Marriage: A divorcee in Michigan, who had suffered through a miserable marriage and a bitter divorce, was left bereft financially as well as emotionally and physically. Friends introduced her to the power of prosperous thinking, and she began to release all unhappy memories of the past, and all bitterness of the present. She began to set a new course for her life. The results? She soon met and married a member of one of the most famous, super-rich families in America!

Inheritance: Ministers are usually expected to be "poor as church mice." Many receive poverty-level incomes, which have to be supplemented by second jobs or personally-depended-upon hand-outs. One such minister began to study *The Dynamic Laws of Prosperity*, from which he learned such an existence was nonsense, and not meant for him as a child of God. He soon came into an inheritance of a quarter of a million dollars! After his "church mouse" existence, that seemed like a fortune.

New Job: A housewife in Arizona wrote: "Within ten days from the time I started practicing prosperous thinking, my husband received a job offer from a former boss. The salary and fringe benefits will boost our income by $5000. In addition, my husband was given a large incentive bonus, and our moving expenses were paid. Furthermore, he was given his full vacation pay when he left his old job."

Magical Results: "During the past six months, since I have carefully applied prosperity principles, some sort of magic has entered my family's life," wrote a California housewife. "Suddenly we were able to meet our bills with money left over to spare. Old friendships were renewed with joy. Then a gift of $10,000 came to us unexpectedly. A myriad of wonderful things have been happening to us ever since."

Depression Lifts and Children Prosper: "What a difference prosperous thinking has made in my life," wrote a teacher from the West Indies. "As I took up this study, my depression quickly lifted. My job as a teacher in a Catholic primary school has given me the opportunity to teach my students that prosperity is God's will for them. That knowledge has added greatly to their enlightenment and happiness."

Conversion of a Communist: "I never realized a single book could change my life so much," wrote a young man in Sri Lanka. "I am a student of twenty-one, and for the last five years I have been a strong Communist. I had studied more than one hundred books written by such authors as Karl Marx and Lenin. But these books gave me no goodness. There was no kindness nor peace in my heart. I was discharged from my job. I found prosperous thinking when I needed it most. I will never succumb to the Communist viewpoint again."

Quicker Results: "Since I began practicing prosperous thinking, problems I thought would take years to solve have been straightened out in months," wrote a businessman in Oregon.

Study Group's Results in West Africa: "A group of business people began meeting weekly ten years ago to study Dr. Ponder's books, and to affirm the prosperous truth together. We have not missed a single week since. Here are some of the results we have experienced:

"A businessman has just been called away to London, England, to take a three-month Senior Management course. He is a Senior Executive in the Federal

Civil Service. A Senior Marketing Manager in a drug store here expects to become an Executive Director of his firm shortly. A Senior Radiographer in the local hospital has been promised a promotion to the post of Superintendent. And I have become the top confidential secretary in one of Africa's most prestigious banks. We are a happy group, progressing at a rapid pace to the glory of God and the honor of man."

Christianity and Prosperity Become Synonymous: A businessman in Singapore wrote: "I have studied success books for years. Yet recently, for the first time, when *The Dynamic Laws of Prosperity* came into my hands, I realized that Christianity and prosperity are synonymous, translating 'the good life' and 'the abundant life' in practical terms. Prosperous thinking challenges all who dare, and I have taken up that dare!"

Little could any of us in my first prosperity class, during the Recession of 1958, have realized where the ideas we studied in that class would lead— merely around the world! Nor could we have foreseen how enthusiastically such simple ideas would be received, nor how dramatically they would transform the lives of people everywhere—including my own. (See the Conclusion: "When the Gold Dust Settles.")

A TWENTY-YEAR DESIRE COMES TRUE

The original version of this book did not contain two chapters that subsequently have been added to this expanded version: One on "Ten, the magic number of increase" (Chapter 10), and one on "Charm" (Chapter 17). Even though the book was a best-seller from the start, I always felt bad that these two chapters were deleted from the original version. Now, years later, I am finally free to include that additional material, which I have always felt was a vital part of the philosophy of *The Dynamic Laws of Prosperity*.

I trust that these additional chapters, and the other material included in Part II, will mean as much to you as they have to me and to countless others over the years.

THRIVE—NOT JUST SURVIVE

A businessman recently wrote: "These days people are constantly complaining about food shortages, housing shortages, and a shortage of money due to rising prices. In my business, we've had to deal with shortages for a long time. But through my prosperity study we've succeeded anyway. I plan to thrive—not just survive!"

Amen.

In the decades since I first wrote this book, we have seen vast changes in some areas of life. But the economic needs of mankind continue much the same now as they did then. The deeper reason may be this: Financial demands of every sort are but an indication that the time is right in the soul growth of mankind for us to raise our beliefs to a higher level. It is as though in this New Age we are being forced to develop our inner powers to meet our outer needs.

So, thanks to the power of prosperous thinking, "There is *still* gold dust in the air for you!"

Now let us go quickly to Part II to continue our journey up the golden path of prosperous thinking. As we do so, may you gather your own God-given gold dust results every step of the way. You deserve no less!

THE AUTHOR

THE PROSPERITY LAW OF LOVE
AND GOOD WILL

— Chapter 11 —

Recently a businessman said to me, "I believe that the greatest prosperity law of all is the prosperity law of love and impersonal good will." He then told me of some of his experiences in business where love, as impersonal good will, had won out in the face of inharmony and apparent failure.

He cited the instance of a wealthy lady customer whom he could always please when her mood was high. But when she was in low spirits, he often received caustic letters or telephone calls, in which she would make unkind remarks about his "mishandling" of her business interests.

His antidote for this woman was to use love as impersonal good will. He stated that when this customer (or any others) "acted up" during the course of his business day, he had developed a special method for "straightening them out." Instead of retaliating or offering a defense when inharmony, criticism or personality conflicts arose, he would sit quietly for a few minutes, think about the person in question, and deliberately think loving thoughts of good will about them. He worked in his own thinking to visualize the person surrounded and enfolded with love, a sense of security, calmness, good humor, impersonal good will.

The result? He states that the results have been so fast and so pronounced that it has often been breathtaking. For instance, that wealthy, moody woman has often telephoned him long-distance to express her profound apologies within an hour after he has visualized her in a loving, kind way. If a telephone call did not come, then she would usually write a note, dating it and timing it within an hour or so after his thoughts and blessings concerning her were realized.

When inharmony arises in business transactions where several people are involved, this man goes over each person in his mind and blesses each one with impersonal good will. He then mentally sees harmony restored in the situation. Soon tempers cool, misunderstandings fade away, and successful transactions proceed.

It is good to use this method at the beginning and end of each day. As you look over your day mentally, for all unpleasantness that occurred, dare to mentally recast that experience. See all concerned as loving, understanding and harmonious, and you will be surprised how often those involved will do an "about-face," and make amends for their previous attitudes.

Dare to begin your day by mentally going over the planned events for that day, visualizing them as pleasant, harmonious and successful. You will begin to experience the paths of prosperity, pleasantness, and peace of which Solomon wrote. Usually, if you mentally plan, visualize and expect a successful day in the early morning hours, there will be little to un-do mentally at day's end.

LOVE NEVER FAILS

No matter how many prosperity laws you know about, if you are not able to live and work harmoniously with others, all else seems of little value. It has been estimated that your financial success is due only to 15 percent of your technical ability, and 85 percent to your ability to get along with people.

The talent for getting along with other people through exercising impersonal good will, which is love in action, cannot be over-emphasized. Perhaps you may have wondered about the causes for employees getting fired—is it due to incompetence, tardiness, dishonesty? Personnel managers seem to agree that more than two-thirds of the people who lose their jobs do so because "they cannot get along with people." Approximately ten percent are discharged because of inadequate preparation for the skills needed. The rest are discharged because of "personality problems." Do you wonder why impersonal good will and the ability to get along with others has such power? Do you wonder why it is that unless you are able to get along with others, both in a business way and at home, all your other training, abilities and efforts are generally futile?

The Bible asserts that "love never fails." (I Corinthians 13:8) Jesus pointed out to the lawyer that love fulfills the whole law (Matthew 22:40), meaning the whole law of healthy, happy, harmonious, successful living. Love has unequaled power, because love is the power that unifies the whole world and everything in it. For instance, the law of gravity is love in action. Love is the equalizing, harmonizing, balancing, adjusting force that is ever at work throughout the universe. Working in these ways, love can do for you what you cannot humanly do for yourself.

At Harvard University, world-renowned sociologists conducted research studies on the power of love. The university established a research center, staffed with serious scientists, who spent their valuable time studying the subject of love. Their findings were that love, like other good things, can be deliberately produced by human beings! According to their findings, there is no reason why we can't learn to generate love as we do other natural forces.

LOVE IS PERSONAL AND IMPERSONAL

How do you produce and generate love? First, by realizing that love is both personal and impersonal. On the personal level, you can generate love as the expression of devotion, tenderness, kindness, approval, and appreciation of those in your family and circle of close friends.

Love on the impersonal level, is the ability to get along with other people, or good will toward all others without personal attachment. For this purpose, affirm often: "I LOVE ALL PEOPLE AND ALL PEOPLE LOVE ME, WITHOUT ATTACHMENT."

A Chinese doctor living in Malaya was especially interested in helping mankind to realize the impersonal power of love for solving all our ills. He sent out over

150,000 copies of a statement about the power of love. In this statement he invited people of all races and creeds to simply think about divine love for five minutes every day. He even provided a synchronizing time table, in case people in various countries wished to meditate upon divine love at the same time. That was one man's belief in the power of love for harmony, justice, and world peace.

HOW TO GENERATE LOVE

If you analyze this thing called love, you will discover that life is a process of giving and receiving love in its many phases. It is those individuals who are not living in the stream of love that feel its lack as a difficulty in mind, body or affairs. Through the deliberate development of love, you can get into the stream of life's goodness, as well as help others to experience it.

It is wonderful to realize, as did the Harvard scientists, that you no longer have to look outside yourself, waiting and hoping that somehow perhaps love will find you. You can begin now deliberately generating love for God, for yourself and for mankind, from within your own being. By doing so, you will unfailingly draw the perfect expressions of love into your own life.

I have discovered that some people feel guilty about their desire for love in its many phases, thinking they should suppress that desire. The time has come for you to realize that you should express the desire for love — from within outward, toward God, yourself, and your fellow man. A loving Father can do for you only what He can do through you. It is through your own thoughts, feelings and expectations that love is born.

As you deliberately express love, it comes back to you multiplied.

Take conscious control of your thoughts and feelings, and begin now to develop an impersonal consciousness of love, knowing that it is the quickest way to solve your own problems, as well as a powerful way of helping mankind. You can do this in a very simple way:

Begin spending a few minutes each day deliberately generating love. In those times affirm: "WITH GOD'S HELP, I AM NOW DELIBERATELY AND JOYOUSLY RADIATING DIVINE LOVE TO MYSELF, MY WORLD, AND TO ALL MANKIND." Ask daily that divine love be made alive in you. Form the mental picture of yourself as healthy, prosperous, illumined, harmonized, blessed, unfettered and unbound. Quietly love that mental picture by affirming: "I LET DIVINE LOVE NOW BE MADE ALIVE IN ME."

In these periods when you deliberately bring alive and generate love, do so in this way: Think of love as being a radiant light that enfolds, brightens, illumines and uplifts you. Think of love as permeating, penetrating, and saturating your whole being. If there are dark, troublesome areas in your life, deliberately think of them as coming alive with the light of divine love and being divinely adjusted.

Continue in your meditation period to put forth the thought, feeling, and enlightened picture of love upon yourself and your world. There is no reason for feeling guilty about loving yourself. You cannot love others or radiate love outward until you love yourself and feel it within. Love begins at home, within you. Psychiatry emphasizes the need for self-love and appreciation. When Jesus said, "Love the Lord thy God with all thy heart . . . soul . . . and mind. This is the greatest and first commandment" (Matthew 22:37-38), He was

referring to man's loving the God-nature within himself, as well as a universal God.

Dare to consciously love yourself, love your life and
affairs, love every little bit of good in all. In your time
of generating love, particularly dare to love any part of
the body that is crying out for healing. Boldly declare
to it, "I LOVE YOU." Dare to direct love to any situation
in your life that seems difficult. Think of the situation
and affirm: "LET DIVINE LOVE BE MADE ALIVE IN THEE
NOW."

When you have sufficiently gained a mental picture
or satisfying feeling of the light of love flooding your
whole being, you can know that you have generated
and released the greatest power on earth into every
phase of your mind, body and affairs. The light of love
shall shine forth as new energy, new peace of mind,
new power and dominion, new poise, new beauty, new
prosperity, new harmony; indeed as new good in every
phase of your life.

TURNING LOVE ON BRINGS
PRACTICAL RESULTS

The Harvard scientists also discovered that you can
actually bombard people, situations, and conditions
with love, thereby producing miraculous changes.
They predicted that "turning love on" might soon become a universal prescription for healing the world's
ills.

There is practical, result-getting power in generating and turning love on. A friend recently spoke of
witnessing her complexion clearing up after daily
thinking of it in meditation, and gently loving it with

the thought of beauty and radiance. Her skin is now radiantly clear and beautiful. A lecturer recently spoke of feeling fatigued during a lecture series. Then he remembered to love his body in his meditation periods, and it quickly responded with new life, energy and vitality.

Not only is it good to meditate upon love, but as you go about daily living, it is good to affirm silently to everything in your world: "LET DIVINE LOVE BE MADE ALIVE IN THEE." To the clothes you wear, the car you drive, the inanimate objects in your home or office, the bills you pay, the income you receive, affirm divine love. Even to the empty spaces in your life, and to the good you seek that has not yet appeared, affirm love.

Everything seems to respond to your thoughts of love. To the people you meet during the day, strangers and friends, as well as to those in your family group, it is good to silently declare: "LET DIVINE LOVE BE MADE ALIVE IN THEE."

I once talked with a secretary concerning the friction and jealousy in her office. Because she was "easygoing," she was being asked to do a large part of the work normally done by two other secretaries, for which they were receiving high praise and pay increases. She had tried at various times to talk with her boss about the unfairness of her extra work, but he had refused to listen. In desperation she came to me, not knowing whether to quit her job, which was generally pleasant and convenient, or to try to "stick it out," unjust though it seemed.

I suggested that she use this affirmation: "LET DIVINE LOVE MANIFEST NOW." I pointed out that it was not necessary to try to appease personalities, or to compromise one's beliefs to satisfy others; that every sign of weakness and insecurity would only lead to further dis-satisfaction and mistreatment. Instead, she should begin radiating peace, power, poise, inner stability, and firmness in what she would and would not do; and as she did, her co-workers would respond with peace, poise and inner stability.

Within a week, the situation began to change. Her fellow workers began to respect her new attitude; they stopped imposing on her, and began to do their own work. Their attitude toward her became one of har-mony and respect. Her boss began to treat her more kindly. Harmony and good will gradually replaced the former tension, bickering and jealousy.

Ella Wheeler Wilcox once said that God measures souls by their capacity for entertaining His best angel, Love. Truly, love never fails.

LOVE SHALL BE VICTORIOUS

After certain points in a law suit were decided against a man, he was faced with financial ruin, and he complained that it was unjust and unlawful. "There is no justice," he moaned bitterly. He then talked with a spiritual counselor who suggested that he use the power of divine love on the situation, by affirming his own right attitudes and emotional reactions: "I LIVE BY THE LAW OF LOVE, AND LOVE SHALL BE VICTORIOUS." It was suggested that every time he thought of the other party in the lawsuit he affirm for him: "YOU LIVE BY THE LAW OF LOVE AND LOVE SHALL BE VICTORIOUS."

After beginning to think in this way, he felt much better about every aspect of the situation. Hostility, resentment, and the desire to get even left him. Suddenly came an unexpected opportunity to do a real favor for his legal opponent. He did it, and immediately he felt better. As his attitude continued to change, he discovered that his opponent's attitude changed also. Each conceded certain points, and soon the case was settled out of court fairly and happily for all.

A woman in a large city opened a restaurant and candy shop in a place where two owners before her had failed miserably. She was a brilliant success. When asked how she had succeeded in the same location where others had failed, she said, "I just love and bless my customers. When customers leave my place not only do I invite them to come back, but I silently send them a blessing of love, and pray for their prosperity and happiness. When no customers are in the store, I view the people passing by on the street with love."

THE HEALING POWER OF LOVE

You can deliberately produce divine love by thinking loving thoughts about yourself and others, and by affirming divine love. But I have also found it a wonderful success secret to speak appreciative, kind, understanding words to people. Kind words produce results after their kind—the kind of results that mean new life, increase, and real happiness for you!

A businessman was hospitalized with a very high fever which medical remedies did not seem to reduce. He also had a heart condition of long standing, and it was assumed that it had actively reappeared. A friend who knew of the healing power of love visited him in the hospital. He soon realized that this man felt greatly unloved because of some tangled relationships in his life.

The friend dared to say to this patient: "GOD LOVES YOU, GOD IS GUIDING YOU, GOD IS SHOWING YOU THE WAY. YOU ARE GREATLY LOVED BY GOD AND MAN." Together they affirmed that God's love was doing its perfect work in this man's mind, body and affairs.

Suddenly an intense feeling of heat passed through the sick man's body, and then it left him. The high fever was gone. Later, his physician declared that his heart seemed fine again. The ointment of love soothed his previously tangled family relationships as well.

A nurse was assigned to a case in which the patient had been suffering from mental illness for a number of months. Shock treatments and drugs had been administered, but had not cleared up her condition. Finally, it was suggested that perhaps a complete rest might be helpful. The patient was taken to her summer home on the coast.

The private nurse assigned to her case had learned about generating love to others. Immediately this nurse began daily meditating upon her patient as loving, kind, whole, well and completely happy again. When she accompanied the patient to the beach and into the water, she would think of her as being immersed in God's healing love. As the patient played in the water, the nurse would go off a distance on the beach and silently and mentally surround the patient with the thought of love and its healing power.

Often the patient pathetically asked this nurse, "Do you think I really can get well? Is there any hope for my condition?" Always the nurse, who knew the power of speaking words of love, declared, "My dear, you are getting well. God's love is doing its perfect work in your mind, body and affairs now, and you are being healed." Over and over daily she reassured the patient in this way. Within six weeks the nurse was dismissed from the case because the patient had responded so beautifully to love's healing power.

It is easy to speak words of love or to meditate lovingly upon those people with whom you are in harmony. But it is those people who seem most difficult, who may even seem hostile, that need your radiation of love most. Their very hostility is but their soul's cry for loving recognition. When you generate sufficient love to them, the discord will fade away.

SHOOT THEM IN THE BACK—WITH LOVE!

A businessman told me that he has a special way of radiating love. In his work as a government employee, his job is to meet the public, handle their complaints, and make things right for them and for his employer, Uncle Sam. The only thing he has to do is to keep everybody satisfied! For anyone else it might seem impossible.

But this man has learned that "love never fails." He meets the public with a smile, no matter what they do. He continues to be courteous and kind, no matter what they say. All the time he silently affirms: "DIVINE LOVE IS IN CONTROL AND ALL IS WELL." When people with problems leave him, he says that is when he really "lets them have it." He declares, "I shoot them in the back—with love!"

Does it pay to shoot people in the back with love? This man claims that the attitude and behavior of many complainants who come to his office seemed to change markedly as he affirmed divine love.

I can vouch that this government employee must be successful, because recently a businessman came to me and said, "I would surely like to know Mr. Black's success secret. He always seems so happy and calm, and yet he has one of the most difficult jobs in this town." He was delighted when I told him that I knew this man's success secret was to shoot people in the back with love! I had the feeling, from the look in his eye, that he went forth to do likewise.

LOVE PROTECTS

A woman in Kansas City protected herself from assault by speaking loving words. One night she was walking down a dark street near the old Unity Society building on Tracy Avenue when a man stepped out of the shadows and put a gun to her ribs, saying, "Give me your purse or I'll shoot you!" She turned and looked him right in the face and said, "You can't harm me, because you are God's child and I love you." After twice repeating his threat, each time getting the same reply, he finally shook his head, mumbled something about "this crazy woman," dropped his gun and fled. That woman met an extreme situation in an extreme way—through the expression of love.

INVOKE LOVE IMPERSONALLY

But you should not go around saying to people outside your family group, "I love you!" Most people would think you meant it in a personal manner, and it could cause embarrassment and misinterpretation. I know of a professional man who made the mistake of telling a number of his lady clients, "I love you," and he is still trying to explain to their husbands what he meant.

In less personal terms, you can assure people of your interest, approval, and sincere appreciation of them. Kindness and courtesy are always in good taste; in such impersonal ways, you can radiate love as good will to others.

A public relations director for a worldwide insurance company recently told me that, in his work with hundreds of employees, he had found that their greatest need is kindness. He believes that you can satisfy the need for kindness in others just by being "decent to them."

WRITE OUT STATEMENTS OF LOVE

Along with meditating upon love, affirming love, and speaking words of love, it is good to write out statements of love, as a method of generating it. A lady once heard that a former friend was viciously gossiping about her. The criticism was severe and unwarranted. A number of people were being telephoned and visited in an effort to cause this lady to lose her job. When she learned of the negative activities which were spreading, she began to affirm that divine love was at work in the situation. Soon a friend, who had just learned of further critical comments, insisted to her, "This situation must be stopped. You must take action!" All afternoon this lady sat quietly and wrote over and over:

"DIVINE LOVE IS DOING ITS PERFECT WORK IN THIS SITUA-
TION NOW, AND ALL IS WELL." That was the only action
she took.

Within a few days she received a gift from the
woman who had severely criticized her, along with a
note expressing words of love and appreciation for her.
Divine love had turned the tide.

The deliberate radiating of divine love is especially
helpful concerning the "little things" in life that can be
quite irritating. A series of little things, little events,
little changes often mold your day and your world.
When you master them, you are approaching mastery
of your life.

PERSONAL EXPRESSIONS OF LOVE
ARE IMPORTANT

We have mentioned a number of ways to generate
and radiate love in the impersonal phases of life, but
let us not overlook the fact that the personal aspects of
love need to be expressed regularly in every family.
Psychologists tell us that everyone needs to feel loved,
appreciated and important; it is a basic need of all
mankind. Often those troublesome situations at home,
in the family group, result from lack of love being
expressed on a personal basis.

For instance, I recently asked a lady who was having
trouble in her marriage, "When was the last time you
looked your husband straight in the eye and sincerely
declared to him, 'I love you and I think you're wonderful!'" Startled, she replied, "You mean I have to talk
like that to save my marriage?" I found myself saying,
"Well, isn't that the way you got your husband in the
first place?"

Wives and husbands should make their spouses feel important and needed. I have counseled with business-men who were involved with "other women." To my question, "Why are you seeing another woman, since you have a lovely wife and a wonderful home?" the usual reply was, "The other woman makes me feel important and needed, but my wife doesn't."

SEX, AN IMPORTANT EXPRESSION OF LOVE

The sexual relationship in marriage is also an important way of expressing love. Indeed, when rightly understood, sex is a vital part of the holy sacrament of marriage. The expression of sex in marriage can deeply enhance the bond of love.[1]

EXPRESS LOVE TO CHILDREN

Children, as well as adults, need to feel wanted and appreciated. Recently a seventh grade science teacher made an interesting experiment with the 12- and 13-year-old students in her classes. She gave 190 boys and girls slips of paper on which she asked them to anonymously write out their greatest problems in life. She read most of their answers to me.

One 12-year-old boy wrote:

My brother is a teenager and all of his friends are teenagers who constantly pick on me. My problem is that I am allergic to teenagers. What can I do about it?

---

1. See Chapter 15, "Sex Is A Success Power," in the Ponder book, *The Prosperity Secrets of the Ages.*

Another student wrote:

My mother and father give me everything I want in
the way of clothes, money and gifts. But they never
have time to talk or visit with me. My friends say that I
am very fortunate to have such generous parents. But I
would much rather have more of their time and less of
their money.

In counseling parents about their so-called "problem
children," one quickly discovers that often the parent's
attitude toward the child is the problem. A change of
attitude on the part of the parent toward the child
is often all that is needed to bring about a happy
relationship. In recent conversation, a very successful
businessman seemed quite troubled about his non-con-
formist teenage son. The man had two sons, one of
whom had grown up to be all that his father had desired—a loving, obedient individual. The other son
had simply refused to be molded to his father's opinion
as to the type of person he should be.

This younger son possessed a highly creative nature,
and was interested in the world of art, music and
writing. However, the father had condemned these ar-
tistic talents in his son, rather than recognizing that
they were God-given. When the father realized that
there was nothing "wrong" with this son, that he was
simply a different type from the older son or from
anyone else in the family, the father seemed relieved
and agreed to praise his son's creative abilities. Later
he encouraged his younger son to take the art courses
he had always wanted.

One of the most loving things you can do for children, your own or another's, who seem to be having
difficulties, is to affirm often for them: "I BEHOLD YOU
WITH THE EYES OF LOVE, AND I GLORY IN YOUR GOD-GIVEN

PERFECTION. YOU ARE GOD'S CHILD AND HE LOVES YOU." It is also good to affirm: "DIVINE LOVE, MANIFEST THYSELF IN, THROUGH, AND FOR THIS CHILD NOW."

CHILDREN THRIVE ON ENCOURAGEMENT

Children especially thrive on sincere appreciation, praise and encouragement, as well as adults; it is a tonic to them. I know of an instance where a little boy was not responding in school at all. His mother became disgusted with him and made an appointment with a psychiatrist, which was scheduled some weeks later. In casual conversation she mentioned her son to me, and I pointed out his sensitivity and his creative abilities. I explained that his differentness, which had so greatly disturbed her, was his potential power for success. I suggested that she take time from her crowded business schedule to daily sit down and talk with him about anything that was on his mind, and especially that she praise his every improvement and his every good attitude.

She immediately began praising him sincerely and daily, and his schoolwork immediately responded. His musical ability also blossomed forth. Soon he was selected as one of six children in his age group from the entire city to perform at a special band concert. The previously planned psychiatric treatment was cancelled.

DISCIPLINE WITH LOVE

This does not mean you should not work to correct negative behavior or to discipline children. You should be firm but loving in your discipline. The word discipline in its root meaning signifies "to perfect." Your methods of correction and discipline should lead to perfection rather than to rebellion, resistance, or further negative behavior. I have found it best to pray for divine guidance concerning each child, rather than to constantly seek advice from other people, or to clutter the mind with too much theory on the subject.

Parents have long believed that they personally had the difficult task of training their children by ingrafting knowledge onto them from the outside, which they felt would equip their children for adult living. When you attempt to rear children from this standpoint alone, it can prove difficult and disappointing for all concerned.

Intellectual education has its place, but it is only a part of a child's real education and development. The word "educate" truly means to "draw out" that which innately exists within. Dr. Emilie Cady has written, "God as infinite love lies within every human being only waiting to be led forth into manifestation. This is true education."[2]

Another way to love children is to teach them that God never intended them to fail or to be in lack. I know of one family group in which the children are developing real self-confidence because their parents constantly tell them they can succeed, and that failure is not necessary. These children are gathered together at bedtime for their prayers. Along with the usual prayers for children, these parents also affirm prosperity statements with their children. They are absorbing

---

2. *Lessons in Truth* (Unity Village, MO 64065, Unity Books) Revised 1953, p. 19.

the idea of wealth and prosperity as their natural right. Every gift that comes to them is received as a "prosperity gift"; every item of clothing becomes their "prosperity clothes." Small wonder that these children are constantly attracting gifts and prosperity to them.

BEGIN WHERE YOU ARE, EXPRESSING LOVE

Remember that love functions on both the personal and impersonal phases of life. If there seems to be a lack of love in your personal life, you can be assured that you will experience love in that department when you persevere in rendering love impersonally as service and good will. If love seems to be missing in the impersonal phases of your life, you can be assured that you will experience understanding, happiness and success there when you persevere in using God's love in your personal life and relationships.

Begin where you are, with the love now operating in your life. Bless it, give thanks for it in either the personal department of your life as happy family relationships, or in the impersonal phases of your life as job success. As you give thanks for every small and large expression of love in your life, you release its multiplying power which can fill every void.

Charles Fillmore commented on the power of love as follows:

You may trust love to get you out of your difficulties. There is nothing too hard for it to accomplish for you, if you put your confidence in it.[3]

---

3. *Talks on Truth* (Unity Village, MO 64065, Unity Books) 1924, p. 59.

Serious scientists have made a special study of love. Jesus Christ, the Master of victorious living, placed it first in importance. One of the early builders of Christianity, the Apostle Paul, ascribed all power to it.

Promise yourself now that you will also begin to deliberately generate God's love to yourself, to family, and to all mankind. As you do, your problems will turn into solutions, and your prosperity will multiply. You can bring this to pass by affirming often: "DIVINE LOVE FORESEES EVERYTHING AND RICHLY PROVIDES EVERYTHING NOW. THE PERFECT RESULTS OF DIVINE LOVE NOW APPEAR."

FINANCIAL INDEPENDENCE CAN BE YOURS

— Chapter 12 —

One of the desires of all prosperous-minded people is to be self-supporting and financially independent. Poverty is a universal fear of mankind, and many people today are experiencing financial lack, despite the unprecedented prosperity of our times.

Once you learn the power which you release through prosperous thinking, it will dawn upon you that the possibility of financial independence isn't so far-fetched after all; you will realize that it isn't just meant for the other fellow, but that it is meant for you, too!

The term "financial independence" does not necessarily mean the same thing to everyone. Basically, to be financially independent means to be financially free. To one person financial independence might simply suggest a well-paying, dependable job, through

231

which he could consistently meet his financial obligations and feel free from daily financial demands. Another person might be thinking in millionaire terms. As you progress financially, your ideas of financial independence expand so that you wish to have greater and greater financial freedom.

Thus, the desire to be self-supporting and financially independent is a divine desire that has been implanted in the intellectual and emotional nature of man to help him to progress, to achieve, and to build a worthwhile life for himself. The desire for financial independence, whether it be for a decent weekly income or for a millionaire's status, is a divine desire that should not be *sup*pressed, but *ex*pressed constructively through the mind of man. When it is so expressed, man is then able to experience the satisfaction and fulfillment that God wants him to have.

DON'T ACCEPT THINGS AS THEY ARE

Perhaps one of the great secrets of attaining financial independence was shown us by the mayor of a New England town when, several years ago, a news story related the remarkable results of this man's first year as mayor. At the time he took office, everyone was saying, "This is a dying city and nobody can save it," and they had facts to prove it. Slums infested the downtown area, the city population was not growing, and business was leaving town. Prosperity seemed to be ancient history for this town. However, within a year the new mayor had inspired his co-workers to adopt a bold program of cleaning up the city. A slum clearance project went to work to clean out downtown slums and make way for apartment houses, shopping areas, parking lots, new office buildings and new business areas.

How was this one man able to inspire so much progress and new prosperity so fast? He stated that the men on his city council were men who dared to "think big," who got the ball rolling. The mayor also mentioned that each night he prayed for guidance. His basic attitude was this: "I won't accept things as they are. Just because they've always been that way doesn't mean they can't be changed!"

Thus, dissatisfaction with present financial conditions is the first step toward attaining financial independence. If you can't settle for things as they are— good! You have the power, through prosperous thought and action, to change them into something far better and more satisfying. This is your key to financial independence, if you dare to use it.

I once observed an acquaintance go from an unpleasant job into his own business, which represented financial independence to him, by boldly following through on "divine dissatisfaction." This man had been employed since World War II in a jewelry store, but always in the back of his mind was the dream of owning his own store. Finally, disharmony and disorder arose where he was employed. After long and faithful service, he suddenly quit his job, although his employers assured him he would not be able to do as well elsewhere. This man silently reminded himself that he had no intention of doing as well elsewhere as an "employee," but that he intended to become independent of bosses and other people's ideas, for he would be an employer himself.

At the time this man quit his job, he had only a small amount of money saved. He also had a family and the usual financial responsibilities. Nevertheless, as soon as he let go of the unsatisfactory financial situation, he began to feel better, more content and somehow freer. Word soon got around. A friend who had a jewelry store in another town offered him a job until he could decide about permanent work. He took the job to assure some income while he quietly made long-range plans.

A little later, still another business friend informed him that he was also dissatisfied with just being a salaried employee. He wanted to go into the jewelry business on a partnership basis. This man had a comfortable savings balance. Together these two men were able to produce the financial assets and credit standing needed to go into their financial venture.

Neither of these men could have managed this financial venture alone, but together they were able to pool their resources, financial assets, talents, and abilities. They formed a partnership and opened their own jewelry store, which has since made them both prosperous. But the first man had to let go, refuse to accept an unsatisfactory business situation first, before the right doors opened.

EMOTIONS ARE YOUR GO-POWER

Another secret of financial independence, after we decide we will not settle for less than the best in life, is the law of concentration and conservation. Conservation of thought, energy and emotional drive are all greatly needed for financial independence. You have perhaps observed that some people seem to prosper for a period. Their business may even "boom," but suddenly the bottom drops out and they experience dire financial failure, from which they seem unable to recover. In almost every instance, if you look closely, you will discover that those people's emotions, attitudes and way of life became scattered, thus depleting them of their previous fine ability to prosper.

Most men's business activities prosper as long as their personal lives succeed. But when marital difficulties arise, their businesses go on the rocks, too. I recently talked with a brilliant man who has made several fortunes and lost them each time his home life was disrupted, as his emotions became upset and scattered.

We are all creatures of emotion and deep feeling, and our deep feelings can "make us or break us" financially. They are your God-power and and your go-power. You should guard them as you would a gold mine, because your emotions are in reality the richest gold mine you will ever own. Scattered thinking, scattered emotions, scattered actions lead to a scattering of your mind power. This in turn depletes your physical energy that is essential for prosperity; it depletes your brain energy that is needed for an intelligent course of action or plan for prosperity; it saps your emotional drive that is needed to put your prosperity plans to work.

DARE TO BE DIFFERENT

Conservation of thought, energy and emotional drive are all necessary for financial independence. In other words, in order to become permanently prosperous, you must dare to be different! At least, for a while. It was General Maxwell D. Taylor, the famous leader who parachuted into Normandy on D-Day, who once said that the time for daring is the moment when the stakes are high. He reminded us that we must be willing to risk much in order to win much; that indeed we must be willing to put all to the test.

But understand—this doesn't lead to a dull life of withdrawal from the world. Instead, it leads to a joyous, satisfying life filled with congenial associations and rich experiences, a life free from nonessential activities. When you decide to become financially independent, you immediately make up your mind to cease caring "what people think" and to dare to concentrate on your goal. As you become more prosperous, you will not care what your previous associates think anyway, because you will doubtless be forming new, more satisfying, and more congenial relationships in keeping with your expanding vision.

THINK BIG!

The most successful people think big, not limiting themselves or their associates to *their* ideas and opinions. If you desire to be free of a lot of limited thoughts and petty opinions, begin to think big. Concentrate on financial independence and you will "lose" the petty thinkers along the way. You will also cultivate enduring, satisfying friends who will help you up the ladder of success.

I once met a quiet little lady who is now president of a large housing project, an apartment project, and a huge suburban shopping center. Twenty years ago, the site now occupied by these homes, apartments and stores, was a large pasture, located about a mile from the nearest highway and five miles from the nearest town.

But this little lady had a dream about her property. Twenty years ago this had seemed a rather foolish dream. She kept building the vision in her mind that one day her land would be the site of one of the most beautiful suburban shopping centers in this country. She quietly and boldly held that vision in mind, impossible though it seemed. Of course, such a fulfilled dream would automatically make her financially independent.

In a few years, a nearby military base was enlarged. As a result of the increased traffic from the military base to the nearest town, a new four-lane highway was built. It happened that this four-lane highway bordered on this lady's pasture.

Almost immediately, real estate agents by the dozen began making this lady offers for the purchase of her land, but she refused to sell. From a practical standpoint, it might have seemed the thing to do because the land was still undeveloped and as such almost worthless. Unlike the realtors who wanted to buy, she had not the money nor the financial assets necessary to develop her land. But still she had her dream, and she courageously held that vision of prosperous financial independence.

The years passed; the nearby town grew and grew. One day this lady noticed a contractor with his equipment and men on the property adjoining hers. Soon she was introduced to this contractor and they became friends. They talked about all her property and of its possibilities for development. She related her dream of owning a beautiful shopping center where the townspeople and the military personnel could shop with ease, without having to get involved in downtown traffic. This contractor was quite impressed with her dream. He explained to her that it was possible for her dream to come true, without her having to sell any part of her beloved land.

He pointed out the possibilities for the formation of a corporation in which she would furnish the land, while he would furnish the services of his contracting company: equipment, personnel for building and supervising the work. He advised that he had a millionaire contractor friend who would be willing to furnish the necessary cash and collateral until the building was completed and could be approved for long-term financing.

In due time they formed a corporation. Upon the advice of her two corporation partners, they first built an apartment project to relieve the critical housing shortage that had occurred in that area. Later, they built homes for rental and sale. Still later, they built a beautiful, colonial-style shopping center that includes everything from a variety store to a drive-in bank. Thus, this woman's lovely pastureland provided for the needs of hundreds of people occupying apartments and homes. Her huge shopping center is considered one of the most beautiful in the South. All because she quietly and boldly held to an image of great success, prosperity and financial independence until others of like mind came along to help her make it come true.

DUST OFF YOUR DREAMS

If you have unfulfilled dreams and visions of greater prosperity and success tucked in a corner of your mind, don't keep them there any longer. Dare to bring them out and dust them off. Dare to begin thinking of the possibilities of financial independence even if, at this point, they seem impossible of fulfillment. Should that old defeating element of fear try to whisper that there's no possible way for your dreams of financial independence to come true, remind yourself of the rich Biblical promises, "Fear not, little flock, for it is your Father's good pleasure to give you the kingdom." (Luke 12:32); "Prove me now herewith, saith Jehovah of hosts, if I will not open you the windows of heaven and pour you out a blessing that there shall not be room enough to receive it." (Malachi 3:10); "All things are possible to him that believeth!" (Mark 9:23); "With God all things are possible." (Matthew 19:26)

Often you may not have succeeded because you felt that somehow you had to succeed alone and the thought overwhelmed you; it seemed easier to settle for failure. But as a very successful engineer said to me recently when I asked him what his success secret was:

> I was never successful until I went into "partnership." God is my partner and the best One I have ever had. His guidance about my financial affairs never leads me anywhere but to greater prosperity. I begin and end my day by asking for, listening for, and expecting specific guidance about all my engineering projects, and that guidance always comes.
>
> Recently, when the president of one of this country's leading corporations said to me, "How do you do it? How do you manage to do all you do and never become ruffled or upset in the midst of such great demands and expectations?" He seemed rather amazed at my answer that it's simple. God is my partner and I leave all the stress, strain and hard decisions to Him. The man answered, "You mean it really works to do

such a thing? That it's practical to trust God in such large financial matters?" My reply was, "Look, if you can't trust God Who is all-intelligence, has all-power and Who runs this rich universe, just whom can you trust?"

Truly, God opens ways where, to human sense, there seems to be no way. Grasp this truth and hold fast to it. Businesses have been saved, fortunes built, discoveries made, inventions perfected and the dead restored to life, after the sentence of defeat had been passed by humanity. Thank God that His goodness does not stop at the limits of our human vision. Keep steady, keep your faith, keep your courage; remember that God opens ways where, to human sense, there is no way!

VISUALIZE FINANCIAL INDEPENDENCE

In other words, you need not undertake the fulfillment of any desire alone. You have the promise, "Ask and it shall be given you; seek and ye shall find; knock and it shall be opened unto you; for everyone that asketh receiveth; and he that seeketh findeth; and to him that knocketh it shall be opened." (Matthew 7:7) Most folks overlook this as a prosperity secret. Often they let riches pass them by, just because they do not ask the help of a Higher Power to learn how to attain their good.

Begin now to visualize yourself, not as just becoming more prosperous, but as becoming financially independent. Emma Curtis Hopkins has written, "Whatever is oftenest viewed with the inner eye reveals its secrets and hands out its gifts."[1] It is a delightful process and very stimulating to the mind, and it really is not daydreaming if you dare to get definite in your thinking.

Mrs. Hopkins has further pointed out, "Success lies in being one-pointed, and in rejecting all that distracts from one's victorious objective."[2] Why be mildly prosperous when, by being mentally "one-pointed," you can be completely free from financial care, so that you will have time and money to develop other phases of your being that can be a credit to you and all mankind? A Texas oilman once made a fortune in a way no one expected. He went into oil fields that had already been drilled for oil and by drilling "deeper" he made a fortune in oil that no one believed was there. In the realm of prosperous thinking, you can, too!

You are actually equipped to master life in its *every phase!* You do not have to compromise in life, if you are willing to let go of the idea of compromise. By ceasing needless activities, associations and relationships; by ceasing to be bothered with needless chatter with scatter-minded people, you will find that financial independence is right around the corner, much nearer than you previously assumed.

CONSERVE YOUR TIME AND ENERGY

Begin to discipline yourself more; conserve your time and energy; associate only with other prosperous-minded people, with whom you have compatible inter-

---

1. See her book, *Scientific Christian Mental Practice*, (Marina del Rey, CA: DeVorss & Co.)
2. Ibid.

ests. As you turn from all that is unproductive or unrelated to your high vision of prosperity; as you stop trying to please others and dare to please the "still, small voice" of progress within your own heart, you are well on the way to financial independence!

Many people want to become financially independent, but they never make the grade because they refuse to discipline themselves and their way of life, even for a time. It may seem to you an extreme idea that you must concentrate, concentrate, and concentrate on prosperity to exclusion of all else, that you should discard negative, failure-minded business associates; that you should begin fearlessly to weed out all undesirable relationships; that you should be careful with whom and how you spend your time, even your leisure time. Once you decide to try this method, you will discover that it is as though you are breaking a hard shell of limited thought, feeling, and activity. When you get past that point, you can begin enjoying a more balanced way of life again. But there is that transition period of having a "one-track mind" that thinks only of success and prosperity, after which you find yourself in a much higher financial bracket. You will discover a new zest in life, and you will be able to relax and really have fun, because you have earned it. But unless you conserve and concentrate prior to that point you'll never attain it.

The truth of this was recently brought to my attention by a news story reporting that a young man, who is still less than 30 years of age, had become vice-president of an insurance company. This young man decided several years ago on an objective, and he quietly started working toward it through prosperous thinking. He spent all of his spare time reading books on success, associating only with others of like mind. For a period his wife felt that perhaps he was restricting himself from social affairs which they both had enjoyed in the past. But when he explained to her why he was devoting his time to concentration upon his present and future success, she was willing to forego most social events that were time-consuming. After several years of hard work and study, this young man has reached such heights that he and his wife can again lead a more social life. Now they can truly afford the enjoyable contacts with prosperous-minded people who are their new friends.

ASSUME YOUR FINANCIAL INDEPENDENCE NOW!

A good way to begin cultivating the expectation of financial independence, and the happy experiences it can bring, is by beginning to be financially independent for the day, week or month now before you. It is always easier for the mind to produce results that are expected in the present or immediate future. For instance, begin your day the prosperous way by affirming lavish abundance for that day, even before arising. Put prosperous thinking first, as well as last, in your day. As you awaken each morning and emotionally prepare to meet the new day, either before arising or with your morning coffee, prepare yourself by writing out, verbally affirming, or silently declaring a number of times: "I EXPECT LAVISH ABUNDANCE EVERY DAY IN EVERY

WAY IN MY LIFE AND AFFAIRS. I SPECIFICALLY EXPECT AND
GIVE THANKS FOR LAVISH ABUNDANCE TODAY!" In this way
you are sending prosperous thinking before you to prepare a satisfying and worthwhile day that will run to
meet you, hour by hour, with its delightful surprises
and satisfactions.

As you daily develop a state of mind that believes in,
expects, and experiences financial independence one
day at a time, your state of mind then automatically
expands, so that financial independence becomes a
weekly, monthly, yearly habit. But you must start some
time in your thinking, and the daily basis is the easiest,
most immediate and most satisfying, because it gives
you proof positive that your prosperity is at hand,
awaiting your recognition and acceptance of it.

A businessman recently told me that his business
doubled after he began to concentrate his attention on
the thought and expectancy of financial independence, rather than on the thought of how hard he had
to work and how useless it all seemed. As a young insurance executive, he discovered that thinking of and
expecting lavish abundance for one day at a time was a
great secret toward financial independence. Several
years ago he began spending an hour each morning
mentally planning his day as he wished it to be. He
held in mind figures of sales he desired to obtain.
Later when he was named supervisor of a group of insurance salesmen, he spent time each morning thinking of them and the amount of sales he wanted them to
make for the day. It was by this daily process of thinking of lavish abundance for himself and his salesman
that he worked his way up to an executive capacity in
his company.

YOU CAN OVERCOME SERIOUS OBSTACLES

In order to become financially independent, to the extent of having a constant financial income, it is necessary to discard a number of negative attitudes. Most people can tell you in a hurry all the reasons why they cannot succeed. Yet as we look about us, we are surprised at how often the people who succeed seem to have serious obstacles to overcome.

There is a lady who is a polio victim who goes to her work as a private secretary in a wheel chair every day. To all appearances, she should have given up years ago when she was stricken with paralysis. But she was rehabilitated and now drives her own car. She has an interesting, worthwhile job. Through her attitude of refusing to give in to disease, she has become independent of the sickbed and makes her own way financially as well. The last time I heard from her she was also thinking of getting married!

One spring day several years ago, a young store clerk talked with me about how discouraged and uncertain he was about his future. I asked him what he really wanted to do, and he shyly replied, as though he had never dared to talk about it, "I would like to attend college so that I may teach." I suggested to him that, through the power of prosperous thinking, all things are possible. I further suggested that he consider becoming independent, that he should positively work toward getting further education, that he should not settle for a clerk's job, if he really wished to become a teacher.

He agreed to begin visualizing himself as attending college in the fall, and to constantly think of lavish abundance becoming visible to meet his every need. At the suggestion that he make plans as though he would attend college in the fall, he immediately registered at the college which he wished to attend. He studied carefully the college catalog, selecting the subjects he wished to take, and memorizing everything in that catalog about the college, history, curriculum, faculty and other features.

As he continued to envision himself as free from what he did not want to do, and as being active in what he wished to do, an interesting thing happened. In mid-summer a relative came to him and explained that for some time he had observed him and felt that his potential was much greater than his present work allowed. This relative then offered to make financial arrangements for this young man to attend college that fall. With great joy this young man then confided all of his hopes and dreams to the relative, who was happy to learn of his foresight.

Recently that young man informed me that he will receive his degree within a few months. All this came about because he dared to become independent in his thinking, and to vision great good as possible for him.

TECHNIQUES FOR BECOMING
FINANCIALLY INDEPENDENT

Begin now to mentally accept the vision of financial independence for yourself and those you hold dear by filling your mind with pictures of the life you would like to lead, rather than being hypnotized by the life you seem to be leading at the moment. But keep your high visions of financial independence to yourself. Start doing whatever little or big thing you can to help your high vision to come true.

Let me share with you a simple, practical technique for helping you to begin today to become more prosperous. If you keep up the practice of this one simple technique, it will lead to greater prosperity, and it can surely lead to financial independence as well! It is this: The ancients believed the number "ten" has a magic power of increase. Thus, beginning right now, whenever you think about money, whether it be income, outgo, the amount in your savings or investments— begin mentally increasing your supply by thinking of ten times that amount coming to you. This is a delightful and fascinating technique for increasing your money.

For instance, look in your wallet. Suppose there is $5 there. Look at it and declare: "I GIVE THANKS THAT THIS $5 IS BUT A SYMBOL OF THE INEXHAUSTIBLE SUBSTANCE OF THE UNIVERSE. I GIVE THANKS THAT TEN TIMES THIS MUCH OR $50 IS NOW ON ITS WAY TO ME AND QUICKLY MANIFESTS IN PERFECT WAYS." Multiply every figure that presents itself to you by ten, and begin expecting the multiplied amount to come to you. In that way, you begin to think of how much you have and how much is coming, rather than the usual deadly thought that you haven't enough. By multiplying everything by ten, your thinking automatically shifts from lack to prosperity. Since the mind quickly responds to *definite figures*, it will seem as though heaven and earth are working to propel money in your direction.

Look at the balance of your checkbook. Perhaps $50 is there. Instead of thinking, "This isn't enough to pay the bills," change the thought to: "THIS IS BUT A SYMBOL

OF THE RICH SUBSTANCE OF THE UNIVERSE THAT IS AVAIL-
ABLE TO ME. I GIVE THANKS THAT TEN TIMES THIS MUCH,
OR $500, IS NOW ON ITS WAY TO ME AND QUICKLY MANI-
FESTS TO MEET EVERY DEMAND." In like manner, when
the bills begin flowing in around the first of the
month, do not think, "This bill of $20 is much too high
this month. We simply must cut down on expenses."
Change the thought to: "$20 IS BUT A SYMBOL OF THE
RICH SUBSTANCE OF THE UNIVERSE THAT IS NOW AVAIL-
ABLE TO ME. I GIVE THANKS THAT TEN TIMES THIS MUCH,
OR $200, IS NOW ON ITS WAY TO ME AND IT QUICKLY
APPEARS, SO THAT EVERY FINANCIAL OBLIGATION IS IM-
MEDIATELY AND COMPLETELY MET WITH THE RICH SUB-
STANCE OF THE UNIVERSE."

After multiplying your money by ten mentally, if
there is a financial need, it is good to go ahead sending
forth whatever substance is on hand to meet it. That
opens the way for the multiplied amounts to begin
flowing in. The outflow makes way for the inflow.

With every financial transaction that presents itself
to you, multiply it by ten, giving thanks that ten times
that much is coming to you for your private use. It is
the quickest, surest, most delightful way to get your
Ph.D. in prosperous thinking!

A saleswoman who heard about this prosperous principle decided to immediately put it to work. The night
she heard it explained, she had a dollar in her pocket.
She took it out, looked at it and thought, "Ten times
this much is immediately coming to me. Ten dollars
now manifests." She then gave the dollar as an offering
at the close of the lecture. The next day she continued
multiplying the total figure of every sale she made by
ten. The result was that she sold more during that one
day than did all the employees on two other floors of

the same store. That night when she arrived home, there were two $5 checks which had arrived in the mail. They were gifts that were totally unexpected. Thus, her dollar had produced ten dollars for her, and her selling power had mushroomed that day through her use of the magic number ten.

You can take this same idea even further, once you get it fully established in your mind and working for you. A doctor who heard this principle explained thought quietly, "Why should I settle for the multiplying power of ten? Why wouldn't the number one hundred, which is ten times ten, be even more powerful in multiplying power?" And so he decided to test it out. He, too, gave a dollar love offering at the conclusion of a lecture he heard on this subject, thinking, "I am giving; thereby invoking the law of receiving. I expect to receive one hundred times this amount, or $100. I give thanks that it quickly appears in perfect ways." The next afternoon, a woman walked into his office, handed him a check and said, "I do not owe you any money because I have not needed treatment from you recently. However, I am greatly impressed with the help you have been able to give several members of my family recently. They have been completely restored to health through your treatment. In appreciation I would like to share a portion of some money that recently came to me unexpectedly." The check she insisted he accept was for $100!

A housewife, upon hearing of the multiplying power of ten, thought as did the doctor, and decided to multiply the dollar in her pocketbook by one hundred, instead of by ten. Within days she received a check for $100 from a business associate who had long been owing her the money!

What freedom this one simple technique gives you from the thought of lack, poverty and "not enough!" It completely changes your attitude to: "This is a rich universe, and there's plenty for you and for me."

FURTHER AIDS FOR ESTABLISHING
FINANCIAL INDEPENDENCE

Along with multiplying every financial figure by ten, or by ten times ten, I suggest that you do a number of other things to aid in establishing your vision of financial independence. Begin now filling your mind with pictures of the life you would like to lead when you are financially able. Study newspapers and magazines carrying luxurious advertisements of the clothes, the homes, the hobbies, and other blessings in life which you wish to have and experience. Build, build, build your inner mental pictures of your life free from financial worry, free for travel, hobbies, worthwhile accomplishments and congenial associations. As for the talents and abilities you would like to develop, begin studying books and filling your mind with the pictures of fulfillment along that line. Think of the organizations you would like to help, and the good you would like your riches to accomplish.

Build the mental picture of financial independence also for your loved ones, in your own thinking. Mentally behold the whole world financially independent. Free yourself, and begin to free mass thought of all that is less than rich, financial independence. Millions of people all over the world are slaves to war, crime, delinquency, ill health, and the godlessness of Communism because they ignorantly believe that their wealth lies outside themselves, leaving them wholly dependent upon others. Dissolve this ignorant, destructive, hypnotic belief for others, as well as for yourself, by daring to accept the glorious truth that financial independence is one of the God-given rights of all mankind, which you can help to bring forth by your own attitudes, actions and reactions.

You should also begin building your expectancy and faith in financial independence by studying the subject of finance, economics, and investments. You should literally pray for financial independence. Realize in your thinking that you are not bound to the wheel of work, day in and day out. You are not a servant to the god of Mammon, but a radiant child of the God of universal abundance!

YOUR TEN LUCKY STEPS

To help you gain financial independence on a steady basis, I wish to share with you the following formula, which I like to call the "ten lucky steps" to prosperous thinking and financial independence:

1. Get quiet, meditate, and ask your loving Father if there is any reason why you should not become financially independent. (This act will remove all uncertainty from your mind, for it is uncertainty that delays your success.)

2. Having decided to achieve financial independence and having gotten a sense of peace about the rightness of it for you, make a mental picture of the highest degree of it that you wish to

experience. Mentally image the amount of income you wish and how you will live when you are independent. Build as detailed a mental picture of financial independence as possible. The more you think about it, the more detailed your mental picture will become. Think of the kind of home you wish, the type of clothes you wish to wear, the activities you wish to experience, the places you wish to visit.

3. Build the mental picture of what you *really* want, not what someone else wants you to have, or what you think it is your duty to have—but what you *really* want. Many people lead miserable lives of failure because they try to please others. Your life is a divine gift for *you* to live, not for someone else to live *for* you. Only what you sincerely want can make you happy. Build mental pictues upon that and nothing less.

4. Say little to anyone about your inner plans, because others can always tell you how they think you should live your life, but they can't live it for you successfully. Keep your success plans to yourself. Do not dissipate them, or subject them to cross-current, by giving others a chance to tear them apart.

5. Proceed as you feel led to take the first steps toward your mental pictures of financial independence. Do whatever little or big things you can to gain the feeling that you are already on the way toward it. Set a time limit and plan to achieve certain things within six months, others within a year, and others within two years. Set a

date when you plan to achieve complete financial independence.

6. Do not become anxious, excited or emotionally upset if affairs do not immediately begin producing the results you desire. Do not try to force or hurry your mental image into fulfillment. Anxious, excited, emotional, hurried, forced states of mind produce violent results that are seldom satisfactory, and they can be most discouraging and destructive.

7. Instead of caring what people say or think, quietly continue to persevere in making your mental image of financial independence come forth, in whatever ways are revealed to you. Remind yourself often that you are working with the rich substance of the universe through prosperous thinking, and that you cannot fail, because the laws of the universe are immutable and cannot fail. Thus, nothing can prevent your success from manifesting, as you keep thinking and working toward it.

8. Realize that your dreams of financial independence have already come true on the mental plane, by the time you desire them or become aware of them. Thus, your great good is as much yours before it becomes visible as it is afterwards, but it is up to you to bring it into visibility. You can do so by declaring: "DIVINE SUBSTANCE, GIVE ME THIS NOW IN THINE OWN PERFECT WAY; OR DIVINE SUBSTANCE, NOW MEET THIS DEMAND IN THINE OWN PERFECT WAY. IT IS MINE NOW AND QUICKLY MANIFESTS IN SATISFYING WAYS." Never say, "It can never happen," but, "This, or something better, now manifests."

9. Remind yourself often that if others have attained financial independence, so can you. What one has done, many can do. What can be done in small degree can, with persistence, frequency and earnestness, be done in an unlimited degree. It's up to you.

10. Remind yourself often that every good thing already exists in the realm of substance. Through your high expectancy, mental images, and prosperous thought and action, you become master of the realm of substance, and can bring forth whatever you wish from it. The history of the world shows that every mental demand of man has been met. Make yours now. Stick to it and you will succeed!

It may not happen overnight, yet it can. It will happen if you dare to persist in expecting, envisioning and mentally accepting the idea of financial independence for yourself and all people. At first, it may take some effort on your part to begin believing success is possible for you, but the fruits of that effort will make it worth every prosperous thought held, every vision entertained, every rich mental picture you have built.

Declare often: "EVERY DAY IN EVERY WAY I AM BECOMING FINANCIALLY INDEPENDENT, WITH THE HELP OF GOD." It can surely come!

THE PROSPERITY LAW
OF PRAYER

— Chapter 13 —

In these modern times you hear much about the power of prayer. Prayer is often described as the mightiest force in the universe. You frequently hear such phrases as "prayer changes things" or "the family who prays together stays together." Everywhere the power of prayer is being written about, talked about and used as never before. Someone succinctly described the power of prayer in this manner: "Prayer is profoundly simple and simply profound!"

Recently the vice-president of a large real estate firm talked with me at length about the power of prayer. He declared, "This is a more spiritual world than many folks realize. People often wear a mask, hesitating to speak of their belief in prayer or of their own answered prayers." He then related how, during a recent period of ill health, his supposedly "hard-boiled business friends" quietly visited him in the hospital, and later at home, to talk with him about the power of prayer for restoring his health. Even after he returned to work, several business friends spent their entire lunch periods with him, relating numerous answered prayers in their own life experiences.

PRAYER IS NATURAL TO MAN

Prayer has been described as man's steady effort to know God. Quite contrary to what most people think, prayer is natural to man, rather than a strange, mysterious practice. Men have always prayed and always will. In his primitive understanding, primitive man prayed to the sun and stars, to fire and water, to animals and plants, to images and myths, but primitive man certainly prayed.

Later, as the intellect of man evolved, his ideas advanced as he conceived of God as a personal deity who had human sentiments and emotions. The early Hebrews prayed to this kind of God, a God with human traits, a God who they felt had to be appeased by sacrificial offerings and implored to bestow favors. Because of their undeveloped spiritual understanding, the early Hebrews felt that God looked upon them as "worms of the dust." There are people today who still pray to that kind of God, not because God has that nature, but because of their limited understanding of the real nature of God.

All men in all ages have prayed in one way or another. At long last, mankind is coming out of a primitive and purely intellectual approach to God into true spiritual understanding. Our methods of prayer are now changing, expanding, and improving. Mankind is finally realizing that God is not a hostile Being with a split personality of good and evil, but that God is a God of love, the unchanging principle of supreme good which pervades the ordered universe. It is easy to pray to and to commune with this kind of God!

PRAY FOR RESULTS

Even though various prosperity laws are discussed in this book, the power of prayer cannot be over-emphasized for permanent, satisfying prosperity. The person who prays daily is certain to succeed, because he is attuning himself to the richest, most successful force in the universe. Jesus promised, "All things whatsoever ye shall ask in prayer, believing, ye shall receive." (Matthew 21:22)

This Bible promise makes it plain that there's nothing wrong with praying for things. Many people have not employed the power of prayer because they have the erroneous idea that it is wrong to pray for things. Jesus did not mean that praying for things was the only form of prayer, or even the highest form of prayer, when He made this statement. But He knew that if you first pray for things, you will learn the power of prayer, and you will then want to go further and deeper in developing your prayer power.

The story is told of a woman who prayed definitely for a husband and got him in six weeks. She then prayed six years to get rid of him! What that woman did not realize was that when you pray for things, you should stipulate the "divine selection," which is always the right, sublime answer to your specific need.

It is right and just that you should pray for things if

you need them, because you are living in a rich universe that desires to fulfill all your needs. Among Biblical figures who prayed for definite things were Abraham, Asa, Daniel, David, Elijah, Ezekiel, Habakkuk, Hannah, Jehoshaphat, Jeremiah, Jonah, Joshua, Moses, Nehemiah, Samson, and Solomon. On a number of occasions Jesus prayed definitely for things.[1]

Tennyson poetically expressed the power of praying for things in his line: "More things are wrought by prayer than this world dreams of!"

Emmet Fox once described the power of praying for things:

> Prayer does change things. Prayer does make things to happen quite otherwise than they would have happened had the prayer not been made. It makes no difference at all what sort of difficulty you may be in. It does not matter what the causes may have been that led up to it. Enough prayer will get you out of your difficulty, if only you will be persistent enough in your appeal to God.[2]

Perhaps you have heard the well-worn phrase, "Pray about it and everything will be all right." But let me share with you four basic ways of praying so that everything *will* be all right:

---

1. See the Ponder book, *The Millionaire from Nazareth* and her books on prayer.

2. *The Sermon on the Mount* (New York: Harper & Row, Inc., 1938), p. 11.

1. GENERAL PRAYER

First, there is general prayer. General prayer is praying to God as a loving, understanding Father in your own private way. It can be on your knees or in any comfortable position. It can be expressed in spoken words or in silent communion. It can be with a prayer book before you, or it can be by browsing through your Bible, dwelling upon favorite passages, or paraphrasing them to meet your need.

SPECIAL METHODS OF GENERAL PRAYER

A good way to begin using a general prayer is to take the Lord's Prayer and consider each line of it silently and verbally. The ancients believed that the Lord's Prayer was all-powerful; they often declared it over and over twelve to fifteen times without stopping. At the healing shrine at Lourdes, those seeking healing were taught to pray the Lord's Prayer fifteen times while they entered the waters. The number fifteen was believed to have the power to dissolve affliction and adversity.

From my own experience I know that deep spiritual power is contacted and brought alive when one repeats the Lord's Prayer over and over, either silently or audibly.

Another effective way to make contact with spiritual power in prayer is to take the name "Jehovah" from the Old Testament or "Jesus Christ" from the New Testament, and verbally and silently declare them over and over. A housewife once told me that her husband became very successful in business, after several previous failures, when she began to daily call upon and dwell upon the name "Jehovah." It seemed to generate spiritual power that released right ideas, right actions and right results.

As for the power of calling on the name "Jesus Christ," Charles Fillmore has written:

> Jesus Christ still lives in the spiritual ethers of this world and is in constant contact with those who raise their thoughts to Him in prayer. . . . The mightiest vibration is set up by the speaking of the name Jesus Christ. This is the name that is named far above all rule, and authority, the name above all names, holding in itself all power in heaven and in earth. It is the name that has power to mold the universal substance . . . and when spoken it sets forces into activity that bring results, as Jesus promised when He said, "Whatsoever ye shall ask of the Father in my name, He may give it you." "If you shall ask anything in my name, that will I do."[3]

Another powerful way to pray generally, invoking the name, presence and power of Jesus Christ, is by mentally imaging Jesus Christ taking care of anything, any situation or person that bothers you. For instance, a woman once wrote describing this type of prayer:

> For twenty years I had as my husband a man whom I had grown to hate. I am married now to the same

---

3. See *Jesus Christ Heals*, page 11 and see *Prosperity*, page 36, both published by Unity Books, Unity Villiage, MO. 64065.

husband, a man who is daily more companionable and loving. Strive as I did, I could not bring myself to love the first man. He seemed dead spiritually, was very selfish, crude, hard, careless, and unloving. I had little ones to care for and was unable to work to keep them, so of course, I had to stay with my husband. Then I began to think of the presence and power of Jesus Christ, and decided to prayerfully image Jesus Christ at work in the situation.

Daily, I began to think of Jesus Christ going to work with my husband. I saw the Christ working in and through him, working with him, even having lunch with him. I visualized my husband and the Christ with him, coming home to his wife and family to well-cooked meals, happy and contented.

Now, as a result of this, although I am still married to the same man, he is truly a different man, one who is kind, thoughtful, happy, and loving. At this very moment, he is sitting out on the back veranda happily whistling "Rock of Ages" as he mends his leather jacket in preparation for work tomorrow. Through prayerfully bringing Jesus Christ into the situation, I have found the companionship I longed for. Truly I love my husband. I feel like telling other wives who continually quarrel with and condemn their husbands just to try my prescription.

Sometimes one form of general prayer will aid you, and at other times some other form will meet your need. In this age when we're hearing a great deal about affirmative prayer, which is often described as "scientific prayer," as well as about meditation and silent prayer, it is good to remember that good old-fashioned earnest prayer, used in a general way, has not gone out of style and still contains great spiritual power.

PRAYER HEALS

I once heard a businessman relate how general prayer met a need in his family. His little son had been ill for several weeks with a serious cough. Medical attention had been of no avail and the cough persisted. One night in desperation this man took his pajama-clad son into the den of his home and sank into the nearest chair. He then offered a short, simple general prayer of thanks that his son was healed of the cough and infection. It might have been a prayer similar to what Jesus prayed before Lazarus came back to life, "Father, I thank thee that thou hearest me, and I knew that thou hearest me always." (John 11:41,42) In any event, the child coughed only twice after that, and recovered completely. That is the power of general prayer!

PRAYER DISSOLVES BITTERNESS

A housewife recently wrote me of some of her experiences with general prayer. She and her husband desperately wished to have a child. For three years they prayed daily that God's will be done concerning it. Their prayer was then answered and they now have a lovely little girl.

In another instance, a housewife had long been estranged from her father who had divorced her mother when she was small. One day, after years of not having heard from him, a letter arrived saying he would like to come for a visit. At first, the old bitterness from the past welled up within this woman as she thought of seeing her father again. Then she knelt beside her bed and prayed that God's good will be done in the matter. She got a feeling of peace and calm, and was led to write him to come. When he arrived, she was amazed at how congenial he seemed with her, her husband and child. She declared, "He was the best house guest I've ever had." They laughed, shared many things, and were quite happy during his ten-day visit. Six months later, she received word that he had passed away in a distant city, and she was so grateful she had prayed for guidance, and had enjoyed that last happy visit with him.

PRAYING FOR MARRIAGE

The assistant secretary-treasurer of a savings bank once remarked that it was time she was getting married. She was an attractive person who had many friends and enjoyed a wide range of activities, but she just never had met the "right man." The janitor heard her remark and informed her that it was quite possible for her to meet the right person and to marry happily. He advised her to pray about the matter. She informed him that she had already prayed many times, but to no avail. Doubtfully, she agreed to pray again if he would also pray with her daily, which he did.

One morning a few months later, she was wearing a lovely diamond as she rushed into the bank and announced to her fellow workers that she would be getting married very soon. She had met her future husband while playing golf at the country club, and it had been "love at first sight." Ever since, she has insisted that her happy marriage is the result of prayer.

PRAYING FOR WORK

A musician was out of a job. The band with which he worked had been asked to go to Florida. Upon arrival there, the job promised them did not materialize, and they were stranded. This musician prayed a general prayer that God's good will be done in the matter. One day he and the other members of the band were at the union headquarters hoping something would turn up, when their agent telephoned from New York and said he had located a job for them in Texas. No one else in the group knew that this musician believed in and practiced the power of prayer. Nevertheless, he felt his prayers for the group had been answered as they proceeded to Texas for a long, successful engagement.

PRAYING FOR PROTECTION

A housewife was in her farmhouse in a dense forest area. While her husband was away on a business trip, a great forest fire arose and raged all around her property. As the fire surrounded her, she could not leave to notify her husband, who was traveling between two points and could not be reached anyway. So she prayed, "Father, it's up to You to save me and our house and property. There's nothing I can do." She then released the matter, went to bed for the night, and slept well. The next morning she awoke early to find only a few stumps still burning here and there. Upon investigation, she realized that the fire had burned right up to her property lines, and had stopped! It seemed a miracle. Later in the day when a forest ranger arrived, he said, "There's only one explanation for this. You must have been praying."

PRAYER IS DYNAMIC

Perhaps you are thinking just now as my young son once did. A friend met him on the street and asked him about me. He replied that I was fine, with one exception: "There's just one thing wrong with my mother." Alarmed, the friend inquired what was wrong. The emphatic reply was, "She prays too much." The friend then asked, "Does anything happen when your mother prays?" to which he brightened up and replied, "Oh yes, *something* always happens when my mother prays."

If you feel that perhaps your prayer experience has not been satisfying or powerful, and that nothing much happened as a result of your prayers, perhaps it is because you would like to develop more specific types of prayer than general prayer.

2. PRAYERS OF DENIAL

The second type of prayer is one little known or understood. It is the prayer of denial.

Many people cringe at the word "denial," believing that its only meaning is "to take away or withhold." But the word "deny" also means "to dissolve, to erase or be free from, to refuse to accept as true or right that which is reported to be true." Prayers of denial are for the latter purpose—to refuse to accept as necessary, true, lasting or right anything which is not satisfying or good.

Prayers of denial are your "no" prayers. They help you to reject things as they are and to dissolve your negative thoughts about them. They help you to make way for something better. Prayers of denial help you to erase, to be free from less than the best in your life. Prayers of denial are expressed in those attitudes that think, "I will not put up with or tolerate this experience as necessary, lasting or right. I refuse to accept things as they are. I am God's child and I will accept nothing but His complete goodness for me."

Mankind greatly needs to use prayers of denial or "no" prayers. So many people lead a pygmy existence of fear, compromise, and dissatisfaction, when they might be enjoying a life of gigantic good, if they only knew how to say "no" to the less-than-best in their experiences.

It is good to follow up thoughts of what you don't want with what you do want; after claiming "No, I will not accept this," you should add, "Yes, I will accept this or something better."

Jesus was speaking of your "no" and "yes" powers when He said "Let your speech be yea, yea and nay, nay." (Matthew 5:37) The prophet Hosea went into more detail to show you how to use your "no" and "yes" powers when he advised, "Take with you words and return unto Jehovah; say unto Him, Take away all iniquity, and accept that which is good." (Hosea 14:2) This passage is a dynamic "no" and "yes" prayer formula. To any situation that is dissatisfying, you can deny it by declaring to a loving Father, "TAKE AWAY ALL INIQUITY." Then follow it up with the affirmation, "I WILL ACCEPT ONLY THAT WHICH IS GOOD."

Long before the time of Jesus, the Egyptians followed the command to take away all iniquity through the power of denial. The Egyptians used the sign of the cross to indicate a crossing out or blotting out of evil, a form of denial which still is used by some churches.

Daniel in the lions' den doubtless used prayers of denial to assure his safety. A famous picture shows Daniel not looking at the lions, but with his back to them, he is shown looking out of the window toward Jerusalem. When the King inquired why Daniel had not been torn to pieces by the lions, Daniel declared, "My God sent His angel and shut the mouths of the lions, and they have not hurt me." (Daniel 6:22)

HOW TO DISSOLVE FEAR, WORRY, TENSION

Prayers of denial dissolve fear, worry, sorrow, sickness, tension and other negative emotions. "No" prayers seem to neutralize the effects of negation. For instance, a man once talked with me about marrying a woman who had just been released from prison. They were very much in love; she had served a long sentence and had been a model prisoner. But he feared "what people might think." I asked him if any of his friends knew of her prison record and he replied they did not, but he feared they might find out.

After praying with him, I had the feeling it was in divine order for him to marry this woman, who was certainly due a second chance in society, after having paid for her mistake. I suggested that he use Daniel's prayer of denial. When any fear or worry tried to come upon him he was to deny it by declaring: "MY GOD HATH SENT HIS ANGELS AND SHUT THE MOUTHS OF THE

LIONS. THEY CANNOT HURT US." He used this prayer, and never had any unfavorable reaction to his marriage.

In speaking of these *second* and *third* types of prayer — denial and affirmation — I should point out that they are as much attitudes of mind as formal methods of prayer. You can use them silently or verbally wherever you are, either as formal prayers or informally as attitudes of mind.

Any secretary knows the feeling when she is hurriedly called in for dictation and informed that she must produce quick results. It can be confusing and upsetting unless one knows how to use "no" attitudes of mind. I recall once, while still a legal secretary, being informed that a long legal contract which had been dictated to me had to be transcribed immediately (if not sooner!) for one of the boss's prominent clients. It seemed an impossible task, so I began thinking over and over, "THERE IS NO NEED TO RUSH. DIVINE ORDER IS NOW ESTABLISHED AND MAINTAINED IN THIS SITUATION." Within a few minutes this client changed his mind about the urgency of this matter and informed the boss he would return the next day to sign the papers. This allowed time to prepare them properly.

So many people get the erroneous idea that somebody else can keep their good from them, and so they unhappily go through life believing it. Prayers of denial can dissolve such false beliefs. When you catch yourself thinking in such a limited vein, change the thought and declare, "NOTHING CAN OPPOSE MY GOOD." As you do, you will find that where people and affairs seemed to work against you, everything will shift and begin working for you.

One of the greatest problems of mankind is how to overcome and dissolve fear. When you can overcome your fear of any problem you have gained control of it; it no longer controls you; and your are well on the way to solving it. A powerful prayer to deny fear is: "PER-FECT LOVE CASTS OUT FEAR."

SAY "NO" TO UNHAPPINESS

A war bride from overseas came to this country with her American husband. For a few years they seemed happy, but then the old memories of her war experiences began welling up in her mind. She became very unhappy, depressed and confused. Finally, her husband had her confined to a mental hospital. Later, he divorced her and married someone else.

In the midst of all this unhappiness, far from her homeland, among strangers, this woman learned of the "no" attitude of mind. She had only one friend outside of the hospital to whom she began to write, "I am not going to remain in my present condition. I know I can be helped. I know I am going to get well." Gradually she began to improve. Soon she was released from the hospital and went to work in another hospital. When she did she declared to her friend, "You see, I told you I had what it takes." She was soon happily married to a doctor whom she met at her new job.

If people only knew how to say "no" to unhappy experiences, rather than to bow to them! The Hebrews were warned repeatedly not to bow down and worship false idols or gods. The gods of unhappiness, lack and limitation are "heathen gods" which are still with us. They cause us as much havoc as did the early Hebrews' worship of false gods.

To declare, "THERE IS NOTHING FOR ME TO FEAR. GOD'S SPIRIT OF GOOD IS AT WORK AND DIVINE RESULTS ARE COMING FORTH" is to dissolve fear, worry, tension and anxiety. To declare (as the scientists know), "THERE IS NO ABSENCE OF LIFE, SUBSTANCE OR INTELLIGENCE ANY- WHERE, SO THERE IS NO ABSENCE OF LIFE, SUBSTANCE OR INTELLIGENCE IN THIS SITUATION OR IN MY LIFE" dissolves uncertainty, confusion and many times dissipates psychosomatic sickness or financial lack. Once when the Asian flu seemed prevalent, I constantly declared, "THERE IS NO ABSENCE OF LIFE, SUBSTANCE OR INTELLI- GENCE ANYWHERE." One day my son came home from school and said, "Mother, I was the only boy at football practice today. Everybody else was home with Asian flu. What is that?"

IMMUNIZE YOURSELF AGAINST NEGATION

The denial attitude of mind does not invite trouble by discussing it. The denial attitude of mind mentally says "no" to talk of others which emphasizes less than the best or that gives attention to what you don't want to experience. Instead of multiplying problems by discussing them loudly and long, instead of fretting about world conditions or the problems of others, do whatever you constructively can to make them right. Use the "No, I will not accept this as lasting, permanent or necessary" attitude toward all.

When people try to upset or bother you with a lot of negative talk, mentally say, "No, no, no, I do not wish to hear this. I do not accept this as true or necessary." Soon they will either switch to more constructive topics, or leave!

In like manner, instead of thinking that you have to "put up with" dissatisfaction in your life as a permanent arrangement, use your "no' power by declaring often: "NO, I DO NOT HAVE TO ACCEPT THIS SITUATION. GOD IN HIS ALMIGHTY GOODNESS IS DISSOLVING AND REMOVING ALL NEGATION FROM MY WORLD. NO SITUATION DISMAYS ME, FOR GOD THE SPIRIT OF GOOD IS WITH ME, UPHOLDING AND SUSTAINING ME AND MAKING ALL THINGS RIGHT."

For financial affairs, here is a prayer of denial: "REGARDLESS OF TAXES, THE COST OF LIVING OR THE RATE OF UNEMPLOYMENT, MY FINANCIAL INCOME CAN AND DOES INCREASE RICHLY NOW THROUGH THE DIRECT ACTION OF GOD."

When you dare to use your "no" power of mind on a loud, boisterous, unhappy situation, you then gain mental and emotional control of it, rather than letting it control you. You are then shown what outer, positive steps to take to meet it victoriously.

3. PRAYERS OF AFFIRMATION

The third type of prayer—affirmations—should be used with denials. When you use denials, you erase, dissolve, liquidate. You then wish to make firm new good, which is done through affirmative prayers.

A traveling salesman once told me how he did this. He had been heavily in debt and had attempted to get a loan from a bank to pay off his debts. Because he lacked adequate security, he had not been able to obtain a loan. In desperation, he decided to say "no" to his indebtedness and "yes" to prosperity. So he constantly affirmed: "GOD PROSPERS ME NOW." Within a few

days after he began declaring this, he made the largest
sale he had ever made, after which he was able to pay
off all his debts, with ample supply left over. Affirmative prayer is fully discussed in Chapter 6, "The Prosperity Law of Command."

4. PRAYERS OF MEDITATION AND SILENCE

*The fourth type of prayer is the prayer of meditation
and silence.* It is often in meditation and silent, con-
templative prayer that you feel the presence of God's
goodness most strongly. In this type of prayer, you take
a few meaningful words and think about them and
feed upon them silently. As you think about them and
contemplate them, they grow in your mind as expanded
ideas that move you to right action, or perhaps as
peaceful assurance that all is well and no action is
needed. If nothing seems to happen in meditation, you
have nevertheless made the mind receptive to God's
good and, at the right time, ideas and opportunities
will be revealed as a result of your spiritual exercise in
meditation.

Perhaps you are thinking, "This is all pretty good
spiritual theory, but how do I know that meditation
and silent prayer will produce tangible, satisfying
results in my work-a-day world?" Moses, Elijah and
Jesus, among others, proved the practical, result-getting power of silent meditation.

Perhaps you are thinking, "But I'm no Moses, Elijah
or Jesus, and I frankly am not sure how to practice
meditation and silent prayer." The truth is that you
meditate whether you've been aware of it or not. Everyone does. The word "meditate" means "to think about,
contemplate, to consider deeply and continuously."

HOW TO MEDITATE

Whatever you think about constantly is the subject of your meditation. In silent prayer it is good to meditate upon the divine solution of any problem. You can begin by taking the term "divine solution" and letting the thought grow in your mind. You can take some spiritual word or phrase, think about it, and let it unfold to you; or you can simply clear your mind, close your eyes, turn your attention within your own being and think of "God," "love," "God is love," "peace," or any such idea that gives you a feeling of oneness with good in a relaxed way.

I often go into silent meditation to get guidance or the feeling of renewal, uplift, encouragement and new energy. If I retire to my room for silent meditation around dinnertime, after a busy day, I find that, after about half an hour of silent meditation, I become renewed and ready for an evening of further work or other activity. Someone has said that "prayer feeds." I can attest that meditation feeds me emotionally with a sense of harmony, uplift and peace; that meditation feeds me intellectually with new ideas, or often flashes into my mind something I need to know about a current situation; and that meditation feeds me physically with a sense of body renewal, new energy, and well-being, dissolving fatigue and tension.

MEDITATION SOLVES PROBLEMS

It is through silent meditation that I often plan my days, my lectures, my writing. It is not necessary to be highly developed spiritually to use the power of silent meditation effectively. I used the power of meditation often while in the business world.

Some of the most thrilling results are realized when we take up a problem, sit alone and meditate as follows: "THE DIVINE SOLUTION IS THE SUBLIME SOLUTION. I ACCEPT AND CLAIM THE DIVINE SOLUTION IN THIS SITUATION NOW." Gently let your mind expand on that thought. The "fear energy" spent in worry and battling with the problem will then be transmuted into "faith energy," giving you the right ideas and the right answer. Always, when you have a problem, if you will go into silent meditation and contemplate the solution from a divine standpoint, you will be shown what to do.

An engineering executive once told me that he uses this method. When his men run into difficulty on an engineering project, he privately takes the problem, goes into his study, silently meditates upon it from a divine standpoint and inevitably receives the solution. One of his junior executives once asked him how he always managed to have right answers just when they were needed most. When he explained his simple method the junior executive skeptically declared, "You mean you *just meditate* upon the solution rather than focus on the problem?" The business world is full of harried, tense people who become that way through trying to solve their problems in external ways, rather than through the "inner short-cut."

Everyone should take time daily for quiet and meditation. In daily meditation lies your secret of power. You may be so busy with many activities and demands that you feel you have no time to "go apart." But the invitation is "Come ye yourselves apart and rest awhile." (Mark 6:31) It is the only way in which you will ever gain definite knowledge, newness of experience, steadiness of purpose or power to meet the unknown in daily living victoriously. As you begin to daily practice meditating, you will discover that some of your activities and demands are no longer necessary; and that it is best to let them go rather than neglect your quiet time of meditation and aloneness with yourself and your Creator.

When you withdraw from the world for meditation it is best not to think of your failures. Instead, calm yourself and center your attention on God and His Almighty Goodness. If possible, let all of the little annoying cares go for a while and turn your thoughts to some of the simple words of the Psalmist. Hold in mind some thought that helps you, be it ever so simple: "I and the Father are one," "Thy will be done in me," "I love you, God," "Thank you, Father," "I am in thy presence, Lord," "This is the day which the Lord hath made, I will rejoice and be glad in it," "Peace, be still."

Until you have practiced the presence of God in this simple way, you can have no idea how it quiets all physical nervousness, all fear, all oversensitiveness, all the little raspings of everyday life. A time of calm, quiet waiting alone with God, is one of restfulness and renewal. This is the "secret place of the Most High" of which the Psalmist speaks. (Psalms 91:1) This is going into the closet and shutting the door, which Jesus recommended. (Matthew 6:6)

THE SECRET OF PEACE, POWER AND PLENTY

Of the four types of prayer: *general, denial, affirmative*, or *meditative*, use whatever type seems appropriate to you at the moment, or perhaps blend the several types. But pray often! It can be the secret of peace, power and plenty.

YOUR GENIUS POWERS
FOR PROSPERITY

— Chapter 14 —

In addition to normal powers of observation and perception, all people possess the deeper mind qualities of intuition and creative imagination, as well as special powers to be discussed in the next chapter. All of these might be considered additional prayer powers which can be activated through our daily practice of prayer and our consistent inspirational studies.

People whom the world considers to be of genius calibre are those who have had the courage and confidence to listen to, and follow the guidance of their intuition and creative imagination. As they follow their inner leadings, the results are usually so wonderful that others believe they have unusual gifts. They do not really possess unusual powers; they are simply actively using their intuition and creative imagination rather than stifling these mind powers, as most of us are inclined to do. We, too, can stimulate our intuition and creative imagination as genius powers for prosperity, success, and more satisfying living.

As you develop your genius powers, you may seem to be listening at times to that "different drummer" of whom Henry David Thoreau wrote. I have always had a highly developed intuitive nature, and it often confused me because I did not understand it. I had been given the impression that if I obeyed it, I was being strange, eccentric, even abnormal. Often as a child I could not explain to other people what it was or why I felt compelled at time to follow its promptings. I found, on the other hand, that if I did not obey the hunch, inner prompting, or "sixth sense" idea that persisted, my world became confused and unhappy. I discovered that when I followed my hunches faithfully, I was inevitably led to the right result.

You will find, on looking over the people in your midst who have been baptized with orginality, that they have let the world's thinking alone; and so creative, new knowledge has been free to express through them. The world needs this kind of original thought in this exciting, progressive era in which we now live.

From a prosperity standpoint, people have not known what to do with their genius powers of intuition and creative imagination. Those who developed that inner feeling or knowing that flashes to all of us at times, were usually considered odd or abnormal by their business associates if they expressed rather than suppressed it. Most of us were taught not to take such people seriously.

YOU ARE EQUIPPED WITH GENIUS POWERS

However, in this enlightened age, we are beginning to realize that, while we are humanly equipped with five physical senses, as mental and spiritual beings, we are born with powers of the mind that are little recognized and little used. It is these unexplored faculties of the mind that seem to have genius power for producing prosperous, successful living.

Because our attention is regularly turned to the outer world of activities, we do not hear or heed the guidance of intuition. A businessman recently said that, if we could make a record of intuitive promptings, we would be astonished at how many times they would have revealed the right path if we had followed through on those promptings.

We have all heard the term "woman's intuition," often used somewhat humorously. The general belief is that intuition is perhaps a peculiar but trivial quirk in women, but hardly dependable enough for men. We are now learning, however, that everyone has intuition, both men and women. If women have seemed to develop their intuitive nature more noticeably than men, perhaps it is because man's attention has been turned more toward the world of business and similar external demands. Such interests can be distracting when we are developing our mental powers. Woman's place has been traditionally in the home, usually a quieter atmosphere, more conducive for responding to the inner promptings of her intuitive nature.

However, in these modern times the situation has changed. The attention of both men and women is given to business and other outside activities. In order to develop our genius powers of intuition, some definite instruction is needed.

YOU SHOULD DEVELOP YOUR INTUITION

The dictionary defines intuition as, "the immediate knowing or learning of something without the conscious use of reasoning; instantaneous apprehension." Literally, your intuition is your inner knowing. Intuition is similar to a radio receiving set through which ideas, plans or thoughts flash into the conscious mind. These flashes have been described as hunches, inspirations or promptings of the "still, small voice" within.

Elijah discovered that the "still, small voice" was the voice of God himself as supreme guidance and wisdom. (I Kings 19:12) The "still, small voice" is a genius power, for it is your God-power.

In this age of general conformity, it is time to realize that true accomplishment comes from "daring to be different," through expressing your distinct individuality. This does not mean you should strive to be a maverick! As Charles Fillmore has written, however, "If you are educated and molded after the ordinary pattern of the human family, you may live an average lifetime and never have an original thought."

The popular belief in recent years has been that, if an individual did not fit into a certain mold of thought and behavior, he was "maladjusted." The dangers of such conformity are now being realized, however pressures toward strict conformity still exist. For instance, several large corporations have recently changed their attitudes. They are finding that conformity in

their employees leads eventually to stagnation and production decline. Certain companies are now seeking
ways to stimulate new individualism. American progress in all fields is a result of ingenuity and individualism. One writer has pointed out that this New
Age demands "daring and persistent individualism,"
and that trait is usually found in a person who has
learned to listen inwardly and who follows his intuitive
leads.

Perhaps you have not followed your intuitive leads
because they have seemed fantastic, and you have
waited to reason through its promptings before you
chose to act. Intuition is not concerned with reason,
for intuition is a faculty of the mind that does not explain. It simply points the way, leaving you free to take
it or leave it, to heed or ignore its promptings. People
of genius have the self-confidence and faith in their inner promptings to follow them without reasoning them
through. That is why they are considered geniuses. Ordinary people usually wait for "proof," and conse-
quently they flounder in the conflicts of intellectual
questioning.

It is through intuition that musicians, artists, writers, and the saints have made contact with the all-
knowing mind of God, and then poured forth inspiration to the world.

There is intuition that comes to you in *inner* ways,
and there is intuition that comes to you in *outer* ways,
but come it will if you allow it to do so.

"YES" AND "NO" PHASES OF INTUITION

There are "yes" and "no" phases of intuition. Often
the "yes" phase of intuition comes in such a quiet, gen-

tle way that you are inclined to disregard its promptings, at least at first. It does not try to convince you of anything. Usually, though, if you disregard it, that same hunch will gently tap at your mind again and again, until you do become aware of it.

The "no" phase of intuition is often more pronounced. For years, it seemed that the only time my intuition ever came alive was when it would emphatically say "no" to me through an inner feeling of restlessness, discomfort, or discontent. The "no" phase of intuition often seems louder and more emphatic. It gives you an uncomfortable feeling that you cannot cast off unless you follow your "no" guidance.

You can learn to contact the "yes" and "no" phases of your intuition and seek its guidance by daily observing quiet times, when the mind is free of bustling thoughts, relaxed and receptive to intuitive leadings. Intuition usually does not force its way, but it patiently waits for a relaxed mood through which to work most effectively. A hunch can work through a busy mind, however, when there is a strong need.

FIVE SIMPLE STEPS FOR UNFOLDING YOUR INTUITION

Here is a definite formula for developing the "yes" and "no" powers of your intuition.

First: Realize that intuition is a spiritual faculty of the mind which does not explain or reason but simply points the way to your greater good. For instance, a secretary applied for three different jobs. One job would pay her very well, another would pay her moderately well, and the starting pay of the third job was rather low, but this job offered the highest potential for advancement and job satisfaction.

Human reasoning tried to tell her to take the first job, with immediate high income. Human reasoning also pointed out that the second job which paid moderately well was a "glamour job" with beautiful surroundings.

But this secretary's intuitions or inner feeling told her that she should accept the third job, which paid less and surely had no glamorous surroundings. But its potential was greater because her employer had an unlimited future in the new business he had just started.

Thus, she followed her intuition, which did not try to reason or prove itself to her, but merely pointed the way. It proved to be the best job she had ever had. Before long, new and glamorous furnishings were added to her office. Eventually her employer rose to the top in his business and her salary was then three times the amount offered at the other jobs.

It is up to you to follow the intuitive path in faith and confidence, in order to claim your good. All that you see in the world about you came forth because of someone's hunch or feeling that it could be done. You can also use your ideas and inner feelings to create a more wonderful world.

Second: As you go about your daily life, whether your work is mental or physical, act as though you were in the presence of Divine Intelligence and Divine Intuition.[1] Train yourself to realize that Divine Intuition is

---

1. See Chapter 8 on "The Wisdom Concept" in the author's book, *Open Your Mind to Prosperity* (Marina del Rey, CA: DeVorss & Co., 1983).

right with you, is interested in you, knows all about you, and delights in guiding and helping you.

As you take this attitude of mind about whatever you are doing or whatever concerns you, you will find new power at work for you and around you. You will discover a new ability to accomplish. You will attract better conditions and happier experiences. The more you think of this loving, all-knowing Divine Intelligence and its intuitive guidance working with you and for you, the less laborious will be your effort to make things right.

To help you attain this attitude of mind, affirm often: "DIVINE INTUITION IS NOW SHOWING ME THE WAY. DIVINE INTUITION IS NOW WORKING IN AND THROUGH ME, IN AND THROUGH ALL CONCERNED, PRODUCING EASILY AND QUICKLY THE PERFECT OUTCOME, THE PERFECT RESULT."

A friend said she used this method when her daughter decided to marry rather quickly. Instead of getting uptight, her mother called on Divine Intuition to arrange everything. The result was that they made all the arrangements over a long weekend: from selecting a church, minister, music and flowers to the selection of wedding attire, attendants, the guest list, invitations, even the choice of china, silver and crystal. My friend later commented, "Thanks to Divine Intuition, we were able to accomplish in three days what would have ordinarily taken at least three weeks." Both the wedding and reception were beautiful, and the bride and groom soon moved into a nice new home.

Third: As you take these steps mentally, you will find you do not have to struggle, even in your thinking, to make things right and better. Instead, you will discover that whatever you think about, give your attention to, or are interested in, begins to reveal its secrets to you. The dictionary further describes intuition as the ability to look at, regard or contemplate. More and more you will discover that the thing you look at and contemplate desires to know you.

You will stop thinking of your desired good as apart, away, or separate from you. You will stop thinking of your desired good as difficult to obtain. You will stop scheming and trying to maneuver and manipulate people or events. Instead, you will begin to realize that through the help of Divine Intuition, all things are already at hand, ready to come forth as ideas, plans and methods of procedure, and in due time, as happy results.

Fourth: After beginning to do everything as though you were in the presence of Divine Intelligence and Intuitive Wisdom, which knows your needs, is interested, is able and happy to help you, you will find not only that your abilities are increasing more and more, but also that you are being instructed from within about many things you need to know!

Suddenly you will "have a feeling" or "get a hunch" about what to do or not to do. As you follow that hunch or prompting, you will be happily amazed to find that Divine Intuition, which gave you the prompting, has already gone before you and prepared the way for its fulfillment! You will discover that as you follow that intuitive prompting in faith, without reasoning it through, your good will unfold to you almost faster than you can accept it.

Thus, a hunch or inner prompting simply indicates that the good which you desire actually desires to be yours. *Desire is God tapping at the door of your mind, trying to give you greater good.* That you deeply desire something is positive proof that it has already been prepared for you, and is only waiting for you to recognize and accept it. This does not mean that you desire or wish to accept someone else's good. You may desire the divine equivalent of someone else's good, and you should give thanks for your own God-given "divine equivalent."

If, after thinking about a hunch, you still need a little more assurance before launching forth into the unknown to attain it, realize that you can get that assurance just by asking for it. Ask for an indication or sign that you are going in the right direction. A powerful attitude of mind to establish at such times is this: "I CHOOSE THIS IF IT IS FOR MY HIGHEST GOOD. IF NOT, DIVINE INTUITION NOW SEND ME THE DIVINE EQUIVALENT." When doubts about your intuitive promptings arise, it is good to ask: "DIVINE INTUITION, JUST WHAT IS THE PERFECT TRUTH ABOUT THIS SITUATION? REVEAL IT TO ME NOW, AND MAKE IT SO PLAIN AND CLEAR THAT I CANNOT POSSIBLY MISTAKE IT."

Fifth: After having made your decrees upon Divine Intelligence in your midst, you must prepare for surprises. Your problems are not always solved in the way you had in mind, nor does your divine heritage of good always come about in the way you humanly expect. If you are not conditioned for surprises at this point, you may miss your good.

This is the point where you make the definite decision that you will choose only the good and accept only the good in the various experiences that follow. Results always follow decisions; things begin to happen that fall in line with your decisions.

In these attitudes of mind, you can develop your intuition in *inner* ways that come as hunches or promptings, or as direct knowledge from the still, small voice within you, speaking as "yes" or "no."

INTUITION ALSO REVEALS
ITSELF IN OUTER WAYS

But intuition can come in *outer* ways as well. After you have asked for guidance, your promptings may come through the words of a friend, a phrase in a book or magazine, or through a series of outer events that take place around you.

For instance, a friend asked for guidance concerning whether she should take a vacation. A few days after asking, she had had no inner leading or hunch about it. But as she leafed through a magazine, these words in bold type caught her attention: "Why don't you go?" That settled it! She accepted the idea that a vacation was possible and thereafter the way was opened quickly for it to be accomplished.

The outer ways in which intuition can prompt you are as varied as they are interesting. A mother was concerned about her son whose behavior was proving quite a challenge. She considered the possibility of sending him to a private school, though he seemed rather young to be away from home. As she pondered what she should do, she remembered to ask for specific intuitive guidance. Shortly thereafter she opened the evening paper to these words which emphatically caught her eye: "Home is the place for troubled children." She took that as her guidance, and dismissed the idea of sending her child elsewhere. She was then

led to give her son more loving attention, to which he
soon responded with improved behavior.

A BUSINESSMAN'S INTUITION SAID "NO"

A businessman recently told me how his intuition
said "no" to him in external ways when he had not
been able to get inner guidance. He wanted to take a
rather expensive vacation trip and did not have the
money, though he could arrange to borrow it. The
urge to take this trip was so strong, even though his
better judgment cautioned against it, that he felt the
need for definite outer indications. One morning when
the urge to take this trip was very great, in spite of the
indebtedness involved, he decided to settle the matter
one way or another. He made the decree that he
wanted to know that very day what he should do. He
then tried several times to telephone me to ask for
prayers for guidance, but he could not reach me.

In mid-afternoon he decreed that if he did not contact me by five o'clock, he would consider that fact as a
definite indication that his answer was "no." I finally
was free at 5:15 and immediately telephoned him.
However, his deadline had been set at 5 o'clock. Thus,
he took that as his intuitive leading that he definitely
should not borrow the money for an expensive vacation. Instead, he remained quietly at home, rested,
and did many things for recreation that his swing-shift
schedule of work did not ordinarily permit. He had
received his answer of "no," and he soon realized that
it was for his highest good. He further realized that the
previous strong desire to take this trip had not been a

deep intuitive leading, but a more superficial quality of human will simply trying to have its human way.

ASK FOR DIRECT KNOWLEDGE
ABOUT EVERYTHING

A doctor has stated that he never treats a patient until he gets an intuitive leading about just what to do. As long as he is undecided about a patient's problem or unsure of the diagnosis, he does nothing more than talk with him and examine him. He has found that it is sometimes necessary for a patient to come for several consultations before he intuitively feels that he is sure of the proper treatment. Since he has a large and very successful practice, he has obviously proved the success power of intuition.

Often I have found that when I ask for direct knowledge or guidance, someone who had no conscious way of knowing I have a need along that line will often telephone, write or make an appointment to tell me just what I need to know.

SOLVE YOUR PROBLEMS INTUITIVELY

When a personal or business problem appears, do not carry it around, nursing it and thinking that you have to wait until a later time to get relief from it. Instead, ask for direct guidance and knowledge and then watch for inner or outer intuition to speak to you.

Begin now to develop your intuition. If you act with perfect faith on the inner and outer intuitive leadings that come, you will never be too late or too early, and nothing will go wrong. Do not get disturbed if things appear to be going wrong after you begin following your strong leadings. Affirm that Divine Intuition is producing the perfect result, and good *will* appear. Sometimes things appear to be going wrong when in reality they are being arranged for the right outcome.

Emerson realized the genius power of intuition when, in his essays, he predicted, "We are passing into a New World. The Spirit will be enthroned in the heart of man. Then will come a philosophy of insight, and out of that the transformation of genius into practical power." Insight is another name for inner knowing or intuition out of which genius power can be transformed into practical power and practical results.

YOUR SECOND GENIUS POWER
IS CREATIVE IMAGINATION

Solomon was surely describing your genius power of creative imagination when he declared, "Where there is no vision the people perish, but he that keepeth the law, happy is he." (Proverbs 29:18)

You can use your genius powers of creative imagination in interesting ways. From an individual standpoint you can develop your creative imagination as a prosperity power in a very simple but pleasant way. We all wish to gain spiritual control of future events and plans for prosperity. Every night before retiring it is good to think of the next day's plans. To release your genius power of creative imagination, I suggest that you then use this technique:

Instead of worrying about how the next day's events will come out or instead of brooding over some troublesome phase of it, simply bring into your conscious thoughts all that you know about the next day's events. Begin with your early morning activities and mentally arrange the events of your whole day as you would like to see them. Every time some distressing possibility wells up in your feelings, take control of it by affirming: "I BLESS YOU WITH GOD'S ALMIGHTY GOOD. GOD'S GOOD IS NOW GAINING CONTROL, AND ALL IS WELL." Pleasantly accentuate the positive developments that you would like to experience the next day and take control of all else by affirming God's good control for it. For the entire day's activities, affirm: "I GIVE THANKS FOR THE DIVINELY SATISFYING FULFILLMENT AND FOR THE DIVINELY SATISFYING RESULTS." Thereafter, dismiss the matter from your mind.

You have used your creative imagination to effect the right outworking of each situation. Circumstances, situations, personalities — all involved — will then gravitate toward the perfect outworking, the perfect prosperous fulfillment. This is a powerful method for using the mind to bring about expanded good in family, business, social or spiritual matters.

CREATIVE IMAGINATION CAN DISSOLVE UNHAPPY MEMORIES

You can also use your creative imagination to dissolve unhappy memories, failures in business, inharmony in relationships, and other negative experiences from the past. In the realm of Divine Intelligence there is no past, present or future. There is no time element at all. Since you live, move and have your being in the midst of this immense intelligence, you can gain dominion over your past, present and future. Thus, you can bring to mind the elements of any situation from the past that you would like dissolved and cleared up forever.

You should bring to mind the time, place and persons involved. You should then mentally go over the elements of the situation, and again affirm: "I BLESS YOU WITH GOD'S ALMIGHTY GOOD." Then mentally rework that experience, seeing it the way you would like it to be. As you do something constructive about a negative memory, the negative thought pattern is dissolved by the loving, positive thought pattern you are putting in its place. Declare to that re-worked memory and all concerned in it, whether or not those involved are still on this earth plane: "I BLESS YOU AND BLESS YOU FOR THE GOODNESS OF GOD THAT IS AT WORK IN AND THROUGH YOU. I CLAIM FOR MYSELF AND FOR YOU THAT GOD'S ALMIGHTY GOOD IS ALL THERE IS IN THIS EXPERIENCE. ALL ELSE IS NOW PERMANENTLY DISSOLVED." If apparent negative emotions and deep-seated feelings try to flare up, affirm to them: "BE THOU DISSOLVED, NOW AND FOREVER."

Through this method you can free your mind from negative memories that have clogged and crowded your mind, perhaps for years. You will thereafter find that you will feel freer, more unburdened than ever before. Soon rich new prosperous ideas will begin filling the space formerly occupied by negative memories. Your creative imagination can in this way uncover new good for you.

ANOTHER CAN JOIN WITH YOU

Through group co-ordination and interchange of ideas, many a person has been greatly prospered.

When even two people begin thinking about an objective in a harmonious way, there is double mindpower at work, so that increased energy and ideas are released upon the objective. Jesus was speaking of this power when He said: "If two of you shall agree on earth as touching anything that they shall ask, it shall be done for them of my Father which is in heaven." (Matthew 18:19)

Any trusted member of your family or a trusted friend is sufficient. The only stipulation for releasing the genius power of good is that the trusted one be in complete harmony with you, and that he or she does not discuss with others your problem or idea. "In quietness and confidence" truly is your strength at such times.

It is good to say to that trusted one whatever is on your mind; to completely unburden yourself to them, and to ask their ideas and their prayer help. Often just by discussing a situation with such a trusted soul, fresh new ideas, a fresh new viewpoint and right results can quickly appear. When two minds are blended toward a single purpose they seem to tune in on a Higher Power that is filled with higher ideas and omnipresent intelligence, which then reveals to them the right way to proceed.

As mentioned in my book *The Dynamic Laws of Prayer* (formerly *Pray and Grow Rich*), I have used this method very successfully for several decades with "prayer partners." Among those who have assisted me over the years are a maid, a business tycoon, and several housewives. What a difference their help has made in my life, both personally and professionally.[2]

---

2. Also see Chapter 5, "Your Secret Weapon for Prosperity," in the author's book, *The Millionare Moses.*

OVERCOME DEPRESSION THROUGH
CREATIVE IMAGINATION

When you are feeling low, depressed, discouraged, and feel that you cannot go on, that is the time to use the creative imagination approach. Talk with some one person with whom you can unburden yourself and let them help you get a fresh, new, uplifted viewpoint. It is at such times that others can rebuild your self-confidence, when you seem unable to do so for yourself.

I recall one instance a number of years ago when a fellow worker had "told me off." She declared that I was a complete failure, could not last, did not have what it takes to succeed and was on my way out. These words came as a great shock to me, since she had previously encouraged me in all my endeavors. Had I not known about the creative imagination method, I might have just given up entirely.

But I remembered that with just one person helping me I could turn the tide and counteract all the negative thoughts that had been directed toward me. In distress I poured out the details of what had happened to a trusted friend who then reversed every negative thing that had been said about me. The friend declared, "Now you know you are not a failure. You have succeeded many times and you will continue to succeed. You know that you have what it takes, and above all, you know that you are not 'on the way out.' Instead, you are 'on the way up!'" The friend then explained that the negative statements about me were quite unimportant. My reaction to them was all that mattered. With my friend's understanding help, I was able to regain confidence in myself. Actually, the only thing that stuck in my memory from it all was the happy, positive statement, "You are on the way up!" Often I have happily affirmed it.

USE CREATIVE IMAGINATION ON FAMILY LEVEL

In recent times you have heard of the "brain-storming" technique, which is a more expanded method for using creative imagination as a genius power for good. Business people sit down, discuss an objective, blend their ideas on how to achieve it, and find that it is accomplished, often with amazing results. Recently a woman reported that her husband's company makes excellent use of this practice. They present a goal, purpose or plan; they then let all the "doubting Thomases" in the group state why it cannot be achieved. After everyone has cleared his or her mind of negative thoughts about the objective, the group leader then declares, "Now we know how and why we cannot achieve this goal. But that is not our purpose. Our purpose is *to achieve* this goal." He then asks for suggestions for doing it and builds a plan of accomplishment from the ideas offered.

A marvelous way to release the genius power of creative imagination in your family group is by having the entire family sit down and agree on group objectives. Often parents struggle hard to provide luxuries for their children; whereas, if they would have the children join them in attaining those desires, the results would come easily rather than through wearisome struggle.

A family that I know does this. They ask each child to write out a list of his desires. They also ask each child to list several desires that the entire family wishes to see come forth. Interestingly, the joint power of agreement on objectives and the joint mind power have produced some satisfying results for that family.

YOUR GENIUS POWERS RESPOND TO HARMONY

Where there is a common purpose you have great power to achieve, as long as you are attuned to others who agree with your purpose. Through this process, you tune in on higher powers and ideas for making your goal a result. Just by thinking about an objective in this way will cause the objective to reveal its own method of attainment, but you must persevere in giving it your attention.

However, harmony, agreement, mutual consent and common purpose are of utmost importance in releasing creative imagination as genius power in a corporate or group situation. If even one of the persons working with you does not harmonize with your objective, that one can so fill the air with thoughts of doubt, fear and antagonism that the negative atmosphere will halt the flow of creative ideas. From a corporate standpoint, you must carefully choose your associates in order to release your genius power of creative imagination.

Both of your genius powers—intuition and creative imagination—respond best to harmonious minds. Your genius powers are delicate powers that come forth forcefully only under receptive conditions of mind and atmosphere.

SILENCE IS NECESSARY

Both your intuititon and creative imagination function well in times of silence and isolation, especially during periods of relaxation and rest. I find that my intuition and creative imagination often supply me with my best ideas and guidance just prior to retiring at night.

Once I was sitting quietly in a relaxed mood at home after a busy day. My son had retired and it was a peaceful time. Suddenly I realized that there was a financial matter that needed my attention, but I had not been sure how to handle it, and so had kept pushing it into the back of my mind. Now it arose in my thinking, and I realized that I had to determine within the next few days just what to do about it.

So I asked: "DIVINE INTUITION, JUST WHAT IS THE TRUTH ABOUT THIS FINANCIAL MATTER? HOW SHALL I HANDLE IT?" Within a flash, a whole series of definite ideas rushed into my mind, giving me detailed instruction of just how to proceed. They did not seem like the logical reasonable ways to handle the matter, but nevertheless, the next day I followed through on the ideas. As I followed my inner leadings, the steps unfolded quite logically and eventually produced the perfect result.

NEVER UNDERESTIMATE THE POWER OF QUIETNESS

Quiet times, reflective times, peaceful times, when your mind is relaxed and somewhat idle, are the times when inner powers are best able to gain your attention and release true genius through you. People who constantly rush about and who never have quiet, peaceful periods of reflection often have to work very hard. If they listened more to their inner promptings, they would receive rich ideas, fresh ideas, intelligent ideas that would make their lives easier and richer.

A business executive recently related to me the wonderful results he once obtained through doing this. He was scheduled for retirement from his company, yet he did not feel ready for the rocking chair. He began affirming that divinely satisfying work would open to him. Since he did not know what contacts to make to produce such work, he made none. Instead, he began spending a lot of time sitting quietly in his office thinking, "Divine Intelligence, just what is the truth about my right place of service?" One day, after returning from his Rotary Club luncheon, he sat down quietly and again began knowing there was a divine solution to this situation; that there was perfect new work for him to do, and that the truth about it was being revealed to him.

His assistant came in to report that someone had telephoned during lunch, and that he should return the call. That call proved to be an offer for similar work in another state. Within a week another offer from still another company came to him by letter. How these two firms obtained his name, he still does not know. He had not mentioned his desire for further work to anyone. Within a short time he resigned from his job, sold his home and made the change to new work in another state which held limitless prosperity for him.

THESE GENIUS POWERS DEVELOP YOUR SELF-CONFIDENCE

You will feel and radiate greater self-confidence about your past, present and future as you develop your intuition and creative imagination.[3] In recapitulation: develop your *inner* intuition as your "yes" and "no" guides through watching your inner feelings, hunches, and ideas that come. Develop your *outer* intuition by watching events, situations and emphatic statements that attract your attention after you have asked Divine Intuition to point the way.

Develop your creative imagination by imaging your good, by mentally seeing the perfect past, present and future; by talking with one trusted person and getting him or her to agree with you on desired results; by forming a creative imagination group, and having them harmoniously agree with you on desired results. This group either can be a business group, family members, or trusted friends. In these simple ways you develop, contact and release your genius powers for prosperity.

Never underestimate your genius powers! They want to work for you to bring you greater happiness, success, and confidence in your ability to receive guidance every step along life's pathway. Why not let them? Declare often for this purpose: "I GIVE THANKS THAT MY GENIUS POWERS OF INTUITION AND CREATIVE IMAGINATION ARE NOW RELEASED, AND THAT I HAPPILY FULFILL MY DIVINE DESTINY."

---

3. See Chapter 16, "The Prosperity Law of Self-Confidence."

YOUR SPECIAL POWERS
FOR PROSPERITY

— Chapter 15 —

In this New Age, the deeper powers of mind, which have remained virtually dormant in earlier eras, are now coming alive more generally in mankind. The scientific world describes these deeper powers of the mind as *telepathy, clairvoyance, general extrasensory perception, precognition* and *psychokinesis*. Let us consider these special powers of the mind not only from a scientific standpoint, but also for prosperity's sake.

TELEPATHY IS AN ANCIENT ART

Telepathy is awareness of the mental activities of other persons, without that awareness being transmitted by sight, hearing, touch or any of the other known senses. In other words, when the mind communicates with other minds without the use of the physical senses or mechanical devices, such transfer of thought between minds is described as telepathy.

There is nothing unusual about telepathy. It was practiced by the native Hawaiians for centuries before the white man appeared on the scene to "civilize" the natives there. In Tahiti there has been widespread use of telepathy for some years. In Africa, news of political decisions has been known to have been received telepathically hours and sometimes days before it was officially announced. The holy men and masters of the Far East also practiced telepathy as a common mental exercise for centuries. In more recent times, Dr. J. B. Rhine of Duke University did much to make telepathy scientifically plausible.

The Bible gives many instances of its use. Surely Jesus did not hesitate to use his telepathic powers for good. When the Samaritan woman said to him, "I have no husband," Jesus replied, "Thou sayest well, 'I have no husband,' for thou hast had five husbands and he whom thou now hast is not thy husband. This hast thou said truly." (John 4:17, 18)

With additional attention to the subject and practice thereof, you can develop more than haphazard telepathic abilities.

If rightly developed, telepathy can help you to experience prosperous, successful living much faster. However, this special power is only one phase of your prosperity powers. Don't become so fascinated with telepathy that you "go off the deep end," by concentrating on it to the exclusion of your other special prosperity powers.

HOW TO DEVELOP TELEPATHY

Perhaps one reason the general public has not taken these special powers too seriously in the past is that they have observed what I have often observed: People who have telepathic or clairvoyant abilities often seem unbalanced and impractical. But your special powers of the mind can and should be developed for quite the opposite reasons: to make your life more balanced, prosperous and successful. You can benefit by using your special powers if you follow closely the suggestions contained in this chapter. For this purpose affirm: "DIVINE TELEPATHY IS NOW REVEALING TO ME ALL TRUTH ABOUT MY SPECIAL POWERS FOR PROSPERITY."

When you wish to make contact with others for your mutual good, and perhaps direct outer contact is not convenient, you can reach them telepathically by affirming: "DIVINE TELEPATHY IS NOW REVEALING TO YOU, TO ME, TO US, ALL TRUTH ABOUT THIS SITUATION."

Recently I wished to make contact with a childhood friend whom I had not heard from for several years. I heard that she had married and had made a number of changes since our last meeting, and I had no idea where she was. Perhaps with some time and effort I could have traced her, but my need was not that great. Nevertheless, I did wish to hear from her again. Several times when the thought of her came into my thinking, I mused: "DIVINE TELEPATHY WILL HAVE TO MAKE THIS CONTACT FOR ME, SINCE I DO NOT KNOW WHERE SHE IS." About ten days later, I was startled to find a letter in the mail from her, answering all the questions about her life that were in my mind, and also giving me her new address.

Often in the midst of a busy day, needs arise that you do not have time to handle immediately. If you think of others involved and bless them with the thought that Divine telepathy is revealing to them whatever they need to know, then they will begin to telepathically receive your thoughts and respond with appropriate actions.

TELEPATHY IS A HARMONIZING POWER

Development of your telepathic power keeps down needless conversations, telephone calls, letters, or fatiguing activity that can be so time consuming. Development of your telepathic ability helps you to maintain poise and to accomplish essential tasks more easily.

A businesswoman had a deadline to meet in completion of a piece of work. The evening before the work was due, she found herself in dire need of some technical help in the matter. The name of a friend who could give that help kept popping into her mind; however, she did not know where to locate that person during the evening, and her residence telephone did not answer. This businesswoman hesitated to trace the friend since she felt it might seem an imposition to ask the friend to spend extra time working so late in the day. Finally, the businesswoman dismissed the idea of trying to reach her friend, casually thinking, "If she is supposed to help me, Divine telepathy will reveal it to her. Otherwise, I give thanks for the divine solution to this situation now."

Within fifteen minutes the telephone rang, and her friend said to her, "I am having dinner in a downtown restaurant. I have a feeling that you need my help tonight. If so, I am available and will be happy to work with you." In half an hour they were busily working together to complete the project.

A minister was in great need, and he wished to talk with a trusted friend who had moved to a distant state. The minister kept thinking, "If only I could talk with my friend about this situation I'd feel so much better. He could help me to get my perspective about it."

Early the next morning his faraway friend awakened with his minister friend on his mind. After a while he thought, "I'd like to have a chat with him," and so he telephoned his friend, who explained to him, "This is uncanny. I must make a decision today, and I kept thinking that a talk with you would help me to resolve everything. I hesitated to call or write because I've called on you so often in the past." They then discussed the problem and arrived at a happy solution.

EVERYONE HAS TELEPATHIC POWERS

We all have telepathic abilities. It is a matter of realizing this fact and then developing our abilities along constructive lines. Of course, as with any power, you must never use your telepathic abilities to coerce or induce others into your way of thought and action. To do so is destructive and will bring destructive experiences to you.

I recently learned of a person who had become so fascinated with these deeper powers of the mind that he made concentrated efforts to develop them. He then began selfishly using them to compel people to do that which pleased him. In several instances he caused others to become emotionally upset and mentally disturbed before he was exposed.

When you use your mental powers selfishly and destructively they will diminish. Not only will you lose them, but you will also personally get a negative reaction from trying to abuse or misuse them on others. In this man's case, his own personal affairs became quite confused and his health was affected. In another instance where mind power was misused on others the person doing so underwent a nervous breakdown, became an alcoholic, and was eventually committed to an institution. By affirming that Divine Telepathy is revealing what is needed for the highest good of all concerned, mental destructiveness is avoided.

Along with affirmation, a practical way to develop your telepathic abilities is by thinking of any situation, person, or condition about which you have some question. Then write down that person's name, along with your question concerning him. Thereafter, sit quietly every day for a while and look at the person's name, think about him, asking your question mentally; get still and listen for ideas to come into your mind, which will reveal the answer. If the answer does not come just then, it may flash into your thinking at an idle moment later. If not, keep up the practice every day and you will be telepathically shown what you need to know. It simply takes practice, and it is a much simpler, less strenuous, and faster method for gaining true information than that obtained through ordinary channels. You can discover a person's real attitudes and motives through this method, even if they may previously have hidden them from you.

YOUR SECOND SPECIAL POWER

Clairvoyance is your *second* special power for prosperity. It literally means "clear-seeing," and it is an awareness of external facts or events without having such knowledge transmitted to you by the five senses. It can include awareness of past, present, or future events. However, scientists have described one phase of clairvoyance as "precognition," or foreknowledge of future events.

Members of the clergy in all ages have been trained to develop their clairvoyant abilities. People in ancient civilizations in China, Egypt, Mexico, even the early American Indians, sought to develop their awareness of events which were happening at a distance.

The Bible testifies to the clairvoyant powers of man. Jesus saw Nathaniel before he came into the Master's presence, as Jesus meditated under a fig tree. (John 1:47) This is but proof that the open, receptive, believing mind is capable of seeing things come forth from the invisible into the visible realm, when it is for a good purpose.

The key to the development of clairvoyance is in knowing that you want to heighten your awareness of external facts and events only through the help of your divine nature. You do not want to become sensitive to the human mental strata of thought, in which float negative ideas about war, crime, disease, and other destructive beliefs.

I once knew a woman who developed her clairvoyant abilities along such negative lines. Tuning in on such negative ideas and conditions was destructive and unbalancing to her. Finally, her husband left her, her children were taken from her, her health failed and her emotions were utterly shattered.

You want to develop your clairvoyant awareness for good only. By affirming the development of your divinely clairvoyant powers, you will grow spiritually, and be led to contribute to the well-being of others.

A number of reports have recently described clairvoyant people who became aware of negative events. No wonder the general public has shunned the idea of clairvoyance, because they do not care to become involved in the world's troubles, having enough of their own!

Becoming clairvoyantly aware of negative events only clutters the mind and prevents your being mentally receptive to the positive, progressive and prosperous things of life. Furthermore, it is not necessary to "pick up" negative thought currents. If you become clairvoyantly aware of their possibility, you can use your "no" power of the mind to dissolve them, rather than accept them as inevitable.

LET CLAIRVOYANCE GUIDE YOU

If you are seeking guidance about some business problem and wish to attain an awareness of external facts or events concerning it, do so in this way: Just as Jesus did under the fig tree, become still and meditate in a listening state of mind. Then let this thought go slowly through your mind: "DIVINE CLAIRVOYANCE IS NOW REVEALING TO ME ALL TRUTH ABOUT THIS SITUA-

TION, CONDITION, OR EVENT, BOTH PAST AND PRESENT."
If there are certain facts or events you should know
about, in your meditation declare: "DIVINE CLAIRVOY-
ANCE IS NOW REVEALING TO ME ALL TRUTH ABOUT THESE
SPECIFIC FACTS OR EVENTS." Then go over the specific
items gently, as best you now understand them. As
your mind absorbs the thought of the item, and also
absorbs the idea that divine clairvoyance is revealing
further truth about it, suddenly the illumining truth
will begin to come. Outer events will probably happen
to substantiate your mental impressions about it.

A medical technician realized that she could develop
her clairvoyant abilities, and she had been declaring
that divine clairvoyance was revealing to her all that
she needed to know. She was planning a trip, and considering new clothes for it. One night in meditation, as
she was thinking of a lovely linen dress she would like
for the trip, she affirmed: "Divine clairvoyance knows
where such a dress is and is leading me to it, if it is for
my highest good to have it."

The next day a friend telephoned from a downtown
department store and said, "There is a lovely linen
dress here on the rack. When I saw it, I thought of
you." Two hours later the technician finished her work
and stopped by that store. Upon arrival, she learned
that someone had already purchased the dress. She
realized that she had clairvoyantly seen the dress, so
she was not disturbed. She nonchalantly said, "If that
dress is rightly mine, I will still have it. If not, the
equivalent will appear."

The next day her store clerk friend telephoned to
say, "The customer has returned that linen dress. It is
here on the rack, and I will put it up for you if you
wish to come and see it." She later happily purchased
the dress, which proved to be identical to the one

which had come to her in meditation previously.

As you develop these deeper powers of your mind, which are your obedient servants and love to work for you, you will find that you do not have to work so hard in the physical world to accomplish right results. The truth of this was revealed to me recently when I had an early morning long-distance call telling me that plans had been changed for that day. It would be necessary for me to make a trip several hundred miles, which I had not planned to make. My first reaction was that I did not wish to make the trip, that it was not convenient in my schedule for that day, and also, I did not desire to drive alone. Then I remembered to meditate and to affirm: "DIVINE CLAIRVOYANCE IS NOW REVEALING THE TRUTH ABOUT THIS EXPERIENCE." A peaceful, harmonious feeling then came to me concerning this unexpected change in plans.

Later that morning, a friend came into my study and said, "I am here to take that trip with you." Surprised, I asked, "How did you know that I might take a trip today? I only learned about it a few minutes ago." This friend replied that, in her early morning meditation, the thought kept coming to her that she would take a trip that day. Knowing the power of ideas, she had made plans accordingly. When she later spoke to my secretary, she heard about my unexpected trip. Not only did she accompany me, but she drove her car, which made the experience an enjoyable one.

CLAIRVOYANCE PROVIDES A SOLUTION

A businessman had been involved in a dispute with two other businessmen. He had tried everything he knew to settle the dispute, but to no avail. One night, while talking with a friend by telephone about the confused situation, he stated that he had done all that he could do, and was going to release the situation to work out as it wished. As he ended the conversation, the face of one of the men involved in the dispute flashed into his mind. The thought came to him that this man would visit him in a day or so to resolve the dispute. He did not tell anyone about this flash of clairvoyance, but he affirmed: "DIVINE CLAIRVOYANCE IS REVEALING ITSELF TO ALL CONCERNED AND PRODUCING THE PERFECT, HARMONIOUS SOLUTION."

Two days later in the late afternoon, as he was finishing a business conference, he walked into his outer office to find that man waiting to see him! The man greeted him cordially, and said, "I got the feeling that if we could just get together and talk, we could resolve our differences." And they did, then and there.

A friend of mine has often spoken of his son-in-law's clairvoyant abilities. This son-in-law always knows if anything seems wrong at home. He often stops everything in the midst of his business day and telephones his wife. At other times, he has remarked to his secretary, "Do not disturb me because my wife is going to telephone me about something important." Always it has proved true.

CLAIRVOYANCE DISSOLVES THE PAST

As previously stated, clairvoyance reveals not only awareness of present events which are happening at a distance, but it can also reveal past events, if they are important to the present. I know of two people, a man and a woman, who have clairvoyant power to "see" into

the past. In each instance, they assure people who go
to them for help that they are never shown anything
about a person's past unless it can aid that person to be
free from the past. The man has often described in detail a person's past actions which are linked to some
present problem.

You can develop this phase of clairvoyance for your
own good if you will declare concerning any situation
which seems shrouded with mystery or uncertainty
from the past: "DIVINE CLAIRVOYANCE, REVEAL PAST AND
PRESENT TRUTH TO ME CONCERNING THIS SITUATION."
You will be surprised how anything from the past
which you need to know will be shown to you.

A man who had had an unhappy past began to realize that certain future events would require that he
return to his hometown, which he had not visited in
years. He wondered how he would be received there.
He decided that clairvoyance could prepare him ahead
of time for the reaction, if he would ask to be shown
what it would be. He affirmed for past and present
events: "DIVINE CLAIRVOYANCE, REVEAL PAST AND PRES-
ENT TRUTH TO ME CONCERNING THIS VISIT. HOW DO PEO-
PLE FEEL ABOUT MY PAST?"

He then got a feeling of peace about the situation,
and dismissed the matter from his mind. A few days
later, he received a letter from a hometown friend
whom he had not heard from in several years. The
friend joyously wrote, "I recently met a relative of
yours on the street. I asked about you, since I had
heard nothing from you in years. He told me of your
accomplishments, and of your plans to come home for
a visit soon. When I heard of all that you are doing,
I was so thrilled that I could not help telling all your
old friends. My friend, they want you to know how

happy they are for you, and they all await your visit with anticipation!"

Perhaps you have unknowingly used clairvoyance when you needed to find a misplaced article. As you would get quiet and think about the misplaced article, often the thought would flash into your mind just where it was located.

YOUR THIRD SPECIAL POWER

General extrasensory perception is your *third* special power for prosperity and success. It is a blending of telepathy, in which you become aware of the thoughts of other people; and clairvoyance, in which you become aware of facts or events that are taking place. Most of us have experienced degrees of this special mind power at times.

For instance, a lecturer was planning a trip to a distant state where a friend had invited him to speak publicly. The date was set and tentative plans were made. A few weeks prior to his departure, the lecturer began to feel uncomfortable about this trip, and wondered if it was wise for him to make it. In meditation he affirmed: "DIVINE PERCEPTION, REVEAL TO ME THE TRUTH ABOUT THIS TRIP. SHOULD I TAKE THIS TRIP OR NOT?"

As he continued to meditate about the situation, he got the impression that great hostility was coming to him from that area. He sensed that someone in the town where he was scheduled to lecture had personal antagonism toward him, and resented his coming. It all seemed preposterous, but he finally wrote his friend about his unusual impressions. Quite naturally, his friend quickly replied that he must be mistaken, that no hostility existed, and that everyone there was happily expecting the proposed lecture. However, the lecturer remained adamant, and he cancelled the trip. While it caused some conflict between him and his friend for a while, the lecturer was relieved.

Every time he thought of the situation thereafter, the lecturer would affirm: "DIVINE PERCEPTION, REVEAL TO ALL CONCERNED THE TRUTH ABOUT THIS SITUATION. LET IT BE KNOWN IF THERE IS ANY HOSTILITY." About six months later he received a letter postmarked in the town where he had planned to lecture. It was an anonymous note, in unfamiliar handwriting, stating certain hostile things about his friend in that town. He mailed the unsigned note to his friend, who recognized the handwriting as that of a friend. The author of the note apparently was jealous of the close friendship between these two men. It was later learned that, shortly after mailing the hostile note, the third party moved away. The lecturer then gave his lecture as originally planned.

HOW TO DEVELOP
EXTRASENSORY PERCEPTION

Most of us have experienced degrees of extrasensory perception (ESP) at times. Have you not sensed that something wonderful was going to happen, and perhaps you were even aware of what it would be? Have you not at other times had a foreboding that something unpleasant was near, which caused you to become restless or unsure?

When you begin to sense that some good is on the way, you have the power and authority to help it to manifest in a perfect way by thinking: "I BLESS YOU WITH THE PERFECT RESULT, THROUGH THE HELP OF DIVINE PERCEPTION." On the other hand, when you feel that something negative is about to happen, always take time to sit down and quietly dissolve that feeling by declaring: "BE THOU DISSOLVED, WITH THE HELP OF DIVINE PERCEPTION." Continue thinking of it as being dissolved, until you feel the burden or unrest subside.

You may not know what it is that you are dissolving, but if it gives you an uneasy, restless, negative feeling, you can be assured that it is not an experience for your highest good. You have the power to mentally dissolve it, for it is in the mental realm that all troubles are first formed. Use of this special power can keep many unhappy experiences from ever occurring, if you dare to take the time to say "no" to them and neutralize them.

A businessman was on a vacation trip. One morning, as he and his wife arose early to drive some 500 miles that day, he had an uneasy, apprehensive feeling. Not realizing that this was his extrasensory perception trying to warn him not to proceed on his journey just then, he drove on anyway. A few miles down the road there was an accident in which he, his wife, and one other person were severely injured. This businessman later confided to me that, if he had understood the meaning of his uneasy feelings, he could have avoided the accident.

YOUR FOURTH SPECIAL POWER

Precognition is another of your special powers for success. While clairvoyance is an awareness of past or present events that happen at a distance, precognition is a phase of clairvoyance which brings knowledge of future events without the use of any physical agent for such knowledge. Sometimes through dreams, inspirational flashes, or in meditation periods, you are shown the action of future events.

I know a child who has often foreseen the events of his life for the coming week. In one instance, this child came to see me and asked, "How is it that I know everything that is going to happen for the coming week?" I suggested that he write down everything he foresaw, and then come back a week later and discuss it.

When he returned with his notes, it was clear that nothing big had happened. He had known how much money his parents would give him. He had been aware of some events that would happen at Sunday School, and the outcome of some sports events at school. He even was aware of how many ice cream cones he would buy at the drug store that week! One night he had not bothered to study for a test because he said that he already knew that he would make 94 on it, which he did.

On his second visit he stated that he could not always see a week ahead, though often he knew what the next day would bring. I suggested that he not discuss his clairvoyant power of precognition with anyone, but that he affirm often: "DIVINE PRECOGNITION IS MAKING EASY AND SUCCESSFUL MY WAY. I KNOW ALL THAT I NEED TO KNOW WHEN I AM SUPPOSED TO KNOW IT, FOR MY HIGHEST GOOD." I assured him that there was nothing different or wrong with him, and that his ability to foresee events in his life was a very special power that everyone has, but that few people have developed.

He was overjoyed when he realized that, if he became aware of some future event that seemed negative, he could mentally dissolve it by saying "no" to it. On several occasions, he did mentally reverse what might have been an unhappy experience by thinking, "No, I will not accept this as coming forth. I accept only that which is for my highest good." He would then think of the results which he truly desired.

A housewife I know says that she has to be careful not to win every bridge game when playing with friends. Because of her ability to foresee results, she has often known what cards were being held, and what the ultimate results would be!

QUIETLY DEVELOP THIS POWER

When you receive impressions or flashes concerning future events and results, instead of running to others and discussing what you have foreseen, it is best to quietly ask for guidance about it. A housewife became aware that her neighbor's husband would pass on within a few months. After praying for guidance as to whether she should tell her neighbor, she felt led to do so, thinking it might explain his recently changed behavior; the neighbor was grateful for her warning, since she also had felt that her husband's life was about over, and that he perhaps knew it, too. She was then able to make his last months on earth much happier, and the shock of his passing did not overwhelm her.

Awareness of future events often comes in dreams. Instead of becoming too involved in dream analysis, however, you can get the true meaning of your dreams by asking: "DIVINE INTELLIGENCE, WHAT IS THE TRUTH ABOUT THIS DREAM? WHAT DOES IT MEAN?"

It has been written of Charles Fillmore, a realtor who became the co-founder of Unity:

> Like Joseph and Daniel, Charles Fillmore felt that God came to him in dreams and visions of the night, and revealed to him much of the truth about which he wrote and spoke. He was always looking forward. He foresaw radio, and talked about it in sermons and articles. He foresaw that the atom would be split and become a source of power.[1]

The Bible is filled with examples of precognition. For instance, the Wise Men were warned in a dream not to return to Herod after they had found the Christ child, but they were told to return home by another route. (Matthew 2:12) The early Christians were regularly instructed through dreams, and they were thus successful in spreading the Christian message abroad.

YOUR FIFTH SPECIAL POWER

Your *fifth* special power for prosperity is *psychokinesis*, which is direct influence exerted upon a physical

---

1. James Dillet Freeman, *The Story of Unity* (Unity Books, Unity Village, MO, revised ed. 1978), p. 18.

object by a person who does not use any intermediate physical energy or instrument. For scientific purposes, this power has been used to mentally influence the fall of dice. You can think of physical objects and influence them for good. From a prosperity standpoint, you can mentally affect your purse, bank account, investments, clothes, automobiles, the buildings and area in which you work and live. In fact, you are constantly molding your outer world thought-by-thought.

YOUR THOUGHTS AFFECT
INANIMATE OBJECTS

"Inanimate" objects have the power to respond to your good thoughts, especially your rich thoughts about them, for they are filled with divine intelligence and seem to "know" what you are thinking about them. When an object near you "acts up," give it the benefit of your blessing with good thoughts, rather than criticizing it.

I know of a new electric typewriter that never worked properly because the employer who purchased it had not truly wanted his employee to have that typewriter; he always found fault with it, after resisting its original purchase.

Everything in your world is filled with intelligence, even the so-called inanimate objects. Treat them intelligently if you wish to obtain intelligent, harmonious results. One housewife has often stated how much more her money seems to buy at the grocery store if she "dresses up" before going shopping. It is as though the substance and intelligence contained in the groceries on the shelves gratefully reach out to her and multiply for her, because of her rich thoughts and rich appearance.

Still another housewife reports how she has used psychokinesis to directly influence and attract physical objects to her. For many years, she and her husband struggled to get the grocery bills paid. They had a large family clan who regularly visited them, which cause their pantry to be "cleaned out" often. This couple loved their kinfolk, but they could hardly afford them!

One day this housewife decided that, through her special power of psychokinesis, there must be some way that she could attract groceries to meet her increasing needs. She began to think of how, through this special mind power, she could influence and attract good food to her kitchen.

She quietly thought of groceries of all kinds, and of where they came from. She thought of seafood passing from the fisherman to market and then to her. She thought of the cattle in the fields passing through the rancher's hands, and eventually to her. Vegetables, canned goods, frozen items, bakery products, and other foods were visualized by her, as she gave thanks for the countless people along the way who prepared such foods for her use. She imaged all types of food coming into her kichen in abundance, with no thought of financial burden or restricted supply.

When relatives came to visit her after that, they brought with them gifts of wonderful food: fresh seafood from the coast; bread, butter, milk, and other dairy products; special delicacies from the bakery, and so on. Never again did she have to worry about the grocery bill, or where the next supply of groceries would come from. It was as though the various food items knew how she loved and appreciated them, and tended to rush to her in abundance, in the highest and best form.

EVERYTHING REFLECTS YOUR ATTITUDE

When you speak negatively of your financial affairs, you are misusing your special power of psychokinesis. Jesus used this special power to wither the fig tree, to prove the effect of words upon physical objects. You mentally and verbally influence everything in your world. A businessman recently spoke of appreciating a magnolia tree which he had purchased for his flower garden. He was told by friends that the magnolia would not bloom for about seven years. Since he wanted to see the lovely magnolia blooms and to enjoy their fragrance, he constantly visualized the beauty of his tree, blessing it with much love and appreciation. After only four years, his magnolia tree burst into full bloom!

Never speak disparagingly of an object. Never speak of an item of clothing or furniture as "this old thing," unless you wish it to age and fade from your world quickly. Remember that everything around you reflects your attitude toward it, and reacts accordingly.

I recall once visiting a lady of lofty, beautiful thoughts. She constantly entertained a high vision of good, and her surroundings were always aglow with beauty and elegance. About a year later I returned to those same surroundings, but she was no longer there. I found the same furniture, drapes, and other features were still in place, but they seemed to have lost their glowing beauty. Some of the furnishings looked rather sad and shabby. Soon I realized that they could not have become threadbare in one short year. That elegant lady's beautiful, appreciative thoughts had literally sustained the furnishings in a state of loveliness.

A good prayer to use when you are trying to radiate an atmosphere of beauty is: "I AM ONE WITH ALMIGHTY GOOD. MY ENVIRONMENT IS GLOWING WITH RADIANT BEAUTY, RADIANT RICHNESS, AND RADIANT GOOD."

PSYCHOKINESIS WORKS EVERYWHERE

You have often felt the power of psychokinesis at work in various environments into which you have entered. They either radiated harmony or unpleasantness to you. Those most active in an environment directly influence the physical objects therein with their thoughts and words of harmony or discord, and you can feel and see the result.

Charles Fillmore has described how you may rightly use the power of psychokinesis for good:

> Blessing the substance increases its flow. If your money supply is low or your purse empty, take it in

your hands and bless it. See it filled with the living substance ready to become manifest. As you prepare meals, bless the food with the thought of spiritual substance. When you dress, bless your garments and realize that you are being constantly clothed with God's substance. The more conscious you become of the presence of the living substance, the more it will manifest itself for you, and the richer will be the common good of all.[2]

BELIEVE IN YOUR SPECIAL POWERS

Do you hesitate to believe that you have these special powers for prosperity? This is the most enlightened age the world has ever known. It has been stated that more progress has been made on this planet in the past one hundred years than in the past ten thousand years! Jesus promised that, when the Spirit of Truth is come, it would guide us into all truth. This is the age when the truth about God, man, and the universe is being explored and revealed as never before.

Never doubt the power of your deeper, special powers for prosperity, new growth, and rich achievement. Dare to think about them, believe in them, and let them begin to unfold their secrets to you. As the need arises, divine intelligence will begin expressing these powers through you with wonder-working power. As they come forth, you will recognize your special inner powers, and you can learn to accentuate their expression by using specific statements given in this chapter.

---

2. *Prosperity*, page 24.

As you dare to begin developing these powers, you will find them to be your special equipment for living victoriously in this New Age.[3]

3. SPECIAL NOTE: When the author first began writing about man's mind powers described in Chapters 14 and 15, they were still considered by many to be extraordinary powers. However, it is now believed that many people born since World War II came forth especially endowed with these accelerated mind powers. And it has been predicted that more and more of the people now being born, and even more of those to be born in the twenty-first century, will have these accelerated mind powers developed at birth. It is felt they are destined to play an important role in bringing forth the New Age of spiritual and metaphysical enlightenment to mankind — the "Age of Aquarius."

THE PROSPERITY LAW OF SELF-CONFIDENCE

— Chapter 16 —

A stockbroker reported that he had studied the prosperity laws from every angle; that he had observed the many prosperous-minded people who buy and sell stocks; that he had read many biographies of successful people; and that from these observations and studies he had decided that if prosperity could be described in one expression, it would be "self-confidence," which means faith in one's innate abilities and talents, and faith in God's help to develop them.

Psychologists state that there is a tremendous power in self-confidence which doubles your powers and multiplies your abilities. My stockbroker friend told me that, after gaining confidence in the laws of prosperity and using them in his work, his income zoomed upward. One month after he began invoking the prosperity laws presented in this book, his income was four times its previous level. His success is even more remarkable when we realize that it happened during a recession period!

THE SECRET OF SELF-CONFIDENCE

Perhaps the most important secret of self-confidence is this: Courses are given and books are written to help you attain self-confidence, and yet you already have it! It is a part of your spiritual nature, with which you were endowed when you were created in the image and likeness of God. The Psalmist reminds you that you were made little lower than the angels and crowned with glory and honor. And the Master Psychologist declared, "Is it not written . . . ye are gods?" (John 10:34)

The truth that we are born with confidence can be viewed by the actions and reactions of most children, before they become filled with the fears, phobias, and inhibitions of thought. Children have the delightful habit of confidently saying and doing whatever they feel led to say and do.

A brilliant child who has no self-confidence does not possess half the potential for living successfully as does the average child with a good degree of self-confidence. I know a Sunday School teacher, who, realizing this, leads her students each Sunday morning in affirming: "GOD LOVES ME, GOD LIVES IN ME, GOD BREATHES THROUGH ME, I AM GOD'S CHILD AND HE LOVES AND HELPS ME ALL THE TIME!" It is interesting to watch her students blossom forth with new courage and confidence, which are reflected in their school work, home life, and social success, as well.

Quite different is the case of a woman with whom I recently talked. She claimed that years ago she employed the power of prosperous thinking with decidedly happy results. But a friend had told her that such thinking was odd and wrong, and that she should have nothing more to do with it. She placed more trust in the advice of her well-meaning, but misguided friend than in her own God-given convictions. The result is that she must now return to prosperous thinking to restore her home life with her husband, to keep the financial wolf away from her door, and to regain her health. Lack of confidence in her own God-given convictions almost ruined her life.

Admittedly, there is a difference between egotism and sincere self-confidence. Egotism is the attitude, "Not Thy will, but mine be done, Lord; I appreciate Your help, but I prefer to handle things my way." Self-confidence means humble faith in your innate God-Self, and in your sincere inner convictions.

Why shouldn't you have great faith and confidence in your deep convictions? After all, the scientists declare that you are filled with innate intelligence. Every atom of your being throbs with active intelligence. The very air you breathe and the world in which you live is abounding with divine intelligence, which seeks to impart to you all you wish to know about everything. That same divine intelligence will perform wonders for you, if you make contact with it in faith.

YOU MUST HAVE SELF-CONFIDENCE
TO SUCCEED

Perhaps you have wondered at times, why some people advance to highly paid positions while others, who have equal or better training, are not promoted. Upon close study, you will observe that those who advance really believe in themselves and in their ability to succeed. They seem to have an inner ear with which they listen for guidance and knowledge. They seem to know that within them is something special, to which they have constant access for wisdom and expanded vision. You will usually notice that they radiate poise and assurance, so that others around them just naturally believe in them and follow their ideas.

One of the superb reasons for developing self-confidence is that it is contagious! It impels and persuades others. Joshua, the first official commanding general of the Hebrews, proved this. Even though the Hebrews had been wandering in the wilderness for 40 years, when Joshua took command after the death of Moses, his first act was to assure the Hebrews that they would pass over the Jordan into the Promised Land in just three days—and they did! It is interesting that the word "success" is found only twice in the Bible, both times in the Book of Joshua.[1]

No one pays much attention to the person who lacks confidence. He does not attract others or convince them of his worth, because his mind is a negative force that repels rather than attracts.

One of the statements we used in our prosperity classes hundreds of times to call forth innate intelligence as self-confidence is this: "NOTHING SUCCEEDS LIKE SUCCESS. I NOW GO FROM SUCCESS TO GREATER SUCCESS WITH GOD'S RICH HELP. I GIVE THANKS THAT MY SUCCESS IS BIG, POWERFUL AND IRRESISTIBLE, AND THAT IT APPEARS NOW!"

---

1. See the Ponder book, *The Millionaire Joshua.*

SELF-CONFIDENCE DISSOLVES INFERIORITY

You cause yourself to perform divine feats of good by having confidence in your divinity and recognizing it often. It is good to declare daily for yourself a statement of faith and confidence such as this: "(state your name), I HAVE CONFIDENCE IN YOUR GOD-GIVEN GUIDANCE AND ABILITIES. I SEE YOU NOW GOING FROM SUCCESS TO GREATER SUCCESS WITH GOD'S RICH HELP. YOUR SUCCESS IS BIG, POWERFUL AND IRRESISTIBLE AND IT NOW APPEARS!"

I have known of several cases where inferiority complexes have been dissolved and self-confidence restored, as the person consistently filled his mind with bold, daring, reassuring affirmations.

Should you wonder if spoken words of good can have such power, you will be interested to know this: One positive statement of good is more powerful than 1,000 negative thoughts; and two positive statements of good are more powerful than 10,000 negative thoughts.

Thus, when discouragment, doubt, or fear of failure try to overwhelm you, affirm: "I AM STRONG IN THE LORD AND IN THE POWER OF HIS MIGHT. ALL POWER HAS BEEN GIVEN ME FOR SUPREME GOOD IN MIND, BODY AND AFFAIRS. I CLAIM AND EXPERIENCE IT NOW."

BUILD CONFIDENCE THOUGHTS
BEFORE SLEEPING

A powerful way to develop self-confidence, which is your attracting power for prosperity, is to feed your mind confidence-filled thoughts as you drop off to sleep. If you fill your mind with happy, expectant thoughts of success, prosperity and good results, your subconscious will take them as orders from you. During sleep, your subconscious will obediently go to work to produce a prosperous tomorrow for you. Thus, you can gain control of each day the night before, by getting into the thought and mood of how you want tomorrow to be for you (as mentioned in the last chapter).

A beautiful young model once told me of the results she obtained in this way. She was low, depressed, and unsure of herself because of a love affair that had ended unhappily. Feeling quite discouraged one night, she picked up a book that someone had sent her about the power of the subconscious mind in sleep.

Realizing her power to transform her unhappy situation by changing her dominant mood and thoughts, she began to think of how thrilled she would be if she met someone nice and congenial. Quietly she began thinking of the type of man she would like to meet. In that mood she relaxed into a deep sleep. Next morning she was awakened by the telephone ringing. The call was from a bachelor millionaire who had been asked by a mutual friend to call her on his next visit to town. He proved to be the answer to her marital dreams!

A prominent metaphysician recommends this powerful affirmation to use before sleeping: "I SHALL GO TO SLEEP BUT GOD IN ME REMAINS AWAKE, BRINGING MY PRESENT PROBLEMS TO A SUCCESSFUL CONCLUSION, IN DIVINE ORDER."

It is good to give yourself assurance by affirming often: "GOD LOVES ME, GOD IS GUIDING ME, GOD IS SHOWING ME THE WAY." Do not wait for others to assure you, praise you, or express their confidence in you. Instead of fretting because they don't, assure yourself that "someone cares"—that One Who made you and Who is ever interested in helping you.

AFFIRMATIONS DEVELOP YOUR CONFIDENCE

To develop your innate self-confidence in your ability to succeed, I suggest that you re-read Chapter 6, "The Prosperity Law of Command," and use the words of command given there. Use affirmations to release your self-confidence in three ways: speak forth affirmations—verbally—at least five minutes a day, somewhere in privacy.

At other times during the day, look at affirmations that you may have written out on cards or in a book. Get them out and look at them when fear or uncertainty seem to grip you. You can do this in the midst of people, ringing telephones and bustling activity, and no one need ever know where your "booster shots" of confidence came from.

A supervisor in charge of a group of book salesmen during a recession period sought to train them to sell encyclopedias, but they regularly returned from attempted sales to complain that times were hard and that nobody was buying. Since he had to remain positive and appear confident, the supervisor told me that the only way he was able to neutralize their pessimism and to convince them that they could sell was by going into another office, getting out his affirmations, and reading them over and over.

He would then square his shoulders, take a deep breath, return and make positive statements concerning his faith in his men, in their sales ability, in their fine product and the customers' need for it, regardless of economic conditions. In this way he restored their confidence in their sales ability, and they began to sell again.

At least once a day, write out 15 times (or more) a favorite affirmation on success, confidence, and perfect results. By writing out words of confidence you help implant the idea more firmly in your subconscious mind, which then works harder and faster to produce happy results. Affirmations are your strongest confidence-builders.

When doubt or fear concerning your ability to succeed seem to come upon you, perhaps you would like to use this series of affirmations that I have used to overcome timidity and a feeling of inadequacy: "GOD'S GOOD IS FOR ME, I OUGHT TO HAVE IT, AND I CLAIM IT NOW!"

Concerning any situation, problem, or personality that tries to tear down your faith and confidence in God's goodness, affirm: "I HAVE UNSHAKABLE FAITH IN THE PERFECT OUTCOME OF EVERY SITUATION IN MY LIFE, FOR GOD IS IN ABSOLUTE CONTROL."

After using affirmations, develop your self-confidence by bracing yourself, and then daring to do the things you want to attempt but have previously feared to try. Declare first: "GOD'S ALMIGHTY POWER GOES BEFORE ME, MAKING EASY, SUCCESSFUL, AND DELIGHTFUL MY WAY." If you began to feel shaky along the way, uplift yourself by affirming: "I CAN DO ALL THINGS THROUGH HIM WHO STRENGTHENS ME. I AM STRONG IN THE LORD AND IN THE POWER OF HIS MIGHT. THE PERFECT RESULT NOW APPEARS!"

STAND FIRM WHEN YOUR
CONFIDENCE-THINKING IS TESTED

Another powerful thought with which to fill your mind for self-confidence is: "INFINITE WISDOM GUIDES ME, DIVINE LOVE PROSPERS ME, AND I AM SUCCESSFUL IN EVERYTHING I UNDERTAKE." A businessman recently pointed out that often after he has affirmed success and then taken outer steps toward it, his faith and confidence are then often tested. He has found, for instance, that after he buys a new stock, its price will sometimes go down for a period, so that it appears he has invested unwisely. During such testing periods, he always affirmed the foregoing words. This practice gave him the faith and confidence in his decisions to hold on, until the stock would rise, and he would realize a good profit from it.

This is an important point to remember after you have dared to follow your convictions. It is as though you are challenged by an invisible force that tests your confidence in your decisions. Often people will try to discourage you. This is the time to hold on to what you sincerely believe is right. You have already laid the inner foundation through affirming success and perfect results. You must now prove to yourself and others that you have what it takes to follow through on your convictions. As you do, the tide must surely turn, and your confidence is multiplied; while the confidence of others in you is often tripled. It is at this point that you can truly affirm, "NOTHING SUCCEEDS LIKE SUCCESS."

When you find yourself in fearful circumstances, it is good to call forth confidence by affirming: "GOD HAS GIVEN HIS ANGELS CHARGE OVER ME, TO KEEP ME IN ALL

MY WAYS." A businessman told me how it seems he had a guardian angel for protection one dark night. Having just cashed his check, he had a pocketful of money. Since a friend had promised to repay him some money, he proceeded into a dimly lit area of town to collect it. As he passed the corner of a darkened building, two men stood in the shadows, one with his arm projecting from the building in such a way that he could reach out and grab a passerby. The second man stood nearby as his accomplice. However, as this businessman rounded the corner of the building, these two men stood perfectly still and let him pass unharmed, though his pockets were filled with cash. This man silently remembered these words from the 23rd Psalm as he had entered this area: "I WILL FEAR NO EVIL, FOR THOU ART WITH ME."

DEVELOP YOUR CONFIDENCE
THROUGH IMAGING

To help develop your confidence in your God-given success, I also suggest that you re-read Chapter 5, "The Imaging Law of Prosperity," and that you make a wheel of fortune, placing on it pictures of the visible good you wish to obtain. As you daily view the pictured results on your wheel of fortune, you are filling your mind with confident images of the good you wish.

One of the statements I once placed on my wheel of fortune was: "GOOD THINGS BEGIN TO HAPPEN NOW," and a series of happy results came forth. Another statement I have found powerful to view on my wheel of fortune daily is this: "THIS IS A TIME OF DIVINE FULFILLMENT.

MIRACLES NOW FOLLOW MIRACLES, AND GOD'S BLESSINGS NEVER CEASE." By filling your mind with mental images, your mind then is given the confidence to make those mental images into visible results.

Truly, the image makes the condition if you will make the mental image. If you do not consciously have confidence that your desires can come true, place a picture of the desired result where you can daily view it. Your subconscious mind will make it so, and your convictions will come to pass.

Another simple way to develop self confidence is to ask directly of a loving Father for guidance about anything that concerns you. As we have previously stated, the divine solution is the sublime solution!

ASSOCIATE WITH SELF-CONFIDENT PEOPLE

Another delightful way to develop your self-confidence is to link yourself with self-confident people. You will subconsciously begin to absorb their air of assurance, which soon will come alive in you.

By making contact with one or two success-minded, self-confident individuals, they will subconsciously inspire you and lift you to higher levels of thought and expectation. Perhaps Jesus was thinking of the power of self-confidence when He said, "If I be lifted up, I will draw all men." (John 12:32)

Other ways in which you can begin developing your self-confidence were explained fully in Chapter 14, concerning the development of your intuition and your creative imagination, along with the five special "super senses" discussed in the last chapter.

CALL FORTH THE GOOD IN OTHERS

Let us consider one final way you can develop your own self-confidence and help bring it forth in others. Begin appreciating, praising, and calling forth the good in others. Speak confidently to others of their good points. Dare to praise them. Speak words of kindness, uplift and success to them. I know of one businessman whose previous failure turned into success, after his wife gained new confidence in his business abilities, and let him know it daily.

I recently heard of a commercial photographer who stated that his great success in photographing prominent models in the fashion world came as a result of his expressing to those models, before he began taking pictures, his confidence in their ability to photograph well. He said that just by assuring them of his confidence in them, they became radiant before the camera, and he could do twice the work in half the time. Few retakes were necessary.

If you think something good about someone, tell them about it! If you have confidence in a person who is still struggling to succeed, let him know it. Don't wait until after a person has succeeded to say in a back-slapping way, "John, how proud I am of you, but then I knew you could do it all the time." Express words of praise and confidence in his success *before* he has succeeded. That's when he really needs it. (More about this in the next chapter on charm.)

Most people wear a mask. If you could see behind the mask of their lives, you would realize what a tonic your kind words can often be. It's like throwing a lifeline to a drowning man. It's better to overdo it, if such a thing is possible, than to let an opportunity to praise another pass by. It could be the turning point in a man's rise to success. And someone will do the same for you when you need it most. Even people whom the world considers highly successful crave words of confidence, thoughtfulness, and appreciation. Wholehearted confidence in ourselves and others has a miracle power when it is expressed.

The truth of this was recently reported by a housewife who wrote:

> Surely no one knows better than I the potency of words of praise and appreciation of others. Before I realized this power I was a chronic grumbler, and the whole atmosphere about me was steeped in fault-finding and complaining. I discovered that words of confidence, thoughtfulness, and appreciation not only helped others, but also eliminated pain from my body and trouble from my mind.
>
> Since I have adopted the method of expressing praise and confidence in others, there has been a great change in my household; especially is this true of my domestic help and my children. I no longer censure my help for apparent carelessness and for accidents, but I praise them for their good intentions, their faithfulness, and their goodness. I have found that the very act of speaking confidently to them and about them calls into activity the very qualities that are needed. I have watched this method work what some would call a miracle.

THE POWER OF SPEAKING
WORDS OF PRAISE

I recently observed the power of spoken words of confidence when I visited a happy family group, consisting of the husband, wife and their five children.

I marveled at the five well-adjusted, well-behaved children. I could not resist asking, "What is your secret for having five such happy, well-adjusted children in this age of common maladjustment?" The wife, who is a quiet introvert, quickly declared, "My husband is the secret. He is *so* wonderful with the children." I thought, "How can your husband be *so* wonderful with the children when he is away at work ten hours a day, six days a week?" But I noticed a look of adoration on her husband's face. He honestly *thought* he was that good with the children!

Later, in preparing for a cook-out the wife said to her husband in sincere appreciation, "My dear, what a wonderful fire you build!" Again I thought, "Whoever heard of praising a man for building a fire!" But it worked—he almost built a bonfire! I have a feeling that if he had built one and set the whole yard ablaze, his wife would probably have responded by declaring, "Isn't my husband the most wonderful fire-fighter?" Small wonder that that family is so happy.

CALL FORTH CONFIDENCE SILENTLY

Along with deliberate words of praise, kindness, consideration, and appreciation of another, it is good to silently declare to him and for him: "_____(call his name), I HAVE CONFIDENCE IN YOUR GOD-GIVEN GUIDANCE AND ABILITIES. I SEE YOU NOW GOING FROM SUCCESS TO GREATER SUCCESS WITH GOD'S RICH HELP. YOUR SUCCESS IS BIG, POWERFUL AND IRRESISTIBLE. IT APPEARS NOW."

This does not mean you are trying to gain hypnotic control of another's mind. You are simply giving him the benefit of your high thoughts of success. To gain control of another's mind is never the object of a prosperous thinker. Hypnosis has its place in medical and scientific research, but is not for general use. One person never has a spiritual right to take control of another's thinking. Such actions usually bring only confusion and unhappiness to all concerned.

Freedom is one of the the great mental laws of the universe, and a prosperous thinker knows it. As long as you simply declare ideas of general success and good for another, there is no danger of trying to mentally control them. Control comes when one tries to get specific, and mentally forces another's actions to his own selfish ways of thinking. Affirmations for yourself do not hypnotize you. Instead, they de-hypnotize you from thoughts of failure and negation which you may have habitually accepted before you realized the power of thought.

A popular business executive for a large corporation attained his success through speaking sincere words of praise, appreciation, and confidence to his employees. In one instance, a young prisoner on parole was brought to him as a prospective employee. This executive expressed his faith in this ex-prisoner's ability to make good. He then hired him. Over the years he constantly spoke words of confidence and expectation of good to this employee. Today that former prisoner is an executive for the same company!

YOUR SELF-CONFIDENCE WILL MULTIPLY

You may never know just how much good your words of confidence can mean, nor how far they can go to produce good for others. The age-old truth applies: when you speak words of confidence concerning others, you cannot help attracting it to yourself, since what you send out comes back multiplied.

Along with these various methods for developing your self-confidence, and with the more scientific methods given you in the last two chapters, there is one other that should never be underestimated. Psychologists declare that prayer is one of the greatest confidence builders in the world, and I believe it. I suggest that you re-read Chapter 13, which gives you the four basic methods of prayer. Through prayer, you tap that *divine something* within you and around you that releases great power and faith. You are then filled with confidence and the zeal to proceed.

Someone has said that it is the man "who thinks he can" that succeeds. Remember the power of putting your best foot forward as a confidence-builder, too. By doing whatever you can to effect the confident feeling and the confident look, you give yourself and others the impression of assured success. Your own thoughts and those of others then multiply along the line of expected successful results.

In the various ways mentioned herein, your thoughts are lifted up, self-confidence becomes a habitual state of mind, which then unconsciously goes to work for you. Then your prosperity can come in an avalanche of praise-filled success!

THE PROSPERITY LAW
OF CHARM

— Chapter 17 —

Sir James Barrie once described the power of charm, "If you have it, you don't need anything else. And if you don't have it, it doesn't matter what else you have!"

The word "charm" fascinates most people. Once, when I was a luncheon speaker for a women's club group in Alabama, the only man present was a business executive who spoke first. Immediately after his speech, the club president said, "We know how busy you are. Please feel free to leave if your schedule demands it."

"Oh no," he replied. "I wish to remain to hear what your speaker has to say about charm. Men are interested in the subject, too."

This was first brought to my attention more than twenty years ago, when I made the original notes for this chapter. Those rough notes were discarded after a final version had been written. In the days before paper-shredders were popular, the janitor found those original notes in my waste basket, and he asked if he could keep them to study. "I want to know more about charm, too," he explained.

In more recent years, I was once invited to speak to five hundred ladies at the Phoenix Country Club on the subject of charm, yet what a ruckus it caused. Why? Many of their husbands wanted to attend, too!

The term "charm" may enchant people because it seems almost indescribable, and its mystery lends fascination. However, the dictionary describes "charm" as "the ability to allure, greatly please, or to delight." That is a phase of charm, but not the whole truth about it. Yet that phase of charm causes most people to want to master its many facets.

THE AUTHOR'S INTRODUCTION TO CHARM

Several decades ago, during my first year in the ministry, I had an experience which caused me to want to know more about this thing called charm. One summer evening I received an urgent telephone call from a young lady who insisted she must see me immediately. When she walked into my study, she was so beautiful and gracious that I must admit I was more impressed with her charm than with her problems—which were not to be underestimated. Never had anyone quite like her crossed my path—either previously while I had worked in the business world, or later as a minister. Perhaps it was a strictly feminine phase of my being asserting itself, but I was fascinated when I learned she was the owner of a charm school, for which she was obviously her own best advertisement.

After counseling with her, we prayed for the divine solution to her problems. As she rose to leave, I secretly regretted that the interview was over thinking, "Here is someone I would like to know better and I will probably never see her again." I naively assumed that people in the glamorous world of modeling and high fashion probably did not pay much attention to religious thought. A few Sundays later, though, I spied her sitting in the congregation. We soon began a friendship that was destined to span several decades and thousands of miles. She, who had come to me to be ministered unto, was also to minister to me through developing my interest in the fascinating subject of charm.

WHAT CHARM HAS TO DO WITH PROSPERITY

You may be thinking, "But what does charm have to do with prosperity?"

Everything!

Why? Because although charm has many facets, if it could be defined in one word only, that word might be "harmony"—harmony of mind, body, in one's relationships, in the events of one's life, and in the atmosphere in which one lives and works. Harmony is a first requirement for true prosperity and success. Whereas, inharmony distracts, repels, and dissipates one's good, harmony attracts it.

Two Texas businessmen developed a conglomerate of banks, insurance companies, and real estate developments from coast to coast. They now enjoy an international lifestyle. Yet they recently explained to a new employee, "Our first requirement is that our employees work quietly, easily, in peace and harmony. We allow no rush, no fuss, no loud jangling of telephones or office equipment, and we allow no gossip between our employees. We have developed a far-flung multi-million dollar business through insisting upon harmony, peace and confidentiality in every phase of our organizaton."

That new employee later commented, "Imagine! Sitting in an office where millions of dollars are being made, yet it was so quiet and harmonious I could have heard a pin drop."

Charm is harmony, and harmony attracts prosperity.

CHARM IS A PROBLEM-SOLVER

That life can be beautiful; that it does not have to be a dull, problem-filled, or a hectic existence is not only the underlying message of many of the world's great religions, philosophies, and metaphysical studies; it is also the basic message of charm.

All normal people seek charm, as harmony, on some level of life. The development of charm can lead to accelerated individual progress, both within and without. One authority on the subject once said she gave thanks for all the unpleasant circumstances of her life, for they had caused her to realize the importance of developing charm.

Regardless of what we call it, more of the charm of life is what mankind longs for. And why not? It is a basic, God-given desire. Freedom from unpleasantness is a universal need that should not be suppressed but expressed in definite, constructive, satisfying ways.

Shakespeare's Macbeth describes a charmed life as "one protected from harm as though by magic."

Charm gives one self-confidence[1] and that "certain something" that helps a person to meet victoriously the obstacles found on life's pathway. Problems have a way of turning into solutions when one is able to meet them with the confidence and inner poise of charm. Such confidence and inner poise can cause life to become an exciting adventure rather than a dull experience. And that's what "a charmed life" is all about. Emerson might have been describing its benefits when he wrote, "Great hearts send forth secret forces that incessantly draw great events."

I once had a well-meaning critic whose "constructive criticism" was anything but. Nothing was right about my lectures, or our meeting place. He complained that the ideas I presented simply did not work for him. When I consulted my prayer group about how to cope with the situation, they suggested we begin to daily affirm for that lonely, unhappy, critical widower, "YOU WALK IN THE CHARMED CIRCLE OF GOD'S LOVE, AND YOU ARE DIVINELY IRRESISTIBLE TO YOUR HIGHEST GOOD NOW."

Sooner than we could have expected, those words worked. He met "a railroad widow" who did not want to marry him and lose her substantial pension benefits. But she was happy to befriend him. They soon were attending my lectures together, and they usually sat on the front row—holding hands.

After her first attendance at one of my lectures, this widow looked at her escort and very innocently said, "Wasn't her talk wonderful?" *That* put an end to his inharmonious, critical attitudes. He was soon leading the happy, companion-filled life he had longed for, and the charm of harmony had been re-established in my lecture experience.

---

1. See Chapter 16 on Self-Confidence.

CHARM IS AGELESS

Margery Wilson has assured us, "Charm belongs to no particular age. Old and young — and all the in-betweens — can be perfectly adorable."[2]

My late mother-in-law, the senior Mrs. Ponder, proved that to me. She was in her 60's when I first met her, and she lived until the age of 89. Yet in all the years in between, she was never anything but a charmer. Although she never took the Dale Carnegie course, she always talked to people in terms of their interest, not hers.

She was "a Southern lady of the old school" with the manners to match. Beautiful she wasn't. Unforgettable she was. Always a member of "the now generation," she never looked backward, but continually forged ahead, even when the infirmities of age tried to catch up with her. Although her last years were spent uncomfortably in pain with other physical disadvantages, she never mentioned it. The disappointments and hurts that life had dealt her at times were never discussed. She was the cheerleader of life and people until the very end. Before I met her I could not understand why her family constantly talked about her with such affection. Once I did meet her, I understood perfectly why they could not stop.

Another charmer was a gentleman of 78. One cold day I was called to the hospital where he had been placed for observation. My schedule had been so full that by the time I visited him, I was feeling tired and depressed.

---

2. Margery Wilson, *Charm* (Philadelphia & New York: J. B. Lippincott Co., 1928).

But the moment I walked into his room, he began relating all the funny experiences he had had in the hospital, and *I* immediately began to feel better. By the time that hospital visit was concluded, I was feeling on top of the world again—thanks to the patient. As I left the hospital, I marveled at the charm of that man. He lived to a ripe old age, and enjoyed every minute of it.

As mentioned in Chapter 11 on love, when a teacher asked her teenage students to write down their greatest problems in life, their anonymous answers indicated that their basic desire was for more harmony in their life experiences generally, and in their relationships specifically. So the desire for the harmony of charm belongs to no particular group. People of all ages crave it, and the many qualities of charm can be developed from the cradle to the grave.

CHARM IS INNATE AND PAYS LARGE DIVIDENDS

When I reflect back over the years on the thousands of people I have met, I only wish I had met more who radiated true charm, sincere and unaffected. Although many of us may have felt that charm has been in short supply in our lives and that it appeared to be a rare quality, it doesn't have to remain so. Charm isn't a quality that a person either is or isn't blessed with at birth (as many of us may have been taught to believe). Instead, charm is innate within each of us, just waiting to be developed.

Charm, like beauty, tends to appear in the eyes of the beholder so its development might take a different form in each person. From my studies of the subject,

I feel there are 3 levels on which charm can be developed, expressed, and enjoyed: (1) Spiritual. (2) Mental-emotional. (3) Physical.

FIRST: SPIRITUAL CHARM

An internationally known beauty expert once said, "Real charm comes from within. It is an inner radiance, an inner glow." Spiritual charm is developed through the practice of daily periods of quietness, reflection, prayer, meditation and inspirational study.

I once revisited a group of people I had known many years earlier. Though they were well-educated and well-to-do leaders of the community, this time they seemed totally unattractive, even dull and boring. When I reflected upon the reasons, I quickly realized why. For many years since first knowing them, I had been immersed in spiritual work, where I had had daily contact with praying people who radiated "a certain something" that prayer-less people do not have.

My former acquaintances were not a part of that later phase of my life. They did not spend time daily in the practice of prayer, meditation or inspirational study, and I could feel it. My contact with them reminded me that there is nothing so unattractive as a prayer-less person. Conversely, the daily practice of developing one's spiritual nature gives a person an attractive, magnetic power — a mystical charm — which nothing else does. I once met a New York policeman who attended Mass early every morning. I learned from him that an inner spiritual radiance has a charm all its own.

During the many years that I conducted lectures in churches of various persuasions, I found that upon entering a church I could usually tell whether it had a prayer ministry, a prayer group, or praying leaders. Those churches which did radiated a harmonious, electric, happy atmosphere. The churches that were run more strictly on a business basis were not so blessed. They often seemed cold, lifeless, and problem-prone. *Prayer, meditation and inspirational study are among the quickest and most permanently satisfying ways of developing the inner radiance, the inner glow, associated with spiritual charm.* And homes, businesses, churches, and other atmospheres can reflect the benefits of spiritual charm, as well as people.

SPIRITUAL CHARM HAS PROSPERING POWER

Spiritual charm has prospering power because it radiates a magnetic feeling that attracts those people desiring greater good in their lives. The exchange prospers. Many people lead such rushed, scattered, confused, inharmonious lives that they scare prosperity away from them. Yet those same people often are attracted to people who take time daily to be holy, or to become whole and well-integrated within and without. Such praying people develop a sense of well-being and inner security that the whole world appreciates and needs.

A doctor once stated that the secret of his large, successful practice was that he spent an hour every morning in meditation. He decreed that the Spirit of the Lord went before him into the new day, making easy and successful his way. He prayed that those people whom he could help would be drawn to him for healing. He gained peace, poise, power and control of his day in that early morning hour. Later, before opening his office, he spent another 15 minutes in meditation with his staff. They affirmed together "divine order" and "divine results" for the day. Throughout the day he often affirmed, "I AM UPLIFTED AND UPHELD BY THE CHRIST MIND, AND NOTHING CAN DISTURB THE CALM PEACE OF MY SOUL."

A lawyer-judge once related that his successful law practice was the result of his daily periods of prayer and spiritual study. "The Bible is filled with 'charm secrets' as reflected in the Psalms, the Proverbs, and the Gospels," he stated. He kept almost as many inspirational books on his shelves as he did law books. When his clients were greatly troubled, along with giving them sound legal advice, this attorney often also suggested an inspirational book for them to study.

The development of spiritual charm has prospering power because it gives you the ability to take control of your world, first from within, and then in outer ways. The development of spiritual charm helps you to make a comeback from life's problems, and it aids you in helping others. Thus, the development of spiritual charm can prove to be one of the best investments you will ever make!

A stockbroker said that he had his biggest month of the year financially after he began using a prayer that flashed into his mind during a period of early morning meditation, "RICH, DIVINE IDEAS NOW COME TO ME, AND I AM IN ALL WAYS ABUNDANTLY GUIDED, PROSPERED AND BLESSED."[3]

---

3. For the development of spiritual charm, study Chapter 13 on Prayer. Also suggested is the study of the author's books, *The Dynamic Laws of Prayer*, and *The Prospering Power of Prayer*.

CET IMMIGRATION
   & CITIZENSHIP PROGRAM
534-5451
WWW.CETWEB.ORG/
            ABOUTCET

M-THRS 11A-6PM

have coffee

THUR

APRIL

at 10:30 A

people and le

Santa Cla

Center ha

SECOND: MENTAL-EMOTIONAL CHARM

The mental and emotional aspects of charm have to do with positive attitudes and constructive emotional reactions to life's various experiences. The instructor who first introduced me to the subject of charm, completely revised her course, after hearing about both the spiritual and the mental-emotional phases of charm. Along with her instructions on the physical aspects of charm, she began to emphasize its other phases. She taught her students to face life positively, joyously, expecting good things to happen, and that there was something good to be gained from every experience.

Once, while visiting one of her classes, I observed a young girl who was trying to learn a new sitting position without much success. Finally she dejectedly declared, "I just can't do it." Her instructor replied, "Never say 'I can't', because you can. And such negative remarks do not bring charming results." The student then tried again and easily succeeded.

After this instructor included the three aspects of charm in her course, her graduates were in great demand for photographic, television and fashion-show work, and a number of them went on to "fame and fortune." As a result of her emphasis upon charm's threefold nature, this instructor became a popular speaker to community groups. The comment most often made by her listeners was, "I have never before been given such a complete and satisfying explanation of what true charm is all about."

In our youthful exuberance, she and I once teamed up to give a special charm course to the ladies of my church, emphasizing its three aspects. The course was

so popular that we could not accommodate all who
wished to attend. The local newspaper heard about
this charm course being held in a church, and sent a
reporter over to check it out. He was so intrigued with
the course that we had a hard time getting rid of him —
graciously. When he wrote a nice article about us, it
only compounded (and confounded) our success.

Although several decades have passed and this
charm teacher has gone on to a happy personal life
elsewhere, she still continues to teach occasional charm
classes. Recently she related this experience:

> I just gave the annual Christmas Party and Fashion
> Show for my models at a nearby country club. There
> were over 300 people attending, and the 20 models in
> the show were making their debut. They were quite
> nervous since many of the people in the audience were
> professional models and talent scouts from New York
> City.
>
> Backstage was mass confusion. I soon realized we
> had to calm everyone down before the show could
> begin. So I gathered all the girls in a big circle and had
> them declare with me the words I had learned from
> you more than 25 years ago, "I WALK IN THE CHARMED
> CIRCLE OF GOD'S LOVE, AND I AM DIVINELY IRRESISTIBLE
> TO MY HIGHEST GOOD NOW." With those words,
> everything was put in order and the show then went
> on — with great success.

CHARM IS KINDNESS

The harmony of mental-emotional charm might be
defined basically as kindness. This phase of charm has
been described as "the ability to make someone think
you are both pretty wonderful!" The writer of the

Proverbs described this phase of charm, "Let not kindness and truth forsake thee; bind them about thy neck; write them upon the tablet of thy heart. So shalt thou find favor and good understanding in the sight of God and man." (Proverbs 3:3,4)

Research has shown that the greatest human need is the need for kindness, courtesy, and to be treated decently. Often people who appear to have no problems may have the greatest ones of all; so everyone needs kindness and consideration. A divorcee was feeling sorry for herself and complained to a friend about the problems of being a single parent to her children. She said, "I wish I had had the nice life of Professor Smith. He is a happy-go-lucky bachelor with no family to burden him."

The friend gasped in amazement, "You obviously don't know much about the challenging life Professor Smith has led. His parents died early, leaving him with six brothers and sisters to raise and educate. He just got the last one through college and into a chosen profession. Professor Smith is only now beginning to lead a normal life."

Because we are all bundles of emotion, a kind word is often all that is needed to uplift, renew and send us forth in a victorious state of mind. Once when I was stranded in an airport on a long layover resulting from a cancelled flight, a little child came over and happily chatted with me. Her visit made my day.

A charming person dares to express kindness by saying nice things to people. If you think a complimentary thought about someone, don't just think it, or tell that opinion to someone else. State it (or write it) directly to the person involved. Dare to compliment people and to pass on compliments to them from others.

As mentioned in the self-confidence chapter, when a person has problems, don't wait until they have solved them to say, "I knew you could do it all the time." If you thought it, why didn't you tell them when they needed to hear it most? Give people a boost *before* there appear to be any signs of victory. That's real kindness, real charm-in-action.

One who is mentally and emotionally charming knows how to take, as well as to give, a compliment. If you play down a compliment, or act of kindness, it may be the last one you ever receive. Graciously accept such words and actions with simple expressions of thanks. If someone compliments an inanimate object, the owner should never reply, "Oh, that old thing?" but might instead say, "Thank you. I'm glad you like it."

This point might at first seem insignificant, even elementary. Yet a compliment or an act of kindness is a big thing to the person who takes the time and trouble to extend it. To be rebuffed can have the same effect as being slapped in the face.

A conscientious neighbor once related how bad she felt after making the effort one cold day to prepare a bowl of hot soup and take it to a sick friend. Instead of saying, "Thank you. It was kind of you to do this," the sick woman declared almost harshly, "Oh, you shouldn't have done it." She doubtless meant to be kind but her words gave the impression of being unappreciative. Her neighbor took her at her word and never attempted another act of kindness in her behalf.

The courtesy of writing "thank you" notes has not gone out of style either. I know of a young girl who may have missed out on a college education because she refused to write "thank you" notes for much lesser gifts, even though she needed them and had never had them before. I know of several other people who missed out on substantial inheritances because of their similar carelessness. In each instance, the donors of the prospective bounty felt if the recipients were so thoughtless about small though worthwhile gifts, they could hardly be wise stewards of much larger ones.

HOW TO OVERCOME THE DESTRUCTIVENESS OF GOSSIP

An important way to impress the kindness of charm is by realizing that gossip is considered a social error as well as a spiritual one. In this age, when there are so many fascinating and constructive things to talk about, to disparage another, or to be a "tale bearer," is unattractive, disappointing, and repels the good of all concerned. We can seal our lips by paraphrasing these wise words from the Proverbs: "Discretion shall watch over me. Understanding shall keep me." (Proverbs 2:11)

During a lunch hour, when an associate tried to "tear down" a mutual friend, a businesswoman simply gave her associate an unbelieving look and said nothing. She then silently declared, "THERE IS NO GOSSIP IN SPIRIT, SO THERE IS NO GOSSIP IN THIS CONVERSATION." The topic was not developed further.

Another businesswoman was on a coffee-break with a group of young co-workers when they began to criticize one of the townspeople who was in the news. This woman silently declared, "No, no, no." At the first opportunity she declared aloud, "I don't believe a word of this is true. I prefer to believe that he is a fine person who is the victim of circumstances." The subject was not mentioned again.

Daniel, in the lions' den, might have been giving a formula for overcoming and dissolving gossip when he declared, "My God hath sent His angel, and hath shut the lions' mouths, and they have not hurt me." (Daniel 6:22)

Once, when I learned I was being criticized for a bold action I had felt divinely guided to take, I began to declare, "THERE IS NO CONDEMNATION OR RESENTMENT IN ME, FOR ME OR ROUND ABOUT ME. DIVINE LOVE AND HARMONY NOW REIGN SUPREME IN ME AND IN MY WORLD, SO ALL CRITICISM NOW CEASES." And it did. Later, when my bold actions had brought equally bold results, those who had so easily gossiped about me, were among the first to compliment my new-found success. Although I appreciated their graciousness in expressing their change of attitudes, I felt it wise to take their compliments lightly.[4]

GOSSIP CAN SUBCONSCIOUSLY
STOP YOUR GOOD

How often workers have unknowingly stopped promotions, pay raises and other recognition they might have received because of their criticism and gossip of their employers. What they did not realize was that

---

4. For dealing effectively with criticism and gossip, study the angel-writing method in the Ponder book, *The Prospering Power of Love*.

their employers subconsciously felt their lack of loyalty and were repelled by it. I once knew a brilliant person with whom I longed to do business, but never did because he was a "tale-bearer." His gossipy ways not only cost him financially, but may have contributed to his bitter, premature death. He would have been wise to have listened to the admonition of Solomon, "Death and life are in the power of the tongue." (Proverbs 18:21)

Husbands, wives, children, relatives and friends also often stop the good that would otherwise come to them, because their criticism of others cause their "targets" to be subconsciously repelled. How often gossip and condemnation have robbed one of the abundance and harmony of a charmed life. "Whosoever keepeth his mouth and his tongue keepeth his soul from troubles." (Proverbs 21:23)

I once knew a well-meaning lady who irritated every friend and relative she and her husband had, because she constantly criticized everything and everybody. She felt very sorry for herself and assumed that people and circumstances had treated her badly when, in fact, it was her own bitter words and attitudes that had repelled the health, wealth and happiness she and her husband longed for.

On an occasion when I spoke on charm, one of the ladies on the speaker's platform whispered to me, "Be sure to tell these women that charm begins at home, and that praise is one of the most powerful forms of charm."[5]

---

5. See Chapter 6 on Praise in the author's book, *The Dynamic Laws of Healing*. See Chapter 8 in her book, *The Millionaire Moses*.

THE MYSTIC POWER OF QUIETNESS

The occult law of quietness especially applies to the charmed way of life. It is one of the least understood and most overlooked laws of success. I once met a businessman, who at first glance, appeared to be charming and succcessful. He was blessed with a lovely wife and family, a nice home and job security. He had looks, charisma, education and a certain degree of spirituality. Yet in casual social surroundings, and certainly without being asked, he proceeded to tell me how much money he made, the size of his house and car payments, and many other personal details of his life. Then he complained about what a hard life he felt he had had.

How often people casually talk away their good. Charles Fillmore explained, "The ignorant open the valves of the mind and let ideas flow out into a realm with which they have nothing in common . . . thus their power is lost."[6] Quietness seals in your good and lets it grow on the inner plane until it is strong enough to produce results on the outer plane. Quietness also exudes a certain mystic charm that has an attracting power.

THE EMOTIONAL BASICS OF CHARM

Basically, charm lies in being your best self and in helping to bring out the best in others. The kind, sim-

---

6. *Prosperity*, page 18.

ple way is the most charmingly correct. A charming person does not take another's time unnecessarily, nor allow others to squander his. Deception and excuse-making are not a part of charm. It's better to say simply, "I was wrong," or "I apologize." Yet a charming person is not a doormat.

In an effort to be charming, people can sometimes be too familiar. Charming people are never too gay, nor are they loud, insincere or affected. There is nothing false or "put on" about true charm. Instead, charm knows how to be kind, yet keep its distance.

A charming person is one who is "altogether," thinking about and doing one thing at a time, with a "no rush, no fuss, no bother" attitude. The charming person avoids becoming angry or too excited, avoids getting too high or too low. The charming person is relaxed and poised, not tense or striving, taking one day at a time and making the most of it, rather than fretting about the past or the future.

Many of the methods mentioned in this book can help you to lead a more charmed life, such as the practice of forgiveness and release, affirming divine love, practicing goal setting, and establishing order in one's inner and outer life.

Margery Wilson once wrote, "Charm is an attitude of mind expressing itself in every detail of every department of life."[7] So the facets of charm are endless.[8]

---

7. *Charm*, page 6.

8. See Chapter 11 on Love. Also suggested is the study of Chapter 9 in, *Open Your Mind to Prosperity*; Chapter 5, *The Healing Secrets of the Ages*; and study of *The Prospering Power of Love*.

THIRD: PHYSICAL CHARM

Physical charm is reflected as radiant well-being. The pagan beliefs of the past taught sacrifice and even torture of the body as a spiritual benefit. But the apostle Paul, instead, described the body's importance, "Know ye not that your body is the temple of the living God which is in you? Glorify God in your body." (I Corinthians 6:19,20)

Some experts claim that we are so emotionally affected by physical appearances that our attitudes toward another person are often formed within the first twenty seconds of meeting them. Thus, let us never underestimate the power of physical charm.

This is indeed an age in which the development of physical charm is emphasized as people are encouraged to diet, exercise, and to participate in various sports. Physical charm has to do with being healthy and making a good appearance. One's tone of voice, grooming, cosmetics, hairstyling, and attire all contribute to physical charm.

A reader of my books recently wrote from Missouri: "Only after my mother had cosmetic surgery and was healing, did she tell me. She said she had not wanted me to feel she was being vain. When I told her she was the child of a King and deserved to be healthy and beautiful, she seemed relieved."

PHYSICAL CHARM HAS NO AGE LIMITS

One of the most attractive, charming and accomplished women I ever met was May Rowland, who for more than half a century directed the internationally prominent "Silent Unity" prayer department of Unity School. She was also a popular writer and lecturer, and she served for many years as one of the School's corporate officers. Although she spent a lifetime in the development of the (1) spiritual and (2) mental-emotional phases of charm, she also knew the importance of (3) physical charm. She deliberately glorified God in the body.

For that purpose she often affirmed, "I AM YOUNG, STRONG AND HEALTHY. MY BODY KNOWS IT, AND MY BODY SHOWS IT." She enjoyed such festive physical activities as square dancing, attending parties, and entertaining in her home on "Unity Ridge." She was an avid believer in proper diet, exercise and fresh air, often sleeping on the screened porch of her Missouri home, even in cool weather. The result was that she looked years younger than her rumored chronological age, and she lived a long, active, fulfilling life that blessed millions of people worldwide.

Her lean, handsome husband, whom she had met on a Western ranch, added great happiness to the last decades of her life. Their retirement years included travel and outdoor living. Even though hers had been a life dedicated to the spiritual activity of prayer, she had wisely balanced it with an appreciation of her physical existence as well. What benefits for her that combination wrought!

After a lecture trip in Florida, my husband and I once rested briefly at the historic Breakers Hotel in Palm Beach. One night, as we were having dinner, we observed on the dining room dance floor a couple who exuded physical charm. They displayed deep tans, beautiful white hair, were attired in colorful clothes, sparkling jewelry, and were reported to be in

their 80's. We were told they were from South America
and that their yacht was docked somewhere in the vi-
cinity. On the dance floor and off, they had a marvelous time. Diners throughout that high-ceilinged,
flower-bedecked, music-filled room were aware of
their attractiveness, charm and glamour. Isn't it wonderful to know that even physical charm need have no
age limit?

THE INFINITE POSSIBILITIES OF CHARM

The purpose of this chapter has been to introduce
you to the potent possibilities of charm. Books which
more fully cover the subject can be found in your library or bookshop. Public courses and instructions are
available to the general public on every facet of charm.
You will also enjoy declaring often the affirmations
that can lead to a charmed life which are found at the
end of Chapter 7 (The Prosperity Law of Increase).

No matter who you are or what your life situation
may be, charm can give you your heart's desire. The
world responds to the person who is developing charm
in its three phases. Indeed, humanity will gladly reward
the charming person with financial compensation,
honor and affection. So dare to develop your threefold nature of charm, in the assurance that the world
wants and needs you that way—and that it will com-
pensate you accordingly!

WHAT ABOUT
INDEBTEDNESS?

— Chapter 18 —

It is not by chance that this chapter follows the previous one, since people facing financial strain often need all the charm they can develop to help them overcome indebtedness.

In a cartoon, several beautiful new cars are seen on display in a showroom. Above them hangs a sign which reads: "Try our credit plan with e-z payments." While a prospective customer stands viewing one of the new cars, a perplexed salesman asks the manager, "How do I go about this? That customer wants to pay cash!"

In this age of credit, what about indebtedness with regard to prosperous thinking? Credit wisely used is a rich asset to financial success; credit that is abused or over-used is a clear path to indebtedness and financial failure. Credit is not desirable if used in desperation to postpone financial disaster a little longer. Neither is it good if used for acquiring items which you cannot pay for without great mental anguish. Credit is intended to be used intelligently toward helping one enjoy the comforts of life in a reasonable manner. Credit may also be used intelligently in realizing profit.

A housewife who suddenly found herself widowed with three children to support, wished to go into business for herself. She borrowed money, invested it, made a profit from the investment within a short time, repaid the borrowed money, and opened her own business with the surplus. The intelligent use of credit proved a financial asset to her.

A good rule to follow in order to avoid the pitfalls of misused credit is this: Do not incur bills that burden you with the feeling of lack and limitation. You may incur reasonable financial obligations if you can do so with an easy mind, in the faith that you can meet them in a reasonable manner.

RESENTMENT AND FEAR CAUSE INDEBTEDNESS

No debt is good if you resent or fear it, because such an attitude causes it to become a burden. The thought of burden often stops the flow of substance into your affairs, as well as hindering the flow of new, prosperous ideas in your thinking. When the flow of substance is halted in either of these ways, you are then unable to meet your bills, and panic and resentment take over.

So long as you do not resent or fear financial obligations, you can maintain mental and emotional control over them in your thoughts, feelings, and reactions.

When you maintain a feeling of control, not feeling helplessly bound to debts, you keep the way open for the rich substance of the universe to flow to you—in expected and unexpected ways—making it possible for you to meet each obligation.

It is axiomatic that if you "look up," you will always be provided for. Surely uplifted thinking, free from fear, resentment, and condemnation, is necessary in order to maintain a debt-free existence.

A housewife related how thoughts of fear, resentment, and condemnation got her into debt; and how by changing her attitudes, she got out of debt. Her husband was a fine salesman whose work took him far from home. Early in their marriage they purchased a farm in the mountains of Kentucky, deciding that it would be an ideal place to rear their children. Since her husband traveled regularly, the wife was responsible for supervising the farm and caring for their growing children. In due time she began to resent her responsibilities. As her resentment grew, it seemed more and more difficult to meet the ever-increasing financial obligations that attended the farm's progress.

Finally, she had to borrow money to pay the workers, to purchase farm equipment, and to meet general expenses of the farm. Soon she was in debt, though the farm had excellent potential. At this point, she heard about the power of prosperous thinking, and began to assess her indebtedness from the standpoint of her mental attitudes. One busy afternoon, when she was wondering how she would meet the payroll that week, she drove up on a lovely hill overlooking a peaceful area where cattle were grazing. There she stopped and meditated for a time on the peaceful beauty of the scene below.

She realized that she had resented her husband's absence from home, though she knew that he was only trying to provide for his family. She further realized that she had been resenting the reponsibility of running the farm alone, although it was a valuable asset. As she reflected in this upward state of mind, a feeling of peace came and the thoughts of burdensome debt, resentment, and condemnation passed. She then silently asked for divine guidance for herself, her husband, the children, the farm, the workers. She gave thanks for financial success and freedom from indebtedness.

When she drove into town the next day, a friend told her that he wanted to buy some farm equipment. She advised him that she had such farm equipment stored away, unused. A purchase was arranged that quickly liquidated all of her debts. Later, as her former resentments were replaced by love and appreciation for the farm, her husband decided to give up his sales work, to move his family into town, and to go into the contracting business. A competent manager was hired to run the farm. As this woman continued to praise and give thanks for her many blessings, her farm and her husband's new business both prospered. She now enjoys a happy home life with her husband and children, along with taking an active part in church and community affairs.

This lady proved to her own satisfaction that thoughts of resentment and condemnation had caused her sense of burden, which in turn had stopped the flow of substance in her affairs. When she no longer resented her obligations, she gained control of them and was able to meet them victoriously.

CRITICISM PRODUCES INDEBTEDNESS

When bills come due, greet them in an unruffled frame of mind, reminding yourself that they represent blessings you are already enjoying. A negative, critical attitude toward bills causes many people to get into debt and to stay there. I know a family that constantly fumed over their monthly bills. Certain bills continued to rise unreasonably; they found themselves further and further in debt. When these people learned of the power of prosperous thinking for getting bills paid, they stopped condemning the bills. Instead, they began to affirm: "WE USE THE PROSPEROUS POWER OF DIVINE INTELLIGENCE IN WISDOM, INTEGRITY AND GOOD JUDGMENT IN ALL OUR FINANCIAL AFFAIRS. WE GIVE THANKS THAT EVERY FINANCIAL OBLIGATION IS PAID ON TIME." Thereafter, their bills decreased to reasonable size again.

It is not only unpleasant and unnecessary, but foolish and dangerous to waste time and energy critizing anything, especially financial obligations owed or owing you. Such a negative practice can lead to permanent indebtedness, and even to utter financial ruin. If you are not willing to give of the substance that comes to you to pay your bills, why should you reasonably expect the rich substance of the universe to flow easily into your life? An ungrateful attitude of mind brings ungrateful, limited financial results.

GRATITUDE PROSPERS

The "attitude of gratitude" keeps prosperity coming to you from every direction. The truth of this was

brought to my attention once while lecturing in the
Palm Beach, Florida area. A minister there told me
that the wealthiest people in his congregation seemed
to be the most appreciative for any spiritual service
rendered them. He stated that often when a person of
average means is hospitalized and requests a ministerial call, their opening remark to the minister is,
"Where have you been? Why did it take you so long to
get here?" Yet he finds on visits to millionaires who are
hospitalized, they invariably are disarmingly grateful
that he had taken time to drop by to see them. He
observed that his millionaire friends regularly wrote
notes of thanks for any kindness received. He felt that
their mental attitude of gratitude and thanksgiving
was a convincing clue to their great wealth.

Never criticize or condemn anything or anyone if
you wish to become debt-free and to remain debt-free.
As stated in the chapter on your special powers for
prosperity, the scientists now believe that everything is
endowed with an innate intelligence that knows what
you say, think, and feel about it. If you speak of
things, people and conditions in a positive, prosperous
way, you gain their subconscious cooperation. Whereas, if you criticize your world, you repel its blessings
and attract only negative, limited conditions into your
life. (This was pointed out in the last chaper on
Charm.)

A merchant found that his merchandise was not selling, though in the past he had been quite successful.
He tried holding special sales, making special offers,
and other methods to sell his merchandise. Many of his
accounts were overdue, on which he seemed unable to
collect. He was floundering deeper into personal indebtedness. Finally, he realized that he had become

quite critical of himself, his business, customers, family, neighbors, community and the world in general. It was then that he asked a friend, who knew of the power of prosperous thinking, to help him get his own thinking straightened out. The friend suggested that he begin using this statement to change his thinking: "THERE IS NO CRITICISM OR CONDEMNATION IN ME, FOR ME, OR AGAINST ME. DIVINE LOVE, WISDOM AND ORDER NOW REVEAL PERFECT GUIDANCE AND PRODUCE PERFECT RESULTS IN ME AND IN MY WORLD."

With the circulation of these ideas in his thinking, this merchant developed a friendlier feeling toward his customers. Along with mailing out monthly statements of current accounts, he decided to send along notes of good wishes to those who had long owed him money. The results were amazing! People with long over-due accounts began paying up! One lady sent him a check on an account she had been owing him for ten years.

The technique of getting debts paid—both those you owe and those owed to you—is first an inner work in the realm of mental attitudes. Others can be so repelled by your critical, unforgiving, condemnatory thoughts that they shrink from wanting to pay you what is owed. As you change your thinking about them, they subconsciously feel it and respond in a more positive way.

DO YOUR PAPERWORK

Instead of fretting about your own debts or those owed by others, sit down and boldly list those obligations on paper. Then go a step further and dare to write out dates by which you wish to see them fully paid. Next, write this affirmation at the bottom of your list and use it daily: "I GIVE THANKS FOR THE IMMEDIATE, COMPLETE PAYMENT OF ALL FINANCIAL OBLIGATIONS. I HAVE FAITH THAT WITH GOD'S HELP ALL OBLIGATIONS ARE BEING IMMEDIATELY PAID IN FULL!"

A businessman, who is self-employed, had tried the usual methods for collecting accounts with little success. He learned of the positive mental technique for handling finances, and he decided to give it a try. He listed each customer's name, along with the amount due, and then affirmed the complete payment of each obligation. Thereafter, when he went forth to collect, he was amazed that no one seemed to oppose him or sought to avoid him. Instead, everyone on the list paid him promptly!

An interior decorator had been out of work for some time, and was $2500 in debt. During a summer slack season she heard a lecture on the power of prosperous thinking for overcoming financial lack. She made a list of her financial obligations, added the above affirmation, and used it every day in thinking of her bills as being paid. Just the act of doing this gave her a sense of accomplishment, which replaced the previous feeling of futility. As she affirmed that her debts were being paid in God's own way, an interesting thing happened: A friend of a former customer telephoned and asked her to do an estimate for decorating a new apartment building. She had never been asked to consider such a large decorating job before. Never before had a client contacted her first; she had always sought out new clients.

Her estimate, running between eight and ten thousand dollars, was accepted. She was given the decorating job and her commission amounted to $2500! Not only did she get her own bills paid, but this proved to be only the first of a series of large decorating jobs that came to her. Previously she had worked hard for small commissions; now she is working steadily for bigger commissions. The work is no different, but the compensation is larger and more satisfying in every way.

ACTIVATING TRUST DISSOLVES INDEBTEDNESS

Here is a pleasant point to remember about indebtedness: if you are in debt, it is because someone believed in you and had enough faith in you to trust you financially. If others are in debt to you, it is because you extended your trust to them. Trust is a wonderful divine element, and it produces divine results when activated. Whenever you think of owing or being owed, give thanks for the trust that brought about the financial transaction in the first place. Know, also, that the same trust which worked in the beginnig can still work to bring forth the full payment due. Re-establish this attitude by affirming: "THE SAME DIVINE TRUST THAT FIRST MOTIVATED THIS FINANCIAL TRANSACTION IS NOW MIGHTILY AT WORK, CLEARING IT UP FOR THE HIGHEST GOOD OF ALL CONCERNED."

A credit manager used this idea to collect substantial sums of money for his company, often after other collectors had failed. In one instance, he was asked to collect a $17,000 account which had been outstanding for several years. When he talked with the man owing this account, it soon became evident that he was in dire financial straits. Nevertheless, this credit manager stated his faith that this creditor would settle the account as soon as possible. He thereby restored good will and renewed trust between the firm and the creditor. In less than two weeks the creditor brought him a check for $4,000. He stated that the credit manager's words of faith in him and his business ability gave him new courage, new hope, new conviction that he could succeed. With new hope came new ideas, which produced for him prosperous results. Soon the entire amount was paid, and the creditor continued to do business with this company.

DISCORD CAUSES INDEBTEDNESS

A harmonious, trustful state of mind is essential to gain freedom from indebtedness, and for collecting debts owed you by others. You will note on every hand that inharmonious people work very hard for their prosperity. The substance of the universe is repelled by inharmoniousness, and quickly dissipates in such an atmosphere. This explains why a certain salesman was not selling. His wife was also failing in her sales work. After a few minutes conversation with them, it was obvious their home life was filled with bickering and contention. They criticized and condemned each other, openly disagreeing about every subject.

It was pointed out that they would have to become more harmonious with each other before they would be able to attract customers and make sales again. They agreed to use this statement together: "THERE IS NO CONDEMNATION OR CRITICISM BETWEEN US. DIVINE LOVE REIGNS SUPREME AND ALL IS WELL WITH US AND

WITH OUR WORLD." Within two weeks, they were both making sales again, and their marriage became happier than ever before.

THERE IS A WAY OUT OF INDEBTEDNESS

Indebtedness may appear to be very big in your world, but it need only be a temporary situation if you dare to begin believing there is a way out. Perhaps the greatest barriers to freedom from indebtedness are fear and desperation. When they are overcome, you are on your way to financial freedom.

I talked with a man whose wife had feared that he was contemplating suicide. He was heavily in debt and could see no way out. He had been in an accident, and it had taken a year of recuperation before he returned to his business. Meanwhile, others, lacking his experience and knowledge, had to be relied upon to run his business. Though conscientious in their desire to help, they almost bankrupted him. Because of his large indebtedness and lack of sufficient collateral, this man had been unable to obtain a loan from the lending agencies to ease the situation. He declared, "If I could obtain even five or six thousand dollars, it would meet the most pressing debts and keep my business solvent until I could get the business activated again." He was feeling quite desperate when he talked with me.

I began to realize that two definite attitudes prevailed which were keeping a solution from appearing: First, this fine businessman had sunk into discouragement and despair. There seemed no way out, nowhere to turn. Second, he felt a sense of great loss about the year he had been ill. He kept telling himself, "If only I had not been in that accident, this would not have happened."

Such attitudes are normal for people in debt, but once those attitudes are changed, the whole situation will change — and very fast! Always, for every problem, there *is* a way out; there is a divine solution. To help establish and maintain the prosperous attitude until it could prove itself, I suggested that he daily affirm: "THERE IS A DIVINE SOLUTION TO THIS SITUATION. THE DIVINE SOLUTION IS THE SUBLIME SOLUTION. I GIVE THANKS THAT THE DIVINE SOLUTION QUICKLY APPEARS NOW!"

For his feeling of loss about the year away from work, these ideas were suggested: "Although it seems dismal at the moment, begin knowing that there need be no permanent loss in this experience. That which seems to have been lost during this year's illness can be 'divinely restored' to you financially and otherwise." To help him establish and maintain this attitude, these words were typed on a card for him to carry in his wallet. Daily, when discouragement or a sense of loss tried to envelop him, he was urged to read these words over and over: "I GIVE THANKS FOR DIVINE RESTORATION IN MY BUSINESS AFFAIRS. DIVINE RESTORATION IS NOW DOING ITS PERFECT WORK FOR ALL INVOLVED, AND THE PERFECT RESULT APPEARS NOW. I GIVE THANKS THAT EVERY FINANCIAL OBLIGATION IS NOW BEING MET IN GOD'S OWN WISE AND WONDERFUL WAY."

For a number of weeks, this businessman daily declared these ideas to himself. No change seemed to be forthcoming, but he persisted in knowing that there was a solution. He persisted in claiming divine restoration.

One day the picture began to change through an unusual series of events. He and his wife attended a family reunion, where his deceased brother's wife called him aside and said, "Years ago, when you first began buying into my husband's business which later became your own, I felt that he over-charged you for the initial downpayment. Now that he is gone, I no longer wish to keep the building which houses your business. I also wish to see financial restitution made to you for that large initial payment. An appraiser tells me that the building is worth $25,000 if I sell it outright. However, I will be happy to sell it to you for $10,000." Further appraisals revealed that this man could obtain a total loan of $16,000. After purchasing the building, he still had $6,000 to clear up pressing debts and have operating cash. As these affairs unfolded, he was filled with new hope, and thereafter he received increased business which helped to bring order and prosperity out of previous chaos and failure. Indeed, divine restoration did take place for him!

KEEP QUIET ABOUT INDEBTEDNESS

Many people who get into debt would not remain in it if they would keep quiet about their financial affairs. By magnifying their obligations, they clutch those circumstances to them ever more tightly. If they would keep quiet, keep going, do the best they could to meet their obligations, and affirm divine guidance, the way would open to clear up all indebtedness.

The well-known Bible story of Elisha and the widow is a subtle example of this. When the widow lamented to Elisha of her sad plight that a creditor was going to take her sons from her, Elisha did not sympathize with her. Instead, he told her to go into her house, shut the door, and start pouring out the oil she had on hand. This was a wonderful Oriental way of telling her to cease her wailing about her debts and financial problems, and to begin using whatever substance was on hand to meet the situation, knowing that as she did her part, substance would multiply to fill every need. (II Kings 4)

A widow likewise proved the prospering power of Elisha's advice in modern times. This woman had had a very troubled life. She was lonely, in debt, unhappy in her work, dissatified with her life in general. While she sought freedom from indebtedness, all the time she bemoaned how harshly life had treated her. Her financial circumstances became more stringent than ever, though she continued to receive pay raises and other financial blessings.

Finally, she realized that, in talking hard times, her very words were her worst enemy. She became silent about her financial affairs. For all the hard experiences of her life, she was asked to affirm "divine restoration" and to dwell upon the promise from the Book of Joel: "I will restore to you the years that the locust hath eaten. . . . Ye shall eat in plenty and be satisfied, and shall praise the name of Jehovah your God, that hath dealt wondrously with you." (Joel 2:25,26)

As she began to meditate on this promise, everything in her life changed. She received a promotion with a pay increase. A friend of long standing, whom she had once aided, decided to show appreciation by giving her $1,000! With this money she paid her debts, and was financially free for the first time in years. Soon she married happily, after having been alone for twenty years. Truly, the years which the locusts of financial lack had consumed *were* restored to her!

SPEAK ONLY IN PROSPEROUS TERMS

Instead of worrying, fretting, or talking about your debts, it pays to affirm prosperous results and to speak only in prosperous terms. A woman who had been out of work due to ill health found herself deeply in debt, but she constantly talked negatively about her situation. One night she and her daughter attended a lecture on prosperity. When they returned home, they decided to use an affirmation given in the lecture: "EVERYTHING AND EVERYBODY PROSPERS US NOW, AND WE PROSPER EVERYTHING AND EVERYBODY NOW." They began declaring these words together each night for five minutes before retiring. Within a week a check for $2500 came to them, representing a sum which had long been lawfully owed them, but their lawyer had been unable to collect it. As they changed their words when speaking about their financial affairs, it was as though all involved suddenly wanted to prosper them, rather than to withhold anything from them.

An artist was in debt because she had been unable to sell any of her paintings for a number of months. One night she attended a prayer group in which the power of praying affirmatively about financial problems was emphasized. At this meeting, it was suggested that each one take an affirmation and use it during the coming week for prosperity needs. This idea seemed a radically different approach to this artist, who had always felt that perhaps it was wrong to pray about money and financial problems. Joyously she began to

declare daily: "EVERYTHING AND EVERYBODY PROSPERS
ME NOW, AND I PROSPER EVERYTHING AND EVERYBODY
NOW." Four days later, she sold a painting for $75—her
first sale in months. Immediately other sales were
made, and soon every financial obligation had been
met.

NO ONE CAN WITHHOLD
YOUR PROSPERITY

Many people also get into financial lack and remain
there because they think someone else is keeping their
prosperity from them. As long as they think someone
else has that power, they themselves are decreeing that
it is true. But once they change the trend of their
thinking, their good can appear in spite of any outer
circumstances.

A widow who had tried in vain for over a year to
settle her deceased husband's estate, was heavily in
debt because an unexpected heir had appeared so that
a court proceeding became necessary. The estate funds
were under court control. For months, she had been
living meagerly from day to day, hoping that the estate
would soon be settled, and that she would receive a
check in full for the inheritance which was rightfully
hers. Each time it seemed near settlement, the case was
delayed because of further resistance from the other
heir.

During a period when her creditors were pressing
hard for payment of some of her late husband's bills,
this woman was given prosperity articles to read by a
friend. In them she found this affirmation: "I DISSOLVE
IN MY OWN MIND AND IN THE MINDS OF ALL OTHERS ANY

IDEA THAT MY GOD-GIVEN GOOD CAN BE WITHHELD FROM
ME. THOSE FINANCIAL BLESSINGS THAT ARE MINE BY
DIVINE RIGHT NOW COME TO ME IN ABUNDANCE, AND I
JOYOUSLY ACCEPT THEM."

Fascinated with the possibility of this simple approach to her problems, this woman sat quietly all
afternoon, writing out and affirming this statement
over and over. As she did, she began to feel a sense of
dominion welling up within her about her financial
affairs. She also began to feel more kindly toward that
unexpected heir, who was trying to force his claim on
her husband's estate. The more she thought peacefully
about him, the more she could see why he felt entitled
to certain financial assets.

Finally, she telephoned her lawyer, told him to use
his own judgment in settling the estate, but to feel free
to give that heir certain portions of the stocks, bonds,
and oil properties which he claimed. Within a few days
the estate that had been pending for months was settled, so that all involved were satisfied, prospered, and
blessed. This woman now feels that her "God-given
good" came to her from the settlement of the estate,
and she did not miss the financial assets shared with
this unexpected heir.

DELIBERATELY THINK BIG

In another instance, a realtor found himself going
into debt because some of his apartments were not
renting during a summer slack period. Friends told
him, "You will never rent those apartments at the
price you are asking. You are thinking too big. If you
cut your rental price, perhaps you may be able to rent

them for the coming season." This man attended a prosperity lecture where he heard: "You can never think too big. Dare to affirm big ideas. Dare to expect big results. Such attitudes are the difference between a prince and a pauper."

This man realized that he must deliberately think big and speak prosperously if he wished to rent his properties and pay his debts. For the rental of his apartments, he began affirming a statement that has prospered countless people: "I LOVE THE HIGHEST AND BEST IN ALL PEOPLE AND I NOW DRAW THE HIGHEST, BEST, AND MOST PROSPEROUS-MINDED PEOPLE TO ME." Though he had shown the unrented apartments several times without success, the very next client to appear was delighted with his apartments, and rented one for the season for $2,000. As he continued using this prosperous statement, his other properties were rented easily. Within a short time he had received checks totaling $8,000, which enabled him to become debt-free.

BEGIN TO PAY CASH FOR MORE ITEMS

Along with getting prosperous attitudes about your financial affairs, it is good to do whatever tangible or intangible thing you can to get the feeling that you are clearing up indebtedness. For instance, begin paying cash for items, though you may do so in a small way. Just by releasing cash for such items, rather than charging them, you begin to get a sense of freedom from debt.

I know of two housewives who decided that the approaching holiday season was the time to prove this. They stopped charging gift items, and began paying cash as they shopped. Later, they declared that spending cash gave them a sense of joy and freedom. In each instance, they found that as they blessed and gave thanks for divine wisdom in using the cash on hand, money kept coming to them for Christmas giving.

One housewife went all through the holiday season without charging anything. She stated that she also gave the best gifts ever. The other housewife finally resorted to her charge accounts for a few gifts, but she had already purchased so many for cash that the few charged did not give her a sense of burden. She did not dread facing payment of them in the New Year, and she quickly paid them as they came due.

DISMISS FINANCIAL MISTAKES OF THE PAST

Another financial attitude that binds many people to indebtedness is this: Like Lot's wife, they continue to look back. They worry about financial mistakes of the past and thus crystallize their thinking, which manifests as present indebtedness. When you look back, there is no room in your thinking for new ideas which could clear up past mistakes and indebtedness.

To forgive yourself and others for past mistakes is essential, if you wish to be permanently free of financial burdens. If such memories try to haunt you, use this statement: "THE FORGIVING LOVE OF DIVINE INTELLIGENCE HAS SET ME FREE FROM THE PAST AND FROM THE FINANCIAL MISTAKES OF THE PAST. I NOW FACE THE PRESENT AND THE FUTURE WISE, SECURE AND UNAFRAID." It will work wonders for you and for others. As stated in the vacuum law of prosperity, it is necessary that we constantly forgive ourselves and others if we wish to be prospered. Re-read Chapter 3 to help yourself and others to overcome indebtedness.

ASK FOR PROSPEROUS IDEAS

Along with establishing prosperous attitudes, and following through with prosperous actions, one should ask for prosperous ideas about financial matters. A businessman had reached the age of 40 and had gone as far as he could with his company, unless one of its owners retired. This fine man did not wish to succeed through such circumstances, but he was growing desperate. Even though he and his wife both worked, they were heavily in debt trying to meet the needs of their growing family. They could see no way to a larger income in their present circumstances.

When this man talked with me he said, "I need more self-confidence in knowing that somehow I can meet this situation victoriously. I suppose I also need more order in my affairs so that I might know which way to turn." It was suggested that he go about establishing order in an easy, quiet, satisfying way rather than to suddenly become aggressive, which might lead to confusion and antagonism with others. It was suggested that he begin spending a few minutes every morning and night to quietly meditate and ask for divine guidance about his financial affairs.

His first reaction was, "What good will that do? You mean God knows or cares about my financial affairs?" It was a revelation and a relief to this man to hear that a rich and loving Father cares about the financial needs of His children. This prayer was suggested for his use: "FATHER, WHAT IS THE RICH TRUTH ABOUT MY FINANCIAL AFFAIRS? WHAT IS YOUR HIGHEST GOOD FOR ALL IN THIS SITUATION?"

At first, no answer to this questioning prayer came, but this man did notice that he was more peaceful than he had been in years. With the increased feeling of peace, he began to feel more in control of himself, his family affairs, and his financial world. One night, as he was decreeing the "rich truth," an idea flashed into his mind with such force that he almost fell out of his chair. It was not a new idea; it had come to him many times before, but he had disregarded it. It was an idea to develop a new department that could mean fresh growth and prosperity for his firm. Never before had he been strongly enough convinced of the power of this idea to approach his superiors.

The next day he found the perfect opportunity for speaking with his boss about it. His boss was both surprised and pleased that this quiet little man was thinking in such big, progressive, and prosperous terms about the company. In due time, he was allowed to develop his idea for a special department; a new title and much better income accompanied it. Other financial surprises followed, with one member of his family receiving an unexpected inheritance. By praying for divine guidance and divine ideas, this man's debts of long standing were paid. A whole new level of prosperous living opened to him and his family.

A good statement to hold in mind for this purpose is: "DIVINE INTELLIGENCE NOW INSPIRES ME WITH PROSPEROUS IDEAS, AND WITH DIVINE ACTION IN PERFECTLY EXPRESSING THOSE IDEAS."

INDEBTEDNESS CAN BE
A BLESSING IN DISGUISE

Indebtedness can be a tremendous blessing in disguise. When unpleasant experiences come upon you, it is often because there are new ways of living and new methods of work trying to open to you. In most instances of indebtedness, those who are financially embarrassed are fine people who are trying to live prosperously on a limited income. However, if they have rich desires, it is because they also have the equivalent talents and abilities that are seeking expression.

Their desire for greater good is very strong, but their bank account has not been equally expanded. Often they are people who are engaged in mediocre work when their talents and abilities, if developed, would bring them a rich income to balance out their rich desires.

HOW TO GAIN FINANCIAL FREEDOM

Dare to use new ideas that come to you when you are working out financial problems. Re-read, study, and follow some of the suggestions for developing your talents and abilities that are given in Chapter 9 on work and Chapter 12 on financial independence. Also note that Chapter 10 points out how people have often tithed their way out of indebtedness when they dared, in faith, to put God first financially. Faith has prospering power.

When you are trying to find your financial freedom, begin to bring it forth by declaring often: "THERE ARE GOOD DAYS AHEAD. THERE ARE RICH DAYS AHEAD." When fear about present problems seems to engulf you, remind yourself: "GOD'S WAY FOR ME IS JOYOUS, A WAY OF SAFETY AND SECURITY. I GIVE THANKS THAT I NOW WALK IN PATHS OF PLEASANTNESS, PROSPERITY AND PEACE." For development of your talents and abilities to bring great satisfaction, declare often: "THE BOUNDLESS, LIMITLESS POWER THAT CREATED THE UNIVERSE IS NOW ACCOMPLISHING IN AND THROUGH ME ALL THAT IS FOR MY HIGHEST GOOD IN MIND, BODY AND AFFAIRS. I GIVE THANKS THAT I AM DIVINELY EQUIPPED TO ACCOMPLISH GREAT THINGS WITH EASE."

HEALTH AND
PROSPEROUS THINKING

— Chapter 19 —

Surely among the greatest blessings of life is health. Without it, nothing else matters very much. With good health, every other blessing is greatly enhanced.

As I counsel people about their various problems, I am convinced that our thinking directly affects our health. Many people who are in poor health, due to worry over financial problems, find it almost uncanny how fast their health improves as their financial situation improves.

A fine businessman, who had enjoyed good health for a number of years, faced serious financial setbacks in his business. Soon he developed gastric ulcers that later were found to be malignant, making several operations necessary. He is now on the way to complete recovery, which his doctors assure is possible. His wife recently stated, however, that every time he incurs a financial loss, he must return to bed. But when he receives good news about his financial affairs, his spirit soars, and he enjoys normal well-being.

The studies of psychosomatic medicine and holistic healing are surely wonderful steps forward in helping people to realize how strongly their mental states influence the condition of their bodies.

PROSPEROUS THINKING IS HEALTHY THINKING

We have shown earlier that you are prosperous to the degree that you are experiencing peace, health, and plenty in your world. In other chapters we have discussed techniques for developing prosperous thinking, so as to assure peace of mind and financial success. Now let us consider prosperous attitudes which will enhance your health. Prosperous thinking is victorious, harmonious, uplifted thinking. A prosperous thinker knows how to free himself of hostilities, resentments, criticisms, and irritated emotions. A prosperous thinker aims toward balanced, normal thinking which reflects his "will to win." Often, it is mental depression and a feeling of defeat that cause ill health.

A lady stated that for the past year she had had a lingering cold. Summer or winter, it held on. She was beginning to wonder if she did not have something more than a common cold, for this one was all too "uncommon"! Her physician assured her, however, that he could find nothing organically wrong to explain the cold.

Since there apparently was something irritating this little lady, something probably of long duration, I asked her to recall various events in her life prior to the appearance of this cold. After a few minutes' conversation, she said that she had held a fine job which she enjoyed. Without warning and without consulting her, her employer transferred her to another department, where she found the work distasteful, even irritating. Because she feared losing her job (because of her age) if she protested, she endured the transfer, with all the discord that went with it, into the new department among bickering fellow-workers. This added to her intense inner resentment and rebellion. Little wonder that inner irritation had manifested as a deep-seated cold which had persisted.

I suggested she begin working within her own thinking to overcome a feeling of hopelessness, helplessness, and defeat, and to adopt a victorious, winning attitude by daily using these ideas: "DIVINE LOVE AND WISDOM GO BEFORE ME, MAKING EASY AND SUCCESSFUL MY WAY IN THIS SITUATION. THE DIVINE SOLUTION NOW QUICKLY AND EASILY APPEARS. I AM NOW GUIDED, HEALED, PROSPERED AND BLESSED!" For several days she fed her mind these ideas, gaining a sense of peace which she had not had during the past year. Just as she was considering approaching her employer to explain her dissatisfaction and to request a transfer, an interesting thing happened: a notice was placed on the bulletin board, inviting the employees who desired transfers to see the manager, since he was considering making some changes. Here was her opportunity to declare her desires, which were granted. As her inner feelings were harmonized, she realized that her cold, which had been steadily dissolving, soon completely disappeared!

INHARMONY CAUSES ILL HEALTH

Truly, where there is a condition of ill health, there is a situation where the ill person has been subjected to internal discord of mind, body or affairs. Prosperous thinking expressed as harmonious thinking, helps to produce harmony in the body as well as in one's relationships and environment.

A pre-school-age child was afflicted with hemorrhoids. His doctor felt that this condition was unusual for a child of his years. He quietly studied the home situation to discover if any inharmony there might be linked with this physical condition. It was soon revealed that the child's mother knew nothing of the power of attitudes to affect one's health. She constantly insisted at each meal that this little boy empty his plate, regardless of how he felt or the state of his appetite. This child happened to be an individual who dared to "have a mind of his own." In several instances, he refused to eat. Thinking it her duty, his mother took him away from the table and spanked him. Such had been a daily event in his young life. It was astonishing that this child had not developed a conditon more serious than hemorrhoids.

After the mother agreed to become more harmonious and less stringent in her demands upon this child, the medical treatment began to render favorable results.

Bickering, quarreling, or general confusion in one's daily atmosphere are reflected in the health of those involved. The body is a very sensitive instrument, plastic to the thoughts, emotions, and words which are expressed through it and to it.

HEALTHY THINKING IS AN ANCIENT ART

There is nothing "new-fangled" about the truths now being uncovered which reveal how strongly thoughts and feelings control the body. Had the ancient Babylonian sciences come down to us intact, our civilization might be even more advanced than it is. Not only did the Babylonians use strange stones of ore for curing cancer, but they were also experts in the use of psychosomatics, various mental techniques, even in hypnotism.

It is believed that Abraham, who resided in the Babylonian city of Ur, learned of their treatment and brought it to the Jews, who effectively used it through the centuries. In any event, the writers of the Bible seemed to understand that disease was caused by wrong thought and wrong feeling, for their writings surely reflect that teaching.

Moses pointed out the definite power of right attitudes and emotional responses for health, and the power of wrong ones for ill health. Miriam, his sister, criticized him for marrying into another race. Because of her critical attitude, the Bible implies that Miriam contracted leprosy, and was healed only by means of Moses's prayer. (Numbers 12)

In another Old Testament story, we find that a wrong attitude killed King Asa, one of the kings of Judah. He did not believe in the possibility of spiritual healing and when his feet became seriously diseased, he died. (II Chronicles 16:12,13) Elisha and Elijah both healed through mental and spiritual methods, as did Jesus, Paul, and the early Christians.

Even witch doctors of primitive cultures realized the need for changing their patients' attitudes in order to heal them. In an effort to attract their patients' attention, they wore masks, spoke incantations, danced, and performed in other ways which seem strange to us today. They believed that if those seeking healing would redirect their minds away from their problems, healing would result.

ATTITUDES CAN HEAL

A housewife once described her improved health after her attitudes changed:

> For twelve years I had a chronic gall bladder condition which was very painful most of the time. For over a year I had had bursitis also, which was getting progressively worse. My husband and I both prayed about my health. We tried all types of medical treatment, but all to no avail, for the pain persisted.
>
> I was beginning to wonder how much longer I could go on. Then we learned about a series of prosperity lectures in our area. After hearing one lecture, which was on prosperity and not on healing, I understood better how to think victoriously. I began to realize that somehow the pain in my body could still be dispelled. For the first time in months, both my husband and I felt uplifted and inspired. And then it happened! Within one week from the time we heard that lecture, my gall bladder condition disappeared and the bursitis pain was also completely healed. I am thanking God daily for the uplifted attitudes which opened the way for healing to manifest in my body.

In another instance, a woman broke her arm. Though it had mended nicely, it remained so stiff and painful that she was unable to drive to prosperity lectures, so she hired a young man to chauffeur her. A

week later, this woman joyously appeared for the second lecture, stating that the painful stiffness had left
her that week, after she had dared to think definitely
about success and prosperity as her divine right. All
week she had been driving her car. She came alone to
other lectures after that, free from all pain. She learned
that prosperous thinking expands one's whole being,
with new, unlimited good, including the area of
health.

AN EMOTIONAL CAUSE OF CANCER

All about us we see the need for transforming negative emotions, if we wish to be healthy, or to regain
health. Cancer has been referred to in recent times as a
"hate disease." Those who contract it often carry their
hate secretly, so that the average person never suspects
the emotional turmoil through which some cancer
patients are passing.

Once I talked with a "self-made" man who had
worked hard to get to the top. He finally made it, and
he was greatly admired and respected by hundreds of
people. His financial achievements, his contributions
in time and talent to the many civic organizations of
his community, and his dedicated church work had
won him wide acclaim.

At the apex of his career, he was informed that he
had cancer. Operations extended his life for several
years. Toward the end of this period, he talked with
me about his condition. At first glance, it would seem
that a cruel fate had struck him down in his prime.
But closer acquaintance revealed that he had been
married several times; that each marriage had ended

in divorce, following bitter hostility; and that he detested his present wife. If she was as bad as he claimed, humanly he seemed to have reasons for his feelings, since she had made his life miserable.

Because of his business success, he felt that divorce or even a separation would be detrimental to his career. So he continued living with her in a state of abject misery, year in and year out. Furthermore, as often happens in such situations, he had turned to another woman for love and understanding he felt he was not receiving from his wife. This other woman was a business executive who was widowed and lonely. As their love affair developed, this woman became so frustrated at not being able to become his wife that her own health declined. Along with a series of health problems that developed, she sought emotional release through drink and drugs. She became so confused that her mind, in due time, no longer functioned clearly, and she lost a series of fine positions.

The only person who seemed relatively unaffected in this triangle was the hated wife. Through it all she remained calm. She did not seem to take on the hate or emotional turmoil of her husband or of the "other woman." In the long run she was the only victorious one.

Her husband stated to me that he could not forgive her or his previous wives for the unhappiness they had brought into his life. He refused to attempt any of the methods of healing mentioned in this chapter, or to invoke the methods of healing through forgiveness. I noticed that when he spoke of his wife, he seemed to exude an invisible poison. It was as though the very atmosphere in the room became heavy with venomous hate. He continued hating her and finally had to return to the hospital for another operation, which proved to be his last. His final conscious words were a curse upon his wife. His hate actually killed him.

The "other woman" did not attend his funeral, enduring her grief alone. Upon the death of her husband, the wife was not only free of his hate, but she also inherited his fortune. At last, she was not only a free woman but a very rich one; she did not hesitate to enjoy her wealth. Within a year she had happily remarried, assured of financial security and true love. By refusing to "hate back," this woman was the only one of the three involved in this situation who came through it victoriously.

FORGIVENESS HEALS

If you are out of harmony with anyone; if you have been caused unhappiness in the past for which you are still holding a grudge; if you feel you have been unjustly treated in financial or private matters; if you feel that some loss has robbed you of the happiness that should have been yours by divine right; if you feel strongly about unhappy childhood and family experiences—you may have every human reason for your feelings, and for continuing to nurse them. You may be able to justify those feelings in a thousand ways. But like the man in this story; like the "other woman," you mainly hurt yourself by doing so. Your health, prosperity, happiness, and peace of mind can and will be destroyed if you continue to harbor negative emotions.

If you now are in a state of ill health, there is some thing, somebody or some memory you need to forgive and release from your feelings forever. Perhaps you are

not consciously aware of what it is. But your subconscious mind, which is the storehouse of your feelings, emotions, and memories, knows what it is. It will
respond with release and healing when you give yourself treatments in forgiveness, as recommended later in
this chapter.

Philosophers and sages of all time have tried to point
out that man's health is controlled by his attitudes
toward himself and others. Hippocrates, the 4th century Greek physician, wrote: "Men ought to know that
from the brain, and from the brain only, arise our plea-
sures, laughters, and jests, as well as our sorrows,
pains, griefs and fears." Plato declared, "If the head
and the body are to be well, you must begin by curing
the soul." The Psalmist warned, "Cease from anger,
and forsake wrath; fret not thyself, it tendeth only to
evil-doing." (Psalms 37:8)

Wise old Solomon surely realized the power of
thought and feeling on the body when he advised, "A
merry heart maketh a cheerful countenance; but by
sorrow of the heart the spirit is broken." (Proverbs
15:13) "Pleasant words are as a honeycomb, sweet to
the soul, and health to the bones." (Proverbs 16:24)
"The light of the eyes rejoiceth the heart, and good
tidings make the bones fat." (Proverbs 15:30). Perhaps
Solomon's best psychosomatic advice was this: "A
cheerful heart causeth good healing. But a broken
spirit drieth up the bones." (Proverbs 17:22)

HAPPINESS HEALS

Truly a spirit that is broken, discouraged, or subject
to depressed conditions usually gets a physical reaction. I once knew a child who for several years was in a

home situation filled with bickering and fault-finding. This child suffered from one ailment after another. Finally his life situation changed, and he was placed in a quiet, harmonious atmosphere. Immediately, his ailments diminished, and he became so healthly thereafter that he never contracted any of the usual childhood diseases.

I know of a family who learned of the power of thought for health or illness. The parents agreed never to speak of negative subjects before the children, never to discuss illness, lack, hard times or troubles of any kind. They made it a point to converse on happy subjects in the home. It became a habit and they became a happy, healthy, close-knit family. This family was free of ill health, and they became very prosperous. Their children grew up without having any childhood diseases. They also developed happy, self-confident dispositions and all married happily. Today, they are enjoying successful lives, even as their parents do.

The bookshelves are now crowded with many fine books by authorities in all phases of the healing arts who point out the importance of healthy, happy emotions for a healthy body.[1]

THERAPY FOR FEMALE TROUBLE

Often we hear about various types of female troubles that afflict many women. In almost every case, the woman with such troubles is also experiencing great emotional unrest, suffering in secret about problems at

---

1. See the Ponder books, *The Dynamic Laws of Healing* and *The Healing Secrets of the Ages*.

home or in her work, which she feels that she cannot discuss. A schoolteacher recently wrote of how her monthly menstrual periods stopped after she was upset by her school principal, who she felt was a tyrant. Through affirmative prayer, she began to hold to the thought that "divine love and justice" would produce a change. Meanwhile, her physician could not locate any physical reason for her difficulties, but he gave her shots to help her through this strained period. In a short time, when her school principal received a transfer to another school, she began to relax and enjoy her work again, and her menstrual periods again became normal.

A housewife had been informed by her physician that she was sterile, after she had taken prolonged treatments to induce conception. Though she and her husband had long wanted children, she finally confessed to me that she had secretly feared the pain and discomfort of pregnancy, labor, and childbirth. She realized that her fear had probably prevented conception. When they investigated the possibilities of adopting a baby, for a number of reasons they decided to wait.

For the first time in years, she and her husband stopped fretting because theirs was a childless home. Instead, they decided to lead as happy and normal a life as possible, and to help care for homeless children in their area from time to time, such as during the holiday season. After the tension about not having children left her, the wife did have a baby in the tenth year of her marriage.

The wonderful part about using mental and spiritual methods for physical health is that it makes the work of your personal physician much easier. He is better able to aid you when your attitudes and emotions are constructive, and often much more than just a physical healing takes place.

THE FIRST STEP IN HEALING

Jesus pointed out that forgiveness is the foundation of healing. He advised the paralytic: "Thy sins are forgiven thee, arise and walk. Go and sin (think negatively) no more." (Mark 2) The greatest of all Healers also pointed out in the Sermon on the Mount how necessary it is to make peace with those with whom we are out of harmony, if we wish our efforts to be fruitful. Every one of us should use the simple method of forgiveness every day to effect reconciliation and harmony with others. Thereby we bring forth physical, mental, emotional, and spiritual healing.

Instead of attempting to painfully analyze your health problems from a psychosomatic standpoint; instead of trying to probe into the mental and emotional reasons for the various health, financial or human relations problems in your life, simply declare: "I FULLY AND FREELY FORGIVE. I LOOSE AND LET GO. I LET GO AND LET GOD'S LOVE DO ITS PERFECT WORK IN ME, THROUGH ME, FOR ME. I LET GO AND LET GOD'S LOVE DO ITS PERFECT WORK IN THE CONSCIOUS, SUBCONSCIOUS AND SUPERCONSCIOUS ACTIVITIES OF MY MIND, BODY AND AFFAIRS. I GIVE THANKS THAT PEACE, HEALTH, PLENTY AND HAPPINESS NOW REIGN SUPREME IN ME AND IN MY WORLD." If you have hostilities toward others, daily declare this forgiveness treatment for them.

I know of two different cases where young women were afflicted with paralysis after entertaining intense bitterness toward their former husbands who had divorced them. In both cases, these young women regained use of their limbs, after they began daily to practice forgiveness. To forgive does not mean that you have to "bow and scrape" to those who you feel have wronged you. You need make no outer contact with those involved, unless an occasion arises that demands it. Instead, you can know that they will feel your mental and emotional forgiveness, and they will release any animosity toward you, when you forgive and release your grudging hold upon them. This is a simple, private, soul-cleansing and body-healing process.

After you begin to daily affirm forgiveness, should you begin to think about people or situations from your past which were distasteful to you, do not be disturbed. Instead of wondering why they have come into your conscious thought again, just know that they are subconsciously receiving your forgiveness. Continue to affirm forgiveness for them, and in due time everything will become quiet and peaceful concerning them. As you get your own feeling of peace, you can know the forgiveness processs has done its perfect work, leaving you free of any thought of ill will. When you ever think of that person or experience, it will be with a sense of peace.

HOW TO LOSE WEIGHT

I once knew a wealthy woman who had tried desperately to lose weight. Several times she used stringent diets from specialists at various hospitals. But once she lost weight she could not maintain it. Finally she wrote of her frustration about weight, wondering why she could not maintain a reduced weight. From personal friendship with her, I knew that she and her husband traveled all over the world; that they had a spacious country estate, filled with interesting objects collected in their travels. Her husband had often complained that these things cluttered the house, so that it was necessary to keep a staff of servants to care for their possessions. This woman had stored many other possessions in the cellar, in addition to crowding all their closets and storage space.

I suggested that she prayerfully consider the vacuum idea (as discussed in Chapter 3) and ask for guidance concerning what she should release from her emotions and perhaps from her life, in order to lose weight and remain slender. In meditation, thereafter, she realized that she had long been holding unforgiving thoughts toward a relative who had caused her much distress. She began to daily declare forgiveness, release, and freedom in that connection.

She also got the feeling that she should heed her husband's request to clear the house of objects which were admittedly congesting the atmosphere. She cleared out closets, cellar and storage areas, called in the Salvation Army, and passed on unused items that could do good where they were needed. Her husband was elated. She said that the very act of release gave her a sense of freedom and peace that she had not known in years. Interestingly enough, she thereafter went on another diet and has been able to maintain loss in weight ever since. She now states that it was the acts of forgiveness, release and a literal, as well as a mental, housecleaning that brought forth her desires.

THE SECOND STEP IN HEALING

There is nothing strange, mysterious, or "new-fangled" about affirmative thought and prayer in connection with healing. The Hindus, Japanese, Chinese and many other nations still use various methods for applying sacred words to alleviate ills. Thoughout the Bible, many references are made to words and their creative power for good. The creation story began with the spoken affirmation, "LET THERE BE . . . AND THERE WAS." (Genesis 1) John emphasized that the word is God-power when he declared, "IN THE BEGINNING WAS THE WORD AND THE WORD . . . WAS GOD." (John 1) Jesus declared that His words were spirit and life. (John 6:63) The writer of Proverbs might have been speaking of the power of words for healing when he wrote, "DEATH AND LIFE ARE IN THE POWER OF THE TONGUE, AND THEY THAT LOVE IT SHALL EAT THE FRUIT THEREOF." (Proverbs 18:21)

There has long been a belief in the religious world that there was somewhere a "lost word of power" which, when found and uttered, would set all things right. The Jews believed that this lost word was veiled in the name "Yahweh," which is Hebrew for the word Jehovah. They felt that its correct pronunciation is no longer known to man. They claimed that the "lost word" was once known to their priesthood. When correctly used, it caused the power of God to become manifest, so that mighty works were accomplished quickly.

Any good word or phrase that gives peace and satisfaction, and that arouses a positive, harmonious response in one's thoughts and feelings, is equivalent to the "lost word" which the Jews sought. That lost word of power can come alive through constructive attitudes and affirmative prayer statements. A teenager, learning of the power of words to produce good results, decided to test its power on a cold which she felt coming on. Over and over she declared, "GOD IS MY HEALTH, I CAN'T BE SICK. GOD IS MY STRENGTH, UNFAILING, QUICK!" The cold never materialized.

Jehovah told Moses to dwell on the phrase "I AM THAT I AM," so that he might gain spiritual power and wisdom to lead the Children of Israel out of Egyptian bondage.[2] Sometimes the lost word of power comes alive by dwelling on the name of Jesus Christ. Jesus spoke of the great power of praying in His Name.[3] Sometimes the lost word of power comes alive through meditating on an appealing Bible promise or upon the Lord's Prayer.[4]

THE LORD'S PRAYER HAS HEALING
POWER

A woman once traveled a long distance to visit a noted spiritual healer concerning a chronic condition that had caused her much suffering. She was surprised, coming into the healer's presence to be invited to join

---

2. See Chapter 9, "The Occult Law of Healing" in the author's book, *The Dynamic Laws of Healing*.

3. See Chapter 8, "The Miracle Law of Healing" in *The Dynamic Laws of Healing*.

4. See chapter on "The Prayer for Miracles" in the author's book, *The Dynamic Laws of Prayer* (formerly *Pray and Grow Rich*). Also see Chapter 5 in *The Millionaire from Nazareth*.

in praying over and over the Lord's Prayer. At the conclusion of their prayer session, the healer told the woman to return to her home and to use the Lord's Prayer many times daily, explaining that it was the greatest healing prayer of all. Feeling a little skeptical of such a simple healing method, she nevertheless followed instructions. In a few weeks her ailment vanished, and it did not reappear.

A schoolteacher, hearing of the healing power of the Lord's Prayer, found occasion to prove it when she was pronounced ill with pneumonia. She sought healing through prescribed drugs, but the pneumonia persisted. One Friday she was informed that there was no substitute teacher available to take her place on the following Monday, when she was scheduled to begin teaching a new specialized course, for which people would be coming from near and far. It was then that she began affirming over and over the Lord's Prayer. As she persisted, by Sunday the fever had vanished, and she was feeling stronger. As she continued declaring the Lord's Prayer, she was able to begin teaching as scheduled on Monday, and her strength returned quickly.

The Lord's Prayer is a powerful healing treatment because it is basically a series of strong, powerful affirmative statements, in which one claims the power, substance, guidance, and goodness of God. Affirmation is not only an ancient healing art, but also a modern, scientific healing technique. Scientists now declare that the body as well as the universe is filled with innate intelligence.

By taking a statement filled with good words and declaring it over and over, man gains conscious attention of the innate intelligence ever active in the subconscious functions of the body. As man continues to speak good words, that innate intelligence is stepped up in its power to respond with conscious as well as subconscious positive results. The body, including our physical affairs, is the obedient servant of the mind, and is plastic to our thoughts and words. When our thoughts and words are uplifting, they are life-giving to our physical world.

GRIPING CAN MAKE YOU SICK

Griping can make you sick, and negative words and feelings can cause all manner of disease. I once knew a secretary and housewife who was a constant griper. She disliked her mother-in-law, who was forced for economic reasons to live with her and her husband. She griped about this, about the weather, the world, especially about her boss. Griping was constant with her, and she repeatedly complained about how bad she felt. She spent hundreds of dollars on medical treatments, on medicines, vitamins, and chiropractic treatments in an effort to be free of the aches and pains that plagued her. As she continued to gripe about everything and everybody, her circle of friends dwindled, her boss refused to give her a raise, and her mother-in-law caused her great anguish. Griping made her sick, and kept her that way. When she was offered the method of affirmative thought and prayer for healing, she scoffed at it, declaring it to be too simple to work. She continued to get a negative result through continued negative thought, a mental method that seemed simple enough to work effectively for her!

YOUR PRAYERS FOR ANOTHER'S
HEALING HAVE POWER

Perhaps you know someone you would like to assist in solving a healing need, but you hesitate to mention it to them, because you feel they might not agree. In that event, begin declaring affirmations for them or ask some prayer group or trusted friend to join you in praying for them. A mother recently proved the power of this for her daughter, who is a successful public relations executive. The daughter suffered a nervous breakdown after her marriage failed. Though she had received the best medical and psychiatric treatment, she still remained in a state of deep depression.

The daughter long insisted that she had no interest in religion, and she had no faith in the power of prayer for healing. When nothing else seemed to bring healing, the mother asked a group which uses affirmative prayer to pray for her daughter. Within a few days her daughter arose from bed for the first time in weeks. Soon she was back at work, although she continued with psychiatric treatments for a time.

She began to feel in command of her world again. She decided to accept a new job involving much more responsibility, in addition to offering her several thousand dollars more annual income. Only at this victorious point was this young woman informed by her mother that prayers had been offered for her healing. Realizing that they surely had led to the turning point in her condition, the young lady executive began using affirmative prayers for her continued health, success and happiness and for some of her business associates and friends as well, with great inner satisfaction.

This book is filled with affirmative prayers and the results they have brought countless people in all walks of life, producing new peace, health and plenty. Be sure, however, to re-study Chapter 6, "The Prosperity Law of Command," in connection with healing through affirmation.[5]

THE THIRD STEP IN HEALING

Mentally picture yourself or the one who seeks healing as completely strong and well. As stated in Chapter 5, "The Imaging Law of Prosperity," mental images make the conditions of our minds, bodies, and affairs, but it is up to us to deliberately make the mental images of our lives as we wish them to be. Otherwise, we get a distorted result from holding distorted pictures in the mind.

Particularly is imaging powerful for healing. By forming pictures in your mind of the results you desire, and by holding to that mental picture, you are releasing your faith to go to work in a simple but supreme way to produce wondrous results.[6]

A housewife recently related how she used the imaging power of her mind to deliberately produce healing. She had suffered a severe knee infection which, after many weeks, continued to be swollen, infected, and very painful. Unable to gain assurance from others as to its healing prospects, this woman decided to invoke

---

5. Also see Chapter 5, "The 'Yes' Law of Healing," in *The Dynamic Laws of Healing*.

6. Also see Chapter 10, "The Imaging Law of Healing," in *The Dynamic Laws of Healing*.

her imaging power, to gain the faith that healing was still possible.

Every day she began sitting quietly for a time and directing her attention not to the swollen knee, but to the one that was healthy and whole. She would place her hand on the healthy knee, give thanks for the health of it, and get a strong mental picture of the knee in her mind. Daily she continued this exercise. When anyone asked about her knee she conveyed the image of healing to their minds by always replying that her knee was healing nicely. At this point, it was strictly an affirmative prayer, a statement of faith.

For several days, there seemed no change in her knee, but this woman dared to persevere in holding her mental image. One morning after weeks of pain and swelling, she awakened to find that overnight the swelling had disappeared, the knee had lost all appearance of abnormality, and was again its proper size. Upon closer inspection, it was as though the skin in that area had been pricked in many places and the infected substance had simply escaped! Her husband, a successful businessman, substantiated her experience to me. They both spoke of how delighted her physician was when he examined her knee that morning, for he assured them they had witnessed a miracle!

MAKE A WHEEL OF FORTUNE FOR HEALTH

If you wish a more definite and tangible method for using your imaging power for healing, I suggest you use the "wheel of fortune" method outlined in Chapter 5.

A doctor once asked me to visit one of his patients who was paralyzed on one side and had not walked for several years. He said that unless her hope could be restored, there was nothing more he could do as a doctor to help her. She had been reading various inspirational books on the power of thought, and he felt that she would be receptive to suggestions along that line to effect her healing.

On my visit, I found her in bed, depressed, discouraged, despairing of complete healing. I told her about the gigantic power of mental images for healing, and suggested that she immediately get busy making a wheel of fortune for her health, which she did. On the wheel of fortune, she placed numerous pictures clipped from magazines, which showed people walking, walking, walking! She placed this wheel of fortune where she could view it for hours every day. I also suggested she employ the forgiveness prayer method mentioned earlier in this chapter. All these things she seemed glad to follow.

When I visited her a month later, she was sitting up in a chair! She had to be put in the chair and taken from it, but she was sitting up. As she continued to image and affirm wholeness, it was as though all the forces of heaven and earth began to work for her to help make it so. A neighbor, who was overseas with her husband, mailed a check to this young woman, suggesting that she use it for physical therapy treatments, which would surely be another step in her healing. A chiropractor, who had treated her in the past, dropped by to see her. He said that he would like to treat her regularly, without charge, in order to ascertain how effective chiropractic would be in such health problems.

Another neighbor promised that when she was ready to begin using a wheelchair, he would purchase one for her; another offered to pay for braces for her feet and ankles, when she had reached that stage. Gradually, as she continued looking at the pictures on her wheel of fortune of people walking, she grew stronger. Finally, another neighbor built a ramp down the porch of her house to the yard, so that she might be wheeled out into the sun and fresh air. At my last contact with this young woman, she was beginning to take a few steps on her own! That is the healing power of the imagination, when invoked constructively and definitely toward a desired result of health.

REDUCE THROUGH MENTAL IMAGES

The imaging method is effective in every phase of health. A businessman who also had been on all types of diets, and had given up, finally heard of the imaging power of the mind for healing. He realized then that, although he had dieted stringently, he had continued to hold the image of himself as overweight; and that his mental image had continued to produce the very thing he did not want.

He then clipped pictures of healthy, vigorous, slender businessmen from magazines, placed them on his bedside table. He would quietly look at these pictures, filling his mind with definite images just before retiring. He also taped a couple of these pictures on small file cards and carried them in his wallet, looking at them during the day. Through this process, he lost 40 pounds while dieting, with a minimum of effort or self-discipline, and since then he has lost more. He now resembles those pictures he still carries in his wallet.

HOW TO STOP SMOKING

I have known several businessmen who used the imaging method to stop smoking. A salesman, a doctor, and a business executive recently stated that it proved to be the easiest habit they had ever overcome. Their method was simple. They did not stop smoking or even try to. Instead, they simply formed mental images of how bad their cigarettes tasted, and of how they finally could not smoke them at all. They would hold this mental image of a bad-tasting cigarette whenever they lighted one. It took several weeks for the mental image to begin taking effect, but it did. Their cigarettes became distasteful, and soon they began to lose the desire to smoke. Within about six weeks, all desire had left and in each instance, they each still had half a pack of cigarettes on hand, which they then threw away. They told no one of their desire to stop smoking or of the method they were using. In that way, no one was able to break down the mental images they were holding; or to attempt to talk them out of using such a simple method.

THIS METHOD EFFECTIVE
FOR OVERCOMING ALCOHOLISM

I have known a number of people who used the imaging method to help bring forth healing in their loved ones. Several people, both men and women, have mentioned recently how they dared to image sobriety in their marriage partners who seemed to have become hopeless alcoholics. As they persisted in imaging them as healed, they gradually improved and finally were free of the desire for intoxicants.

I had lunch recently with one such couple. A few years ago, the husband was considered a "has-been," but he is now a successful business executive and one of the most poised, peaceful and charming men I have ever met. He said to me, as the subject was discussed:

> "I knew all the time my wife was 'up to something' in trying to effect my healing, but I didn't know what she was doing, and since it was proving painless for me, I did not care what her method was. I got to feeling so much better that I only hoped she would keep on until I was completely well again. Thank heaven, she did!"

His wife had formed the mental image of a sober, happy, prosperous, victorious husband and she held to that mental image day in and day out, month in and month out. Her husband is today the wonderful man she imaged!

THE BIBLE TEACHES THIS
HEALING TECHNIQUE

A number of great healers in the Bible wisely used the imaging power of the mind to produce healing. An interesting case is noted in Jesus' healing of the man blind from birth. When his disciples asked Jesus who had sinned to produce this blindness, instead of giving such an analysis, Jesus turned to healing him. His method was clear enough to one who understands mental processes. First, Jesus spat on the ground and made clay of the spittle. He then anointed the man's eyes with that clay and instructed him to "go, wash in the pool of Siloam." This statement set up the mental image of an expected healing in the man's thinking, and it motivated him to then act upon the image. Thus, he followed through on that mental image of healing: he "went, washed, and came away seeing." (John 9:7)

The early Christians undoubtedly realized the healing power of the imagination. When Peter and John were going up into the temple, they encountered a beggar at the temple door who had been lame from birth. In response to the beggar's request for alms, Peter fastened his eyes (imaging power) upon the beggar and along with John said "Look on us!" The beggar did so, expecting to receive a donation from them.

It was then that Peter declared a strong affirmation which instilled the image of healing within the beggar's mind: "Silver and gold have I none, but what I have, that give I thee. In the name of Jesus Christ of Nazareth, walk!" To help the beggar accept that mental image of healing, Peter then took him by the hand, raised him up, and immediately he did walk and was healed. (Acts 3)

A HEALING PROPHECY

Thus, along with the usual methods for obtaining and then maintaining good health, adopt the techniques and methods suggested in this chapter. Let them prove their power for you!

For this purpose I would like to share with you a favorite affirmation for health: "I GIVE THANKS THAT I AM THE EVER-RENEWING, THE EVER-UNFOLDING EXPRES-

SION OF INFINITE LIFE, HEALTH, AND ENERGY." For wholeness in mind, body and affairs, which is truly health personified, I suggest: "I AM THE RADIANT CHILD OF GOD. MY MIND, BODY AND AFFAIRS NOW EXPRESS HIS RADIANT PERFECTION!" Truly, as you adopt prosperous thinking for health, it can and shall be so. "Then shall thy light break forth as the morning, and thy healing shall spring forth speedily." (Isaiah 58:8)

THE PROSPERITY LAW
OF PERSISTENCE

— Chapter 20 —

Jesus was describing the power of persistence when He declared: "No man, having put his hand to the plow and looking back, is fit for the kingdom of God." (Luke 9:62) In other words, when you realize that prosperity is your divine heritage, you should persist in claiming it.

A businessman who often sends me books and articles on prosperity recently sent this statement by Calvin Coolidge:

Nothing in the world can take the place of persistence. Talent will not; nothing is more common than unsuccessful men with talent. Education will not; the world is full of educated derelicts. Persistence and determination alone are omnipotent. The slogan

412

"Press on" has solved and always will solve the problems of the human race.

When discouragement tries to beset you; when it seems as though your efforts toward success have been in vain, remember to hold onto that statement: "NOTHING IN THE WORLD CAN TAKE THE PLACE OF PERSISTENCE."

PERSISTENCE IS YOUR "CAN-DO" ATTITUDE

I know a young man who had tried everything and had failed at everything. Yet he had tremendous talent, ability, and charm. He knew that there was a right place for him in life, but it had just not appeared. Finally, he decided to enlist in the Navy, and that was the turning point for him. Everything he has done from that point on has proved for him a great success. He has received a number of promotions and official recognition for his Navy work. Recently his commanding officer wrote a letter praising him for his "can-do" attitude. The letter stated that his attitude had led to definite success in the face of challenging difficult assignments. His commanding officer advised him to continue his "can-do" approach to all of his duties.

The prosperity law of persistence might easily be described as the "can-do" attitude. Many people have just the opposite approach—the "can't-do" attitude, which is a guarantee for failure. As you observe successful people about you, you will discover that they have cultivated the habit of persisting in the face of apparent failure, so that they seem to enjoy insurance against it. No matter how many times they experience setbacks, they persist toward their goal and they inevitably achieve it.

There is nothing half-way, lukewarm, or half-hearted about persistence. It is bold, daring, fearless. It does not hesitate, but goes after what it wants, and keeps plugging until it gets results. A good statement to use in the face of distressing lulls or setbacks is: "I AM NOT DISCOURAGED: I AM PERSISTENT, AND I GO FORWARD." Remind yourself often: "I AM NOT ON THE WAY OUT. I AM ON THE WAY UP!"

When Jesus spoke of putting your hand to the plow and not looking back, He was describing the mighty power of persistence. A plow is an implement used to cut up, turn up, or break up the soil for planting. Your persistence is your mental plow which helps you to break up those old failure attitudes of mind, which have previously kept success from you. Once you have broken up the feeling of defeat, you are then ready to launch forth with the "can-do" attitude that will surely show you how to succeed.

DON'T SURRENDER TO DEFEAT

The average person surrenders too easily to appearances, when often just a little more enduring persistence is all that is required to turn the tide from failure to success. The word "persist" literally means "to refuse to give up." It also means to "continue firmly, steadily, insistently." When you are discouraged and unable to see any good ahead, declare: "I REFUSE TO GIVE UP. I

SHALL CONTINUE FIRMLY, STEADILY, AND INSISTENTLY UN-
TIL MY GOOD APPEARS." Keep plowing that hard ground
of failure and limitation until you break it up completely with your victorious attitudes of mind, supported by your outer actions aimed at success.

Once an old friend met my late father on the street
and inquired about me. After my father told her of
my work as a minister and writer, she happily wrote
me a note and said, "I used to wonder how such a little
girl could think so big, but I'm glad that you did!"

Often all it takes is a little more persistence in thinking big, working steadily, and expecting big results in
order to bring them forth in your life. A recent advertisement carried this caption: "People who chase
dreams are the most likely to catch them."

PERSISTENCE PRODUCES SUCCESS

The story of Jacob wrestling with the angel until the
break of day shows the power of persistence in producing success. He vowed to the angel, "I will not let
thee go, except thou bless me." (Genesis 32:26) The
angel renamed him "Israel," which means "Prince of
God." You can, like Jacob, become a "Prince of God"
through persistence.[1]

When you meet disappointment constructively, you
will go forward to great good. It is as though by your
refusal to give up, "the years that the locust has eaten"
(Joel 2:25) are restored to you. Indeed, through persistence, so much good can be added to the present

---

1. See Chapter 5, "The Persistent Millionaire, Jacob," in the
author's book, *The Millionaires of Genesis.*

moment that it blots out the emptiness, discouragement, and failure of the past.

FAILURE CAN BE A PRELUDE
TO SUCCESS

Often, failure is success trying to be born in a bigger
way, and persistence helps you to experience that
greater result. For several years I wrote inspirational
articles for the Unity publications. Then at one point I
"hit a snag." Everything I wrote and submitted was re-
jected, and I wondered if my writing career was ending
so soon. I went through a disheartening period, constantly battling with the feeling of failure, and wondering what it all meant.

Months later, as I began to evolve the laws of prosperous thinking, it became evident that the rejections
of my articles were an indication that I was not thinking big enough. The time had come for me to write
books instead of articles. Those rejection slips were
nothing but success trying to be born for me in a bigger way. It was then that the ideas began to form for
the writing of this book, and for the many books that
have followed.

My first reaction was, "If you can't even write
articles that are accepted for publication, how can you
possibly expect to write books that will be accepted?"
But prosperous thinking insisted on the opposite attitude—my previous failures in writing magazine articles were but an indication that the time had come to
aim higher. Had my articles continued to be accepted,
I probably never would have pushed past that level. So
I was able to establish and maintain the attitude: "I

REFUSE TO GIVE UP. I SHALL CONTINUE FIRMLY, STEADILY, AND INSISTENTLY UNTIL THE GOOD APPEARS IN THIS EXPERIENCE." Someone has said that success is failure turned inside out. I believe it!

REFUSE "NO" AS AN ANSWER

The enduring achievements of mankind have come about because men have steadily refused to take "no" for an answer. I recall a favorite phrase used by one of my high school teachers. She often talked to us about the power of "going the second mile" in life. At times those words have floated up in my memory when I was tempted to stop at the end of the first mile, to sit down and quit.

When inner methods of persistence are used, external persistence is not often needed. When you learn the power of prosperous thinking, you learn how to work things out in your mental attitudes first, rather than expend effort in running hither and yon attempting to manipulate an outer result. The inner will produce the outer—but you must first persistently produce the inner.

After you are convinced of an idea, you should persist in your conviction. If outer doors seem to close to you, do not hesitate. Persist in inner preparations. The inner realm of thought controls all outer action. When you get the right attitude, the outer world of results and personalities must conform to it. That is the law of mind-action.

In the face of apparent defeat, declare: "IT IS MY DIVINE DESTINY TO SUCCEED, AND IT IS GOD'S BUSINESS TO HELP ME. I EXPECT AND CLAIM HIS DIVINE HELP NOW." It has been said that he only is beaten who admits it. The timid seldom attain great fulfillment.

PERSISTENCE WORKS BOTH WAYS

Persistence works both ways. We have all used persistence to fail when we should have used it to succeed. If you persist in expecting and talking failure, there is no power in heaven or earth that can prevent failure from appearing in your world. The story is told of one negative thinker who said to another, "Did you know that a depression is on the way?" His friend replied, "What do you mean 'on the way'? I've been living in a depression all of my life!"

On the other hand, if you persist in expecting and talking about prosperity and success, there is no power in heaven or earth that can prevent them from appearing in your world. I once observed a group of men and women persist in affirming and expecting success when everyone around them was decreeing hard times and recession. Their results were proof positive of the prospering power of persistence. A businessman in the group, whose stock market profits had been quite low during the previous year, found that his stocks began to increase, as he persistently affirmed it. In the next two months, he made more money on the stock market than he had made during the past twelve months!

The owner of a cleaning plant watched his business increase weekly after he began decreeing success in the face of apparent recession. In fact, while three other cleaning plants in the same area closed down, within a few weeks this man's cleaning business increased $400 per week over previous income.

A housewife who received an annual income from a relative's estate had not received her yearly check at the usual time. After deciding to persist in expecting a successful result, the check finally arrived. It came late — but it was written for three times the amount received the year before!

Another housewife was decreeing success persistently during this period. Her husband received the best job he has ever had, as an engineer in the missile program. Furthermore, his new employer insisted that his starting salary would be more per month than he was asking.

ONE RIGHT ATTITUDE IS ENOUGH

Physical science has discovered that everything can be reduced to a few primal elements, and that if the entire universe were destroyed, it could be built up again from a single cell. In like manner, you can expand or rebuild your financial world from a single right attitude to which you persistently hold. By refusing to give up or give in to failure, failure is finally worn out by your persistence and gives up its power to success.

The Apostle Paul proved this. Although he has been described by historians as a "versatile genius," I believe his greatest genius power was that of persistence. In his time, Christianity was still considered illegal. Often Paul was imprisoned, beaten, and persecuted for being a Christian missionary. He braved criticism from all directions, betrayal among his followers, privation, and even shipwreck to do the work which he felt was important. Had it not been for Paul's persistence,

Christianity might never have spread from the Holy Land, and in all probability would have died out in the first century.

There's something about joyous persistence that seems to produce good results much faster. I have often heard the story of my grandfather who used the power of joyous persistence to get cotton picked on his South Carolina plantation at the turn of the century.

When the day grew hot and the cotton-picking had slowed down, he would join the workers in the fields. As he picked cotton, he began to sing. The workers then began singing, too. He would sing a little faster and pick cotton a little faster; everyone else did the same. It proved an effective and happy method for stepping up production in the cotton fields!

MEET HARD EXPERIENCES WITH PERSISTENCE

Spasmodic efforts count for little. When hard experiences appear on your pathway, meet them on their own terms with persistence, expecting success to come out of them. You should not use gentle methods when there are hard conditions. To use gentle methods on hard experiences is like trying to plow hard soil with a dull blade. You make little progress when you try to solve difficult problems in half-hearted ways. Meet hard problems by persistently refusing to give up to them. Insist upon receiving a blessing from those experiences. Face them with dauntless courage and daring.

If you ever have had the breath knocked out of you, you probably found the process of normal breathing was not sufficient to restore proper breathing. Instead you had to fight for more air. In like manner, in times of apparent failure or discouragement, if you do not vigorously persist in believing that you can and will succeed, you are likely to curl up forever in the clutches of defeat and failure.

William James, the American psychologist, evolved the theory of getting your second wind, mentally, emotionally, and physically. He wrote of persevering until you reach your second wind. Often he kept going when fatigue assailed him, only to find that suddenly new reserves of strength were tapped so that he gained his second wind, and later his third and even his fourth. New energy would flow in to produce new power and victory. It was as though an unseen partner had taken over.

In times of emergency or deep need, untapped, dormant power is often released in man—power that would never be released unless there were an urgent need. You can know that such a time of challenge is but an indication that great power within you wishes to be released to aid you, to work for you and through you.

REVISE YOUR SUCCESS PLANS

Thus, when discouragement overcomes you, when despair says, "It can't be done, you'll never make it," that is the time to review your plans, to write them out and revise them, as suggested in Chapter 4. That is the time to image and re-image your good as mentioned in Chapter 5. That is the time to affirm: "THIS IS A TIME OF DIVINE FULFILLMENT. MIRACLES NOW FOLLOW MIRACLES AND WONDERS NEVER CEASE TO MANIFEST AS THE DIVINE PLAN OF MY LIFE."

That is the time to declare: "THE WORK OF MY HANDS AND THE PLANS OF MY LIFE ARE NOW MOVING QUICKLY TOWARD A SURE AND PERFECT FULFILLMENT. I ANTICIPATE THE GOOD. IN GOD'S RIGHT ACTION I NOW PLACE MY FULL TRUST."

That is the time to affirm often: "I AM A PART OF ALL THAT IS GOOD, AND GOOD SHALL BE VICTORIOUS." That is the time to talk with a trusted friend and get a boost, or to form a small creative imagination group which will work with you toward success, rather than entertaining any possibility of failure. That is the time to browse through the Bible for inspiration and guidance. That is the time to read the 23rd Psalm and meditate upon the meaning of its words: "The Lord is my shepherd; I shall not want." Read the 91st Psalm, "He will give his angels charge over thee, to keep thee in all thy ways. They shall bear thee up in their hands, lest thou dash thy foot against a stone."

PLOD ON TO VICTORY

Remind yourself of the times you "came through" to victory in the past. When discouragement and despair try to keep you from persisting toward your goal, remind yourself of the successful people who succeeded in spite of being maimed, blind, deaf or psychoneurotic: Toscanini was so nearsighted that he could not see the score when conducting; Lord Byron had a club foot; Homer and Milton were blind; Sir Walter Scott was an invalid; Beethoven was deaf; Dostoyevski and de Maupassant were epileptic; Franklin D. Roosevelt did not have free use of his legs.

Shakespeare might have been describing the power of persistence when he wrote, "There is a tide in the affairs of men when, taken at the flood, leads on to fortune." Bring forth your floodtide of good by affirming from the words of Jesus, "ALL THAT WHICH THE FATHER HAS GIVEN ME NOW COMES TO ME." (John 6:37)

Remind yourself that it is not always the people with the most education or talent who make the grade. It is the "plodders." It is the people who doggedly refuse to give up, whether they seem to have talent or brillance. The story of the hare and the tortoise is the story of persistence winning out over great odds. As with the tortoise, you cannot be defeated if you just never give up.

It is not usually the men of flashing mind power who are the heads of the great corporations and industries; on the contrary, it is the men of patient, plodding character. They cannot be defeated because they never give up.

It is not necessary for you to have money to get a start in life nor that you inherit property, family name, or privileges of any kind. Neither is it imperative to have an extensive education. The one thing you do need, however, is a goal and a persistent, plodding determination to reach that goal, no matter what.

DON'T LOOK BACK—LOOK FORWARD

If disappointment tries to sidetrack you along the way, meet it as best you can and then just keep going. No negative experience can stop you for long if you don't look back after such episodes. Learn a lesson from Lot's wife, who became hard and crystallized when she looked back. (Genesis 19:26)

Instead, get your vision back on your goal, and begin moving toward it in whatever way seems most logical at the moment. If you have been sidetracked and can't do anything directly to work toward it, there are little things you can do that give you the feeling you are moving toward it. Do them; they will lead to the bigger opportunities along the way. Just one step at a time, big or little, is all that is necessary. Take it, and it will lead to the next and the next.

I once heard a man tell a story that impressed upon me the importance of persistently looking ahead. As a boy, he and his father started to town by horse and buggy on a warm Saturday. At the first crossroads, they stopped to listen to a candidate for political office giving a speech. The candidate told the people he should be elected to office because his father and grandfather before him had been political leaders in that area. Since he came from a political family, he claimed that he was best qualified to serve the people.

As the boy and his father drove on toward town, they came to another crossroads where a second political candidate was making a speech. He, too, claimed that his family had long been in politics, which he felt gave him a favorable background for serving the people.

At the next crossroads, they heard a candidate speaking. He stated, "I have never run for office in my life. No one in my family has ever served in a political office. However, I believe I can ably serve the people of this area, because I feel that where we are going, rather than where we have been, is of great importance!" That man won the election!

You can win, too, no matter where you've been or what your past experiences have been, if you will decide what you wish to achieve and persist toward it.

With Paul, the persistent soul should declare often, "Forgetting the things that are behind, I press forward toward my goal." (Philippians 3:13) As Shakespeare's Cassius declared, "It is not in our stars, but in ourselves, that we are underlings."

PERSISTENCE ALONE IS ALL-POWERFUL

If one does not persist, one does not achieve lasting success in any field. If one does dare to persist toward success, regardless of lack of education, background, talent, influence, money, or reputation, one can and will succeed. Dogged determination outlasts and outgames talent. Persistence is a characteristic to which success invariably surrenders.

Calvin Coolidge offered this gem: "Persistence alone is omnipotent." Defeat may test you; it need not stop you. Regard apparent failure, disappointment, or defeat simply as signposts that success is just around the corner. Use them as greater incentives to forge ahead and suddenly there will loom upon your pathway your heart's desire or something better.

BE PREPARED IF SUCCESS COMES SUDDENLY

Success has a way of coming in a hurry after a "long haul" of plodding along quietly. As you persist toward your goal, get ready for fast, exciting, success-filled results. Have your plans carefully in mind of what you will do when success arrives, because just when it seems least possible, the tide will turn for you. Then it will be necessary that you take a deep breath and proceed to accept your floodtide of good, step by step, as already planned.

As fulfillment comes, you must not let it "throw you." Be alert and ready to accept it; otherwise, it may evaporate before you, leaving you to begin all over again. Once success arrives, it is wise to persistently accept it and quietly maintain it; otherwise, it can slip from you.

Persistence is the keynote to realizing your heart's desires and to maintaining them. Dwell often on the promise of Jehovah to Isaiah: "I will go before thee and make the rugged places plain; I will break in pieces the doors of brass, and cut in sunder the bars of iron, and I will give thee the treasures of darkness, and hidden riches of secret places." (Isaiah 45:2,3)

It can and shall happen, through the omnipotence of persistence, perhaps just when it seems least likely. Through persistence, you can be one of those happy, victorious people who not only chases dreams, but who catches them! The persistent man also perseveres long enough for his dreams to catch up with him!

Conclusion . . . .

WHEN THE GOLD DUST SETTLES

You will recall our salesman friend whose answer to the question "How's business?" was always, "*Business is wonderful, because there's gold dust in the air.*"

While you have been reading this book, I trust that some of its gold dust power has already touched you, even as it has touched me. I began writing this book while serving the Unity ministry in the Deep South. Many months later, I concluded these pages in the heart of Texas, where I continued to lecture and write. With me in my happy new life was my college professor husband, whom I had married while writing this book. Truly it seemed that my dreams had come true!

Then—suddenly—my husband was gone, a heart attack victim at the age of forty. It was a hard blow. There were those well-meaning people who bluntly asked, "If all that you write is true, why did this happen to *you?*" Well, life progresses through change and we must flow with it, even when there are unexpected (and unwanted) turns in the road.

In the years that followed, I delivered my "gold dust lectures" far and wide, participated in countless radio, television and print interviews, managed to write more than a dozen books, and founded several churches. I have continued to receive lecture invitations, on a worldwide basis, too numerous to accept. The teachings in this book have gone from reaching 50 people in my first prosperity class, to reaching into all 50 of the United States, and more than 50 other countries.

When I finally felt guided to settle in the Palm Desert-Palm Springs area of the Golden State of California, listings in *Who's Who* and the *Social Register*, and receipt of an honorary doctorate followed. The gold dust is settling.

Little did I realize, when I began working with the power of prosperous thinking, how much my own life could change as I developed and wrote down these ideas.

At the time I began to develop the material in this book, while teaching a prosperity class during the Recession of 1958, my son and I were living in one room. Several years later, most of the first edition of this book was written at odd moments, mainly in the middle of the night, from my tiny "gold dust study" in Alabama. The book was finally finished in my apartment overlooking the University of Texas in Austin.

Now, as I complete this revised version several decades later, the scene has changed again. From my writing studio in my desert home, I am surrounded by the mystic glamour and prolific tropical beauty of Southern California. Tall palm trees and majestic purple mountains hover in the background of this celebrity-studded area. How grateful I am to have completed this updated edition in such surroundings with adequate time and staff to assist me; and with a comfortable lifestyle to cheer me on.

Others might consider my progress normal for most people with my long work record. However, because of my meager beginnings, and the humanitarian professions I have long worked in—ones in which a person is traditionally overworked and underpaid—I feel that only my discovery and use of "the dynamic laws of prosperity" could have rescued me from a life of obscure poverty and despair, and made my present blessings possible.

It can prove so for you, too! Regardless of what life has dealt you in the past, or what limitations you may feel in the present, continue to study these prosperity laws and to apply them daily. Continue to invoke prosperous thinking deliberately and definitely. Do so with real joy and with great expectations. As you persist, your own divinely-intended gold dust can still appear as greater peace, health, and plenty in your life. Accept gladly those gold-dust results. They are part of your divine heritage prepared for you by a rich and loving Father.

They will not only make your life happier and more worthwhile, but you will become a greater blessing to your fellow man in countless wonderful ways in this exciting New Age.

In this joyous assurance, I wish to affirm for you a scriptural blessing, which was given during another era in man's continuing effort to prove the rich promises of God:

"Beloved, I pray that in all things thou mayest prosper and be in health, even as thy soul prospereth."

(3 John 2)

Catherine Ponder
P.O. Drawer 1278
Palm Desert, California 92261
U.S.A.